Annette Wolter

Parrots

**How to Take Care of Them
and Understand Them**

With 66 color photographs
Drawings by György Jankovics

Consulting Editor:
Matthew M. Vriends, Ph.D.

W9-BUI-923

BARRON'S

Contents

About the pictures:
This Australian galah quenches its thirst in flight. It flies down, drops its head, dips its beak into the water to drink, and immediately takes off again.

You will learn everything you need to know about correct care and maintenance of parrots from the renowned expert Annette Wolter. In the chapter on species you'll find descriptions and pictures of 34 popular parrots, large and small. A parrot lexicon, enchanting color photographs, and informative drawings round out this complete Pet Owner's Manual.

About the Nature of the Parrot

In nature, parrots form a lifelong bond with a member of the same species. Thus we strongly advise against keeping a single parrot if you have little time to devote to the bird. It's better to buy two birds, preferably a pair, in this case.

Everyone knows the wonderful large macaws and the decorative Amazons from South America, the clever gray parrots and the charming lovebirds from Africa. The enchanting cockatoos, the magnificently colored loris, the beautiful parakeets from East Asia, Indonesia, and Australia as well as the playful and curious keas from New Zealand are also members of the large family of parrots. Altogether there are about 326 species with 816 subspecies. The largest among these are the macaws, with a body length of up to 39 inches (1 m); the pygmy parrots are the smallest at 3½ to 4 inches (8.5 to 10 cm).

Where Parrots Live

Most parrot species live in the tropical and subtropical regions of Central and South America, Africa, the entire Asiatic area, and in Australia. A very few species are also to be found somewhat more northerly or southerly.

Parrots live in a wide variety of habitats, such as mountains, virgin forests, deserts, grasslands, palm groves, scrub, eucalyptus-scrub plains, and cultivated areas, on rocky cliffs, along river courses, and sometimes even in cities.

Parakeet or Parrot?

Although the budgerigar, rosella parakeet, and cockatiel are parrots, many ornithologists and parrot fanciers place the parakeets in a separate group. Physical differences can be very difficult to perceive. Most parakeets, however, are much smaller than parrots, have a particularly long tail, are swift, nimble, tireless fliers and, kept as house or aviary birds, require different setups from those for parrots. Therefore this book excludes the parakeets from its discussion of the birds of the large parrot family.

Typical of All Parrots

Body build: The body build of all parrots can be described as decidedly stocky. It is just that the varying lengths of the tail feathers give the macaws, for example, the optical effect of elegance, whereas other parrots with short tail feathers sometimes even look awkward. On the other hand, their heads, large in comparison with the body, with their expressive eyes and large beak, are unmistakable.

Beak: In all parrots the powerful, down-curving upper beak encloses the funnel-shaped lower beak. Depending on their type of diet, some species have very long, sharp upper beaks; in others the profile is gracefully rounded off by the beak, as in the cockatoos, for example. In all parrots the beak

Parrots like this yellow-naped Amazon are very wasteful with their food. They often only eat a small part of the fruit and carelessly let the rest drop.

*I*t doesn't matter whether you choose a male or a female.
Both will become equally tame and—according to their ability—will learn to speak, imitate sounds, or whistle tunes.

The African gray parrot has caught sight of "its" human.

serves for taking in food, for defense, and as a third "foot" for climbing.

Cere: This is the fleshy or waxlike swelling at the base of the upper part of the beak.

Toes: Of the four long toes, which are furnished with sturdy claws, the two middle ones face forward, the two outer ones backward. Thus the parrot's foot is especially well adapted for climbing and for grasping its food. Not all parrot species, however, use their foot to clutch food tightly.

Plumage: Many parrots have splendidly colored plumage, especially most of the macaws. The varying tones of green of the Amazons' feathers are interrupted by striking blue, yellow, or red areas. The African gray parrots draw attention with beautiful white markings and their luminous red tail. Countless other examples could be given.

The colors of the plumage serve as camouflage. In the tips of sunshine-flooded trees in the tropics, for example, green parrots with yellow accents look like leaves that are reflecting the sun. The colorfully marked areas of the plumage also play an important role in courtship and the communal life of the flock (see Courtship and Mating, page 61).

Common Characteristics

They are wasters: Parrots' carelessness with food originates in their life in the wild. Usually the supply of food is abundant in nature. This "extravagance" is easily seen in parrots

Its posture reveals what it wants . . .   *. . . and that's to be scratched.*

that subsist mainly on fruit. Usually they eat only certain parts of the fruit, for example, the seeds or the juice. The rest they carelessly drop.

Loyalty and affection: Parrots form a strong attachment to a member of the opposite sex, often when young, and retain this loyalty for the rest of their lives. Thus they are monogamous (see Monogamy, page 59). When one parrot is kept alone, it bonds so closely to "its" human that a separation may cause serious psychological disturbances, even death. Whenever a firmly bonded pair is separated—for example, if one bird is sold—both birds grieve and often pine away to an early death.

Life expectancy: Unfortunately there are no precise statistics on the life expectancy of parrots in the wild. It is known, however, that parrots in zoos or in human captivity have lived to be very old. Many Amazons and African gray parrots have reached an age of 40 to 50 years; a bare-eyed cockatoo and a great sulphur-crested cockatoo lived to be 80 years old. Smaller parrots are said to have a life expectancy of 20 to 30 years, and the little parrotlets live about 18 years.

Behavior and character: Even in captivity, parrots display their lovable, peaceable natures and their great ability to express themselves. When the contrary is reported of a parrot, you may be certain that this animal has had harsh treatment or has suffered separation from a favorite human or fellow parrot.

About the pictures:
A well-branched climbing tree is very important for parrots. From it they can participate directly in family affairs and use up energy by climbing.

7

*M*ost people think parrots are among the most fascinating birds in the world. As pets, however, they make heavy demands on their keepers. You absolutely must devote at least three hours of your time daily to a parrot that is kept singly, and this has to be quality time.

Intelligence: Parrots are among the most intelligent birds in the world. There are many impressive examples of their good memories, which go back for years. Parrot fanciers report almost incredible tales of their wealth of inventiveness, their reasoning power, and their learning ability. Their love of play, pranks, and stunts and their cunning cleverness demonstrate their intelligence and compensate for many abilities that must remain un-exercised in captivity.

Ability to imitate: Parrots are able to imitate sounds. Many parrots have become true masters of mimicry. They can even associate certain situations with others in terms of their general meaning. The imitation of weeping or laughter, or the pop of a drawn cork or the cat's meowing also has the de-sired effect. The parrot's ability to imi-tate is related both to its keen sense of hearing and to the highly differen-tiated sounds that in the wild enable the entire flock—pairs, parents, and offspring—to live together amicably.

Housemate with Demands

Parrots place great demands on their keepers. You must devote at least three hours daily to a singly kept par-rot and occupy yourself intensively with it. If an older parrot is no longer able to bond to humans or if you sud-denly have less time, the only solution is to provide the bird with a partner of the same species (see page 32). Ideally, you should acquire a young pair that will readily become attached to humans but also maintains its pair bond at the same time.

Things That May Get on Your Nerves

The loud voice: A single bird bonds closely to one or a few humans and simply "showers" its keeper with love. In extreme cases, the parrot will begin to scream piercingly as soon as its "partner" busies him- or herself with something else besides the bird.

Always being there: Along with this vast love comes the bird's wish to be a part of all that goes on and the perpetual request to be scratched.

The mess: Feather dust, shed feathers, and excrement are found wherever the bird is. Its careless deal-ing with food causes plenty of rubbish. You also have to remove the traces of beak activity, which result from the bird's pecking away at cardboard, branches, baskets, and other things.

My tip: If the droppings fall on a smooth surface, remove them immedi-ately with paper towels and wipe the surface down afterward. If the drop-pings fall on textiles or rough sur-faces, let them dry, brush them away, vacuum, and remove any remaining spots with soapsuds.

Destructiveness: The curious par-rot investigates all reachable objects with its beak. Thus it can easily hap-pen that one good piece or another gets broken.

Never-ending childhood: For all its intelligence and learning ability and despite its age, which may already be considerable, mentally the parrot re-mains on the level of a preschool child. The bird will be your child all its life.

Arrangements: A parrot needs fresh fruit, vegetables, and other food daily. During your vacation or absence from home for any other reason, you must always arrange for a responsible caretaker for your parrot.

What to Consider in Making a Decision

1. Are you and your family ready to accept responsibility for a parrot over what is often a long life?

2. Do you have enough room to give the bird the living conditions it requires?

3. Do you have enough time for it?

Male and female black-masked lovebirds do not differ outwardly.

4. A parrot makes a great deal of mess.

5. How will you react if the parrot doesn't learn to talk?

6. What will happen to it if you ever have to be away from home?

7. Are your children still small? If so, the beak of a large parrot could be dangerous to them.

8. Are there other animals living in your household? You can accustom a dog to a parrot, but not a cat. A parrot can be dangerous to small mammals and small birds.

9. Consider that the parrot will cost money.

10. Is anyone in the family allergic to feather dust?

The colors of a parrot's plumage serve as camouflage and also play an important role in courtship and in the communal life of the flock. For instance, in sundrenched treetops, a parrot with areas of green and yellow feathers looks like foliage that is reflecting sunlight.

A black-headed caique in its natural habitat.

Equipment and Purchase

Buy the Cage First
Even before the parrot comes to live with you, its cage must be completely furnished and standing in its permanent spot in your home.

The right cage: The parrot cages available from pet shops measure 16 × 16 × 31 inches (40 × 40 × 80 cm) and are suitable as hospital cages or for the acclimation period. One or two medium-sized parrots such as Amazons need a model 39 to 59 inches (100–150 cm) high, with a surface area of 20 to 39 inches (50 × 100 cm).

Important: Round cages are not suitable.

Bars: The bars should run crosswise on at least two sides of the rectangular cage so that the parrot can climb well. The bars should be spaced at least ½ inch (15 mm) apart, at most 1 inch (25 mm).

The cage door: It must be large enough for a bird sitting on your hand to be taken out or placed inside. The fastening on the door must be "beakproof" or secured by a snap hook.

Bottom pan: It should be made of unbreakable, heat-resistant plastic and have a sand drawer. If there is a floor grating over the sand drawer, it must be removed.

Feeding dishes: The two dishes that usually come with the cage aren't enough, and they are usually too small for the larger parrots. Buy two additional dishes of stainless steel to hang in the cage. These are easiest to clean and they retain their attractive appearance for years.

Perches: Most cages have plastic perches; replace these with natural branches. Natural perches are better for the parrots' feet and the bark provides an excellent source of nutrition and entertainment.

The Indoor Aviary
An indoor aviary is an appropriate and roomy environment for parrots. A wide variety of different designs and sizes are available. You can also assemble individual prefabricated elements to your own design. Your pet dealer will be glad to advise you. Even the roomiest aviary, however, should not be the parrots' only environment. Parrots absolutely must have opportunities for flying free and for personal contact with you.

Location for Cage or Indoor Aviary
Put the cage or indoor aviary in a room where you and possibly your family, too, spend most of your time. A bright, spacious corner of the room, not too near a window but if possible with a view of the outdoors, is the ideal spot. Make sure that the cage or aviary doesn't receive any direct sunlight and is not standing in a draft. Drafts will make parrots sick. The cage must be placed so as to be completely stable, on a special cage stand, a solid table, or a shelf made from a thick board. Fasten the board to the wall at about eye level with a mounting designed for that purpose. The bird wants to be able to look a human in the eye; it becomes uneasy when anything hovers over it.

Food dishes of stainless steel or plastic, with practical mounts for fastening to cage and aviary bars.

Important: The kitchen is completely inappropriate as a permanent location for a cage or aviary. Above all, cooking steam and drafts are very harmful to the health of your parrot.

Practical Tips for Arranging Cage and Aviary

Remove floor grating: The grating over the sand drawer has to be removed. Many species like to "burrow" with their beaks in the sand or the litter (pine bedding, corn cobs). Spread either bird sand or litter in the drawer or line it with absorbent paper.

Provide perches: First, the doweled perches that usually come with the cage should be replaced with natural branches of a similar diameter (see page 11). Notch the branches and attach them securely to the bars of the cage; in addition, tie them on firmly with heavy string. All branches need not be of the same thickness, nor need all run horizontally. The parrot doesn't find "standardized" branches in nature either. Climbing on irregularly shaped branches is good foot exercise.

Important: Most of the branches should be thick enough so that the claws of the bird don't touch when they are grasping a branch.

How many perches? Put up a branch in front of the food bowl so that the parrot can enjoy its food in comfort. A branch placed as high as possible in the cage will serve as a sleeping place, for parrots prefer to sleep on a high lookout. However, the bird should never be bumping against the cage bars when it is in its sleeping place, and there must still be room enough for it to stretch out a wing and a leg or lift its wings. If there is still room between the branches for one or two more, fasten them stepwise halfway up the cage. Please bear in mind

that you don't want to inhibit the bird's freedom of movement with too many perches.

Where to get natural branches: Pet stores sell suitable natural branches. If you want to provide your own, use only fruit-tree branches—which are ideal—and beech, willow, and other branches if they are guaranteed free of pesticides and exhaust gases. Even branches from parks, gardens, or woods must be carefully washed and scrubbed to remove deposits left by acid rain, for example.

Nonpoisonous wood: Hardwoods also suitable for perches are birch, maple, elm, ash, beech, oak, and walnut; for gnawing you can also offer twigs of soft wood from poplar, willow, elder, linden, and chestnut trees.

Filling food dishes: After buying your parrot, before you put it in its cage, fill a food dish with the mixed seed that you've bought with the bird. A second dish will be filled with water; in the third dish put a mixture of carrots, apples, bananas, and a cracked or only slightly cracked walnut. In the fourth bowl put some peppers, Chinese cabbage, spinach, or beets—mince fruits and vegetables coarsely (see page 37).

Toys: The parrot also needs some diversion in its cage or aviary. Branches for gnawing should be available from the very first. Cut twigs into pieces about 8 inches (20 cm) long, bundle them, and hang the bundle from the cage bars so that the bird can reach it from a perch. Items such as a thick hemp rope with knots, large-linked stainless chains, empty spools, a bundle of bark (willow!) strips, empty cardboard tubes, or wooden playthings from the pet store (see How-To: Climbing Tree, page 26) make good toys.

*P*arrots have a pronounced need to exercise and to fly. Living in a cage exclusively is a torture for parrots and sooner or later will result in physical ailments.

Ideally equipped indoor aviary.

Important Facts about Species Protection

oung parrots quickly become tame and bond closely to their human mate substitute if they have no partner of their own species. Love for the human can become so strong that the parrot will start to scream piercingly if "its mate" isn't paying attention to it.

The Washington Endangered Species Convention (CITES) regulates the protection of threatened animal and plant species all over the world. The parrots are included in Appendices I, II, or III, depending on the degree of their need for protection. Parrots that are endangered are listed in Appendix I, and trade is permitted only in exceptional circumstances. Various macaws, for example the hyacinth, the Lear's, the Spix's, the scarlet, and the military, are on this list. Appendix II lists species that could become endangered unless their trade is regulated. In fact, the list is contentious because all parrots not in Appendix I are in Appendix II, except the budgerigar (parakeet) and the cockatiel. They are in Appendix III and may be regarded as in no danger. This also applies to captive-bred birds. You can buy the parrots sold in pet stores without concern so long as the bird is wearing the leg

At ease, the rose-breasted cockatoo preens its feathers.

band prescribed by law (see page 16) and you receive the required CITES certificate (see page 16).

The Difficulty of Choosing. . .
. . . will certainly be spared you, for today hardly anyone can find a large number of parrots to choose from in a pet store. The parrots available commercially mostly come from domestic breeding. If you know which species of parrot you want, your best course is to contact a bird society in your town.

A representative of the society will try to get the desired species from a domestic breeder or give you the name of a breeder to whom you can turn. In some cases this may become a test of your patience, for captive-bred offspring of many species are still rare.

Is the Parrot Healthy?
A healthy parrot exhibits the following characteristics:
- All the feathers are already fully formed, lie smooth, and are not stuck together.
- The feathers around the cloaca—which is the term for the anus of a bird—are not smeared with feces.
- The eyes and nostrils do not secrete any fluid and are not encrusted.
- The horny scales on the feet lie smooth.
- Two toes on each foot point frontwards, two backwards; none are missing; all have claws. (A missing claw or even a toe would be only a blemish, not necessarily a sign of illness.)
- The droppings consist of a dark and a white excrement and are medium firm.
- A healthy parrot shows interest in its surroundings, preens its feathers, eats, drinks, or sleeps while resting on one leg.

All alert, the rose-breasted cockatoo observes what's going on.

A sick parrot gazes indifferently straight ahead, has ruffled feathers, or sleeps resting on both legs. The droppings can be watery, reddish in color, or even foamy. Bare spots on the body can indicate feather plucking, but they are still not proof that the parrot is a slave to this bad habit. In this case you should discuss the situation with your avian veterinarian, who will give you the facts.

15

Young Is Better Than Old

It's better to buy a young parrot, because it will quickly become friendly. The age of a bird bred in captivity is known. Young birds raised by hand are usually already used to people and bond closely with them. Parrots that have been fed in the parents' nesting box must gradually get accustomed to people first. If a young bird has already bonded to a mate of the same age, the pair should not be separated under any circumstances. Getting such a pair would be a piece of luck for you. The young birds can easily accustom themselves to life in human society, become tame, and still have a partner of their own species.

What Sex?

It is completely unimportant whether you choose a male or a female. You can even put together birds of the same sex without any concern, if they get along well together. The gender plays a decisive role only in breeding. Very few parrot species can be sexed by means of external characteristics (see Popular Parrot Species, page 64). As a rule the sex of a parrot can only be established by endoscopy, an invasive procedure.

The Formalities of Purchase

The CITES certificate: As the owner of a parrot belonging to an endangered species you must show proof of legitimate ownership. The so-called CITES certificate, a quasi identification card, fulfills this requirement. The papers are filled out and given to you when you purchase the bird. You should not buy or sell any parrot without this document and without the official leg band. For more information, contact the American Federation of Aviculture (AFA), Box 56218, Phoenix, AZ 85079-6218.

The leg band: According to law, each parrot from an approved, officially supervised quarantine station or breeding operation must, at a certain age, receive the prescribed leg band. Today, of course, psittacosis (see page 49) is no longer a serious danger, but the authorities still want to be sure that the quarantine period (30 days) has been observed according to the law. To permit the origin of sick birds to be traced if the need arises, all parrots and parakeets receive a metal leg band. Unfortunately, the leg band can be removed legally only if it causes injury to the bird. For example, many parrots get the band caught on something, try to free themselves by tearing at it, and thus injure their foot. If the foot then swells, the band cuts off the blood circulation and can result in the loss of the foot. Therefore you should continually monitor the banded leg in order to notice any changes immediately. If necessary, have the band removed by a veterinarian, have the need for this procedure vouched for in writing, and safely store the band. It constitutes a record.

The purchase agreement: Today it is routine in every well-managed pet store for the buyer to be presented with a detailed purchase agreement. This contract should indicate the following: The date of purchase, species or subspecies of the bird, sales price, and addresses of the buyer and the seller. The sex of the bird also should be noted. If an exchange, loan, breeding associations, or gift is involved, there should be an agreement in writing with the details covered as specifically as in a purchase agreement.

A thick, knotted cord hanging from the cage will be used by many parrots for climbing and also for working with their beaks.

The more occupation the free perch offers, the more it will be used.

Cautious Acclimation

alking frequently with the parrot promotes the bird's trust and ability to speak. It learns to know your voice and may in time try to imitate short sentences.

After buying your parrot, bring it home the shortest way, preferably in a transport container. Make sure that the bird is protected from heat, cold, and damp. At home, the cage that has been prepared ahead of time must be standing ready for your parrot, food and water dishes filled.

The First Hours at Home

First step: Hold the opened transport box in front of the open cage door so that only one way is open to the bird. It will certainly move from the darkness to the light and climb into its cage. Once it is inside, immediately shut the door and withdraw. It's best to leave the parrot alone for the next few hours so that it can become familiar with the equipment in the cage without being disturbed. Besides, the bird first must get over its being caught in the pet store or by the

Once the parrot has learned to climb onto the stick, it can be transported without difficulty.

breeder, the transport, and the change of environment: These terrifying experiences cause the parrot tremendous emotional stress.

Second step: A few hours later or the next day, sit down near the cage, some distance from the bird but in sight. Speak softly and reassuringly to the parrot. Use only short sentences, calling it by name often. Always speak or whistle when approaching the bird, because birds are mistrustful of silent creatures.

The First Days with the Parrot

Probably the first few days will be marked by caution on both sides. You don't want to frighten your parrot in any way or make it anxious, and it wants to keep as much distance between it and you as possible. Still, you must reach into the cage twice daily to provide fresh foot and clean the cage. A good way to lessen these terrors for the bird is to be absolutely punctual. If you always carry out routine procedures at the same time, they soon become part of the inevitable course of the day for the bird.

Cage chores: In the morning and afternoon, remove the food and water dishes from the cage and put them back freshly filled. Every morning, using a spoon designated for that purpose only, take out the droppings on the cage floor and spread some fresh sand or bedding, or change the paper. Talk with the bird during the entire procedure. Avoid hasty movements, even if the bird tries to peck at you. In that case, incidentally, you should react immediately with a quiet but firm

"No, no." In time the bird will understand that "No, no" entails a taboo.

"Go-getter" or "scaredy-cat": Once your parrot has overcome the worst of the stress, it will busy itself with the cage, testing out all the perches and beginning to gnaw on branches. Soon you'll be able to tell from its reactions whether you've gotten a lively "go-getter" or a distraught bundle of anxieties. If the parrot tries to nip you while you're tidying up the cage, it's just a "go-getter" trying to catch you. On the other hand, the "scaredy-cat" avoids you as well as it can but bites when it feels threatened. The first time your parrot raises its voice loud and long, it may be a protest against being left alone or fear for its life. The "go-getter" keeps on screaming with all its might when you speak to it. The "scaredy-cat" falls anxiously silent when it hears your voice.

Note: You can stop loud cries of protest by laying a cloth over the cage for a few minutes. Surprised, the bird will be quiet and soon will understand that the cloth appears only when it screams loudly.

Undisturbed Nights

In nature, parrots seek out their resting places and begin their night's rest when darkness falls. In captivity, the parrot may be quite lively under electric light, or become sleepy in spite of the light when its internal clock announces "sleep time." If the parrot wants to sleep, it withdraws to its favorite sleeping spot and pays no more attention to the goings on around it. Even television, music, or conversation hardly disturb it if it needn't look directly at a nearby TV screen, if all noise is somewhat subdued, and if no very bright light shines directly on it.

In a comfortable resting posture, the beak is tucked into the back feathers. When sleeping, the parrot usually draws one leg up into the belly feathers.

Please bear in mind:
• Before you turn off the light, make sure the parrot is sitting on its sleeping perch. It can't find the perch in the dark and will climb restlessly about the cage or even flutter, which could result in injury.
• If street lights shine too brightly into the room or car headlights could frighten the bird, darken the room with curtains or shades; otherwise, the bird won't be able to rest.
• In a completely dark room, however, it's better to leave a dim light burning so that the parrot can orient itself if it wakes during the night and is frightened by something.

The First Weeks with the Parrot

If the first few days with the new family member pass without extreme excitement, the bird will soon curiously observe what's going on around it. No one can say how much time it will take for the parrot to get used to living with you. Sometimes a few days are enough, sometimes it takes several weeks. Try to avoid anything that

About the pictures:
Friendship between cat and parrot is extraordinary. When you have a parrot, there should be no cats living in your home. In normal circumstances the two don't get along with each other, and an encounter can end fatally for the parrot.

When accustomed to each other from an early age . . .

could shake the trust of the parrot and make it anxious.

To foster trust:
• Speak with your parrot as often as possible. While doing so, call it by name and sing or whistle little melodies to it. Perhaps it will try to imitate you someday.
• Avoid disturbances and hurried movements in the parrot's vicinity. Loud slamming of doors, barking dogs, or noisy housework make it anxious.
• Don't come near the cage with unusual, striking objects, for example, a big, black hat, curlers in your hair, or an open umbrella.
• Place unfamiliar objects with which the parrot soon will become acquainted near the cage in the bird's

sight for a while—for instance, the spray bottle from which it soon will have its first shower bath (see page 28). If the bird already knows such objects by sight, it won't react with panic when they are employed.

Exercise and Occupation
Your parrot must be patient about flying, because it is better that it stay in the cage until it is hand tame. Nevertheless, it may beat its wings powerfully while sitting on its perch. Naturally this causes dust and noise, but it is good for the bird. This way it trains its flying muscles and compensates for the lack of opportunity to exercise. Keep the bird busy by bringing it fresh twigs (see page 12) to gnaw daily. The nutrients it gets from

. even cat and parrot can become friends.

gnawing on the bark promote good health.

Hand-taming

"You catch more flies with honey than with vinegar," goes the well-known saying. You can make your parrot hand-tame in a similar way. First observe which fruits and vegetables it chooses from its food bowls. Then offer it these treats in your hand from outside the cage, through the bars. You may also give the bird a little piece of bread crust, some white bread, a dry cookie, or a tiny piece of hard cheese. Large parrots get bigger pieces, small parrots only small ones. This way your parrot learns that your hand brings it good things. With some parrots, however, it may take weeks before they dare to take something from your hand. Then you attempt the next step. Using a small twig, try to scratch it very gently on the neck, against the lie of the feathers, through the cage bars. Try scratching the bird as often as possible, until it willingly holds still and visibly enjoys the sensation. Further hand contacts should follow only when your parrot is no longer spending all its time in the cage (see The First Flight, page 22).

Offer your parrot treats such as a dry cookie or a little piece of white bread on your hand. This way the parrot will become hand-tame eventually.

21

Life with a Parrot

Once your parrot has overcome its fear of your hand and no longer huddles anxiously in a corner of the cage when you approach, you may prepare for its first outing.

Preparing for the First Outing
At the beginning it's enough if during its first outing your parrot only gets thoroughly familiar with the room where its cage is located.

Remove hazards: Even before you open the cage door, you should make the room "birdproof." You can find out what things might be dangerous for a parrot outside its cage from the table on page 35.

Close the windows: Make sure ahead of time that all windows and doors in the room are closed. Even "cracked" windows must be closed, because they won't keep a parrot from escaping.

Draw the curtains: Pull the curtains or blinds over the windows. A parrot doesn't recognize the clear windowpane as a spatial boundary. It can bang against the glass with such force that it drops to the ground unconscious or with a broken neck. If you have no blinds or curtains, pull the shutters or jalousies down, leaving about 12 inches (30 cm) of the window uncovered and, if necessary, turn on the lights in the room. Then increase the uncovered window surface a little bit more each day until the bird has perceived the window as a boundary. This usually takes only a few days.

Offered damp leaves in a large, shallow dish, some parrots enjoy using them to take a "dew" bath.

The First Flight
When the cage door is open, sit down a little distance away and observe your parrot. At some point it will dare to leave the cage and take off from the cage roof or the door opening. Then it depends on where it can make a good landing. If it flies to the climbing tree (see How-To, pages 26–27) or to the cage roof again, you need do nothing. The bird will climb into the cage again, investigate the bird tree, or start on the next circuit. If it lands on a high vantage point such as a lamp, a cabinet, or a curtain rod, it won't soon want to leave the security of its place. If it lands on the floor, however, it's a different matter. From this perspective everything is above it, and this makes a parrot anxious.

Note: Parrots whose wings are clipped (see page 25) cannot fly. Either they flutter to the floor during their first flight or they leave the cage climbing. Once on the floor they can no longer fly up. Therefore try to get the bird to climb on a stick and carry it to the cage or the climbing tree.

Back into the cage: Take the stick and hold it out to the bird with your arm outstretched so that there is a substantial distance between you and it. It may climb onto the stick immediately because it offers a perch. If not, place the stick in front of the bird at an angle so that the wood gently touches its underbelly. Press the stick gently against the bird, and this will probably induce it to climb on. If your parrot has found a high lookout as a landing place, let it sit there for a while. If it doesn't come down on its own after an hour, try the trick with

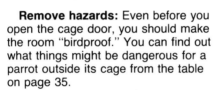

22

the stick. If that doesn't work, let the bird sit there, even overnight if necessary. Eventually it will get hungry and make its way back into the cage by itself.

Absolutely to be avoided: Don't chase the bird now. That could destroy the trust you've already gained.

Important: Practice the stick-climbing procedure daily from now on. If the stick is a commonplace object for the parrot, the bird can even be quickly transported on it, if necessary.

The Greatest Danger: Escape

Every escaped parrot is in extreme danger. Depending on the time of year, the birds find no food or unwholesome food outdoors or they fall victim to predatory birds. If you discover at once that your parrot has escaped, there's still a chance to find it nearby on a tree or a bush. You can then try to lure it back into the cage with flattery, a treat, or—in the best of cases—its avian partner. If that doesn't work, and there's a garden hose handy, spray the parrot with a gentle stream of water until it is so wet that it can't fly and allows itself to be caught. These methods are not guaranteed to be successful, however.

Therefore, my advice is: Have at least one window in the bird's room fitted with a spot-welded screen of ½ × ½ inch (13 × 13 mm) mesh for smaller species, 1 × 1 inch (25 × 25 mm) for larger ones. This way the room can be aired at any time, and in good weather the window may remain open for hours at a time.

Training

After your parrot has gotten somewhat familiar with the environment outside its cage, to a large extent let it decide

for itself whether it wants to stay in the cage or sit on a free-standing perch. With its beak, it thoroughly investigates everything that looks interesting, and it will certainly gnaw on wallpaper, books, wires, rugs, house plants, or anything else to find out what they are like. Small objects that capture the parrot's fancy will be transported into its territory in its beak. All these are grounds for not leaving the bird alone outside its cage without supervision for the time being. Still, you should allow it these explorations under your supervision as often as possible. This is the only way the bird can really get to feel at home in your house. It's best to try to stop behaviors that can endanger the parrot or the furnishings with "No, no." If this still has no effect, use the stick to immediately put the bird in the cage for about 10 minutes. It quickly will grasp the connection and gradually will avoid forbidden things. Not all bad habits are curable, however.

Let It Come!

It's best to keep yourself completely detached when the parrot comes near

When your hand is accepted as a place to sit and is gently nibbled, great confidence exists.

23

you. Speak to it, but don't touch it. If the bird bends its head before you with softly fluffed-out feathers, this is an invitation to scratch. Accept the offer. The time of greatest trust has arrived when one day the parrot plucks at your arm, gently nibbles your hand, or climbs over your arm to your shoulder. From then on you may stroke it too or scratch it in hitherto unaccustomed spots.

The Sharp Beak

Sometimes it happens: Your parrot pecks at you and catches you painfully with its beak. The causes of this "crime" are uncertainty, anxiety, or a sensitivity. In scratching, for instance, you can sometimes touch an in-growing feather quill so clumsily that it hurts the parrot, which instinctively protects itself by biting. With increasing familiarity, however, it only nips or bites for fun, because it looks forward to the "Ow-ow" cry or enjoys your fright or because it wants to "punish" you. You'll notice that the pecks are only symbolic in that case; they very seldom wound painfully. Some parrots simply take fiendish pleasure in nipping strangers. The lovable Amazon male Jo-jo first says "Ow, ow" before he bites and immediately begins to weep heartbreakingly. Don't become annoyed with the parrot for nipping or pecking; take it as a joke that unfortunately hurts sometimes.

Important: Small children and strangers should not be permitted close contact with the parrot. Children

Goffin's cockatoos skillfully use small objects for their activities.

can easily be injured by the parrot. Also, it has no inhibitions about using its beak on strangers.

Wing Clipping, Yes or No?

Small parrot species: First, a clear *no* to wing clipping for all small species, which fly skillfully and nimbly, gladly and often. Examples of these are Senegal parrots and Meyer's parrots, lovebirds, parrotlets, and caiques. The *no* also applies to all parrots that are kept in an aviary flight in the hope of breeding them.

Large parrot species: Although well-acclimated large parrots rarely fly extensively in the house, birds capable of flying enjoy the opportunity to do so now and then. Especially charming are flights from room to room or floor to floor. Because you can't arrange a large apartment or an entire house to be absolutely "bird-proof," flying involves great dangers for parrots (see Table of Hazards, page 35). As contrary to nature as it may be to make a parrot unable to fly by clipping its feathers, this may actually be a blessing for a pet bird. A parrot that can't fly can still, for example, climb about in the yard under supervision, go for walks on the shoulder of its owner, and sit on a terrace or balcony on a free-standing perch. Besides, it needn't spend nearly so much time in the cage, because it can get into less trouble than a flying bird.

Cockatoo on the high wire.

My tip: If the bird is left on the terrace or balcony without supervision, it can still escape by fluttering over the railing. Even on the ground floor there are dangers that threaten it (cats, dogs, traffic). If it flutters down from a higher floor, the fall can be fatal. Consequently, stretch a cat net (available in pet stores) in front of the railing.

About the picture: *This cockatoo performs its acrobatic trip on the high wire almost every day at the top of the circus tent. Many pet parrots also enjoy learning little acrobatic stunts. For one thing, it makes a change for them, for another it gets them attention.*

How-To: Climbing Tree

Climbing tree and free-standing perch

No cage, no aviary can be a permanent location for a parrot. It needs to fly every day and to satisfy its curiosity outside the cage. To give the parrot a resting place in the room and opportunities to land and occupy itself, it needs a climbing tree or a free-standing perch. In the ideal situation, a climbing tree or free-standing perch already will have been in the room for some time so that the parrot knows it by sight.

The climbing tree
Drawing 1

If you're handy with tools, you can build a climbing tree yourself. You need a strong limb, branched if possible. Get a large wooden tub and a sturdy Christmas tree stand. Put the stand in the tub. Anchor the branch firmly with the screws of the Christmas tree stand. Weight the tub with heavy stones to keep it from tipping. Put a layer of pebbles over them, a layer of soil over that, and on top of it all a layer of bird sand. To make a properly branching climbing tree, additional perches made of natural wood (see page 12) may be fastened in the tree. Like the perches in the cage, the perches in the climbing tree must be replaced from time to

time, because parrots gnaw the branches extensively. For smaller parrots it's enough if you introduce items such as mirrors, bells, a wooden toy with lava stone (from the pet shop), or a bundle of twigs (pieces 8 inches [20 cm] long). Large parrots also receive a small basket made of woven fibers (in their natural state, no dyes or paints) in which the bird can always find fruits and vegetables, and two feeding bowls. Put seed (see Basic Feed,

page 37) in one bowl, fresh water in the other.

The free-standing perch
Drawing 2

If you can't or don't wish to build your own, fall back on the offerings of the pet store and buy a free-standing perch for parrots. Attach this perch to the cage roof. Expand the perching and climbing possibilities with additional natural branches, ladders, and boards, so that various planes are created. For fastening, use heavy string that you've dampened before tying. That way the joints will be good and strong. Replace the natural branches if the parrot has gnawed them heavily. "Furnish" the free-standing perch the same way I've described for the climbing tree.

The proper place for the climbing tree or free-standing perch

For large parrots like Amazons, gray parrots, or cockatoos, place the climbing tree or free-standing perch so close to the cage that the bird can reach it by climbing out of its cage. For smaller species like parrotlets,

1 Climbing tree for parrots. With some handyman's skill you can make one yourself. If the branch doesn't extend over the edge of the tub, everything that falls to the ground will land in the sand of the tub and can easily be removed.

lovebirds, a Senegal parrot, or a Meyer's parrot, put the bird tree or free-standing perch in another corner of the room, because the small parrots love to fly. Offer them no food whatsoever on the climbing tree or free perch, but only things to keep them occupied, so that they always will have to fly to the cage if they want to eat or drink. The location of the free perch or climbing tree must meet the following specifications:

- Draft-free;
- No direct sunlight, but bright and if possible with a view out the window;
- One wall should offer rear cover. It's best to place the climbing tree in a bright corner that provides cover on two sides. Protected areas can also be created by suitable houseplants.

Plants in the bird room

Even if your parrot remains outside its cage all day long, you don't have to do without house plants in the bird's room. House plants create a homey atmosphere for the parrot and can allow it privacy or rear cover. However, it should not be able to reach the plants or they will be victims of its beak and won't live long. This is somewhat difficult, because birds able to fly can also reach plants even if they're placed in high, smooth-sided stone pedestals, which a parrot cannot climb. Therefore it's all the more important to banish poisonous plants from the bird room. If you use plants, choose only fast-growing, inexpensive ones that are easy to replace.

2 Free-standing perch for parrots. This free-standing perch is one you can buy. However, it is somewhat scantily furnished. You can quickly provide more perching places for the parrot with a few natural branches. If you also add a small basket of untreated fiber with fresh vegetables in it, the parrot always has healthy "snacks" at its disposal.

Poisonous house plants: Chinese primrose, nux vomica tree (*Strychnos nux-vomica*), periwinkle (*Catharanthus*), crown-of-thorns, all *Dieffenbachia* species, yew, hyacinth, myrtle (*Vinca minor*), all members of the nightshade family—for example, Jerusalem cherry—Madagascar palm (*Pachypodium*), narcissus, oleander, berries of the spicebush (*Ardisia*), poinsettia, garden croton (*Codiaeum variegatum*), desert rose, berries of the ornamental asparagus.

The following plants are not poisonous, but they contain substances that irritate the mucous membranes and can cause injury to a parrot: Ivy, monstera, flamingo flower, golden trumpet, aglaonema, philodendron, schefflera. Use *caution* with all cactus and plants with thorny parts; the bird can injure its eyes on the thorns.

27

How to Clip Wings

Shorten six to eight feathers of the secondary and primary flight feathers by clipping every second one, beginning with the second from the end. Using scissors, cut off these feathers about ¾ to 1 inch (2 to 3 cm) above the quill (see drawings at left). There is also another method of clipping, which you can see in the upper drawing. Make very sure that the feathers are completely grown out and are no longer sticking in the "blood shaft." As long as blood can be found in the shaft, the blood feathers, as they are called, are still growing and are being supplied with nutrients from the bloodstream. If a blood feather is injured, the result is unnecessary pain and loss of blood.

My tip: If you've never clipped a parrot's wings, have your avian veterinarian or an experienced aviculturist show you how it's done before you try it yourself.

Important: Always clip both wings in the manner described, never just one. With both wings clipped, the bird can still flutter to the floor without danger or get to safety from pursuers by beating its wings. If only one wing is clipped, the bird will lose its balance when fluttering and can have dangerous falls. The shortened feathers grow back over the course of weeks or months. You have to monitor their growth, because one day your parrot will be able to fly again. The danger of escape would then be doubled, because precautionary measures were no longer being taken.

Required Humidity

Parrots come almost exclusively from climatic regions with high humidity. The humidity provides for the waxy gloss of the feathers and makes the plumage glisten. The dry air in our homes and the completely different

Clipping wings: In the upper drawing the secondaries and the inner primaries are shortened on both wings. The lower drawing shows a different method of clipping. Here every second one of the primary and secondary feathers on both wings is clipped.

climatic conditions make parrots' plumage dull. The dust of the powder down produces itching and causes the bird to fidget more. Only sufficiently frequent dampening can maintain the health and beauty of the plumage and promote the well-being of the bird. At least twice a week you should provide your bird with a lukewarm bath or shower.

A bath for small species: Many small parrots dip their belly, head, and both wings alternatively in water with joyous excitement. If the birds are tame, you can offer them a large clay flower pot saucer of lukewarm water outside the cage. They can better spread their wings in this than in a little bathhouse. If the saucer isn't adequate for the larger small species, provide a rectangular plastic dish, such as a cat pan or the drawer of a hamster cage.

The shower bath for large parrots: Most large parrots don't bathe but enjoy a lukewarm shower from a plant mister. If you're spraying your parrot for the first time, stay about 2 yards (2 m) away and just spray it gently at first. You'll quickly be able to tell from the bird's reaction whether the bath gives it pleasure or is irritating to it.

If it trys to avoid the spray and retreats to the farthest branch, the bath isn't welcome at the moment. If the bird extends its wings, however, and turns and twists so that the water reaches all possible areas of its body, the bath is already overdue. The bird must not become wet through; there should be only a fine film of water on the feathers.

Many love a dew bath: Regardless of their size, many parrots love a bath in damp weeds or leaves. This preference certainly goes back to the way of life of parrots in the wild. Early in the morning they search for food in the

A *climbing tree for stays outside the cage is essential for parrots. It offers a change from life in the cage and lets the parrot practice its climbing skills.*

This parrot loves to use this sturdy climbing tree

dewy grass, and while doing so they dampen their feathers. If you fasten a bundle of still-damp weeds (see page 39) to the roof of the cage, for instance with a wooden clothespin, they will energetically try to dampen themselves with it. Their pleasure will be still greater if you offer them a large shallow dish of wet leaves so that they can wallow around in it (see drawing, page 22).

My tip: Don't use leaves of green head lettuce for the dew bath. It has been sprayed to kill insects and prevent rapid wilting. These chemicals are soluble in water and can harm the bird.

Important: Never use a plant mister that has come into contact with any plant-protective agents. After every bath provide an even temperature without the slightest draft!

Care Plan

Daily

Remove all leftover food and droppings from the cage floor and from the floor around the free-standing perch. It's best to spread a sheet of washable plastic on the floor underneath the free-standing perch. Cover the bottom of the cage with fresh sand, litter, or clean paper.

Wipe off dirty branches with a damp cloth, rubbing them with sandpaper first, if necessary.

Empty all bowls, wash with hot water, dry, and refill.

In the afternoon, check to see if there's still enough seed and water in the bowls and refill if necessary.

Weekly

Wash bottom pan and sand drawer with hot water and rub dry.

Wash any toys in the cage or climbing tree—mirrors, bells, and such—with hot water and dry.

Monthly

Empty the cage and with its bottom pan removed wash it in the bathtub in hot water and rub dry.

Replace gnawed branches in the cage and on the climbing tree with fresh ones, washed in hot water and dried well.

Perches of natural wood must be replaced from time to time.

Important: Do not use any dishwashing or cleaning materials, because they are poisonous to the bird. Hot water is completely satisfactory and is harmless.

Everyday Parrot Life

Preening: In the course of a day the parrot draws every single feather through its beak in order to smooth it and remove all dust. With its beak it keeps removing a little oil from the preen gland at the base of the tail and applies it to the feathers while preening so that they become water-resistant and shiny. This persistent preening continues at intervals throughout the day and is performed, with interruptions, for 20 to 30 minutes at a time.

Food intake: When it wakes in the morning the parrot needs to eat and drink at once, because after the long night the bird needs energy. You should make sure the parrot finds seed on hand in the morning—at daybreak if it is in an undarkened room—even if you don't get up before it does. When you later bring the day's ration of fresh fruits and vegetables, it will certainly examine the offering curiously and taste some here and there. During the day the bird goes to the food dishes often and eats something, but it usually feeds extensively in the mornings and in late afternoon.

Beak activity: The more suitable material you place at your parrot's disposal, the less it will attack the furniture. Besides fruit, vegetables, and fresh branches daily—in spring with young buds and leaves on them—you can also offer it cat grass or weeds and chickweed you've sown yourself in flowerpots (see Diet, page 41). Nuts should be cracked enough so that the bird is successful when it tries to open them; otherwise it will drop them carelessly. Large parrots like to work on a dog bone of buffalo hide, empty wooden thread spools, or a piece of wood, soft or hard, depending on the strength of the beak. All parrots love to destroy baskets, large and small, and tear up postcards or empty paper towel tubes.

Rest periods: All day long parrots interpolate rest periods into all activities, during which some really sleep, with their beak tucked into the back feathers, usually resting on one leg, or they doze a little with eyes half open.

The dreaded screaming: A contented parrot won't allow the full strength of its voice to be heard very often once it has become domesticated. Nevertheless, sometimes it may utter jungle screams, usually when it wants something or feels neglected. If you can't find out why your parrot is screaming so murderously and the noise gets on your nerves, cover the cage with a cloth until the bird grows quiet. If it isn't in the cage, usually a little talk with the parrot, a round of scratching, or a treat will help.

Parrots Are Smart

Parrots are indisputably among the most intelligent birds in the world. The smartest parrots include the cockatoos, macaws, Amazons, and African gray parrots. Almost all parrots learn to imitate all kinds of sounds and to overcome the circumstances of their environment somewhat, and many also show evidence of discerning action and intelligent individual initiative. The parrots' good memory alone may be interpreted as proof of intelligence. The ornithologist von Lucanus kept an African gray parrot and also had a tame hoopoe, which was called Höpfchen by its owner and by the parrot. When Höpfchen died, nothing more was said about the bird. After nine years von Lucanus again got a hoopoe. When the African gray parrot saw this bird for the first time, it cried excitedly, "Höpfchen, Höpfchen."

Pleasure in tricks: Many domesticated parrots enjoy learning little tricks

When cockatoos preen they often apply a small branch to their head with their foot so they can give the feathers a more thorough working over. Employing a tool for this activity again demonstrates the intelligence of this bird.

31

and thus generating excitement. I saw an example of this years ago with a pair of Meyer's parrots belonging to friends. Every time the dinner table was set, the small parrot got a little bell out of the cage. It held it in his beak by a chain, flew to the lamp over the dinner table, hung there head down from the lampshade, and rang the little bell until all the family members were gathered around the table.

Parrot Speech

Parrots have a characteristic vocal communication system that is understood only by other parrots. Still, you can soon interpret some sounds clearly, for the parrot's repertoire of sounds also serves to express its moods even when it is a house pet. It can growl with contentment, hiss excitedly, crunch its beak in relaxation, and utter soft sounds as well as screams. In general these natural sounds are mixed with those that the parrot hears often in its environment and imitates. Parrots are known to mimic the meowing of a cat, the barking of a dog, the crying of a baby, and many other sounds. Parrots do more than mimic sounds, however; they also learn to say words and short sentences. Usually they begin with expressions that go with certain recurring situations. These could include the "Hello" on the telephone, the good night and good morning greetings, names that are often called, frequently spoken curses, or short phrases. Because such expressions are always used in particular situations, the parrot naturally says them at the appropriate moments. For example, I always say to Moses, "I'll be back soon," when I leave the room. When I stood up to leave today, Moses said immediately, "Come back soon"; the parrot never has picked up the "I'll."

According to parrot experts, the parrots most capable of speaking are, in order of their proficiency, the African gray parrot, yellow-naped Amazon, yellow-fronted Amazon, blue-fronted Amazon, and some cockatoos. Even if your parrot doesn't learn to speak, but instead whistles melodies it has heard or imitates sounds, don't be disappointed.

How to Encourage Speaking

If you want your parrot to speak, you should speak with it often, clearly, and slowly. It's best if you always say the same phrases when you bring the bird something to eat, when you go away, and when you come back again. Accompany tasks that you carry out in sight of the bird with little commentaries. You'll soon hear how much of this your parrot takes in and when he repeats it. Naturally the parrot pays the greatest attention to your words when it isn't distracted by anything. If it turns out that your parrot has no talent for speaking, try whistling or singing. Many parrots listen attentively to a song, sung or whistled, and immediately try to imitate at least some tones.

Getting Two Parrots Used to Each Other

Often older parrots are no longer able to get used to a human. It can also happen that you suddenly have considerably less time for your single parrot than you used to. The best way out of the dilemma is to get a second parrot as company for the first one.

What To Do?

Of course, it's ideal to get a parrot of the same species as a partner for your parrot, but a parrot of a different species and approximately the same size could also be a possibility. Go to the pet dealer from whom you bought the parrot or directly to a breeder. Even if the kind of parrot you want really is available, don't under any circumstances buy it right away. It is entirely possible that the two birds won't be compatible. Try to make an arrangement with the dealer or breeder that will allow you to find out whether the two parrots get along. A responsible pet dealer or breeder will allow you this opportunity.

This blue-fronted Amazon is on the hunt for a suitable nesting hole.

The Moment Has Arrived

At first, you absolutely must have a second cage (bought or borrowed) for the new arrival. Place both cages, each containing a parrot, next to each other. Both cage doors should remain closed. The birds can now see and hear each other without coming into direct contact. The next day you may let your parrot out of its cage again.

Now you can observe the reaction of your bird to the newcomer more clearly than before. Does it ignore the new bird or does it keep approaching the other cage? Does it initiate voice contact or does it try to touch the new parrot through the bars of the cage? As soon as the new arrival has gotten over the change of environment and seems calm, you may also allow it the freedom of the room. Please observe all the precautions that you had to take with the first outing of your own parrot (see Preparing for the First Outing, page 22). The birds are now sure to approach each other, cautiously at first. The new arrival is at a disadvantage in any case. Wherever it goes, it is in the established territory of your parrot. Now much depends on the nature of your parrot. If there is actually fighting, interfere by having your parrot climb onto the stick and removing it. If the other bird flies after it, let them both go at it again. Small disagreements are necessary for them to get to know each other.

If there is no aggression at all and the two birds sit side by side and scratch each other, it's all set. The birds can now be housed together in one spacious indoor aviary (see page 11). Keep monitoring the new pair for a while before you leave the parrots alone together for any length of time. Under no circumstances should it become established behavior for one to chase the other, bite it, or constantly drive it away from the food dish. If this situation does occur, you must return the new arrival.

What to Do with the Parrot When...

You want to travel or have to go to the hospital unexpectedly. You need to think about this problem ahead of time, even if it isn't at all likely, because it isn't so easy to find a good bird-sitter. The following solutions are possibilities:

At home in its own familiar environment, the parrot naturally feels best. Then, however, a reliable person must substitute for you and live in your home while you are away.

Boarding the bird, perhaps with friends or relatives, is also a possibility, but you then must transport not only the parrot but also its equipment. The bird needs some familiar things, especially its cage and free-standing perch, to be able to settle into the strange environment.

Important: In both cases your parrot should get to know the bird-sitter ahead of time and also like him or her. Besides precise instructions for daily care, you must also provide food and give the sitter money for fresh food.

My tip: Bird clubs, veterinarians, and animal shelters will provide addresses of bird lovers who regularly take care of birds.

Pet store dealers will sometimes take care of a parrot for a fee. There, of course, the bird has no personal attention and may not fly, but the store offers your parrot plenty of variety on weekdays. Find out what arrangements are made for care in case the store is closed during the weekend.

Traveling with the bird: This works only when you have a large car and are not going abroad, because import regulations in all countries forbid entry to parrots. In the car, drafts should be prevented during the journey. In a hotel or motel, the parrot must always remain in its cage for safety, because the personnel will not pay attention to closed doors and windows while cleaning. A tent is unreasonable for a parrot; on the other hand, the bird can be comfortable in a vacation house.

Hazards for a Parrot

Hazards

Bathroom: Flying away through partly open window, drowning in open toilet.

Open doors: Used as perching place; pinching of feet can occur when door is being shut.

Floor: If the bird is playing on the floor, it may be killed by being stepped on.

Containers of water: Birds slip into a basin, bowl, large glass, or vase and drown (soapsuds look like solid surface).

Cupboards, open drawers: Unnoticed, the bird is closed in and suffocates or dies of hunger.

Poisons: Fatal poisoning possible from alcohol, lead, pencil points, felt-tips, strong spices, verdigris, adhesives, varnishes, glues, solvents, plant fertilizers, plastic wrap, cleaning agents, mercury, strong-smelling sprays, detergents, strong cigarette smoke.

Heating elements: Fatal burns from landing on hot stove elements.

Candle flames: Fatal burns from flying through the flames.

Wastepaper baskets, decorative containers: sliding in, dying of hunger or heart attack from fear, because the bird cannot climb out by itself.

Bright sun, overheated car: Heart attack from heat accumulation.

Electrical appliances and wires: Electrocution.

Temperature changes: Abrupt swings in temperature lead to colds or heat stroke.

Avoiding Danger

Keep the bathroom door closed. Allow bird in the bathroom only when you are there.

Always make sure first when the bird is perching!

Practice the utmost caution.

Cover containers, do not allow the bird to fly free while house is being cleaned.

Never leave open, even a crack.

Keep all the substances or objects named out of the bird's reach. Remove any residues. Please also check to see that no poisonous plants are kept in the bird room (see page 27).

You may give your parrot a sip from the glass if it has water, juice, or milk in it.

Leave a pot of cold water standing on any unused hot stove element. Birds should never be allowed to fly in the kitchen unsupervised.

Avoid using candlelight where birds are flying free.

Use wickerware, cover smooth interior surfaces with wire screening. Fill decorative containers with sand.

Provide shaded spots; ventilate cars.

Install them so as to be unreachable for birds.

Maintain average temperatures between 41 and 86°F (5 and 30°C)

Many large parrots grasp food with their foot and raise it to their beak.

Proper Diet

What Parrots Eat

For parrots in their natural habitat, the variety of food available is huge. They eat seeds, grains, nuts, fruits, grasses, weeds, tubers, roots, bark, young shoots, pollen, buds, and flower nectar, and some species also eat insect larvae, insects, and water snails. Every species has developed particular preferences for the various food plants, though it is not known exactly which ones. At one time wild-caught birds were the only ones offered for sale. It was very difficult for parrot keepers to get such birds used to their new, relatively restricted diet.

Today almost all young birds have been accustomed by the breeder to a diet of the available seeds, nuts, plants, and fruits. They don't miss the food supply of the natural environment because they don't know it at all.

Basically I can only advise you to feed your parrot as great a variety of foods as possible. Dr. Wolfgang Aeckerlein, a well-known German parrot authority and veterinarian, is of the opinion that singly kept parrots in particular are apt to be fed too unvarying a diet. An unbalanced diet that consists of the usual grain feed with a piece of apple now and then results in vitamin-deficiency diseases and damaged liver.

Seeds as a Staple

Pet dealers or breeders usually recommend a seed or grain mix when you buy a parrot. This mixture will do as a basic staple. The size of the seeds will probably be right for the beak strength of your parrot. Observe carefully whether your parrot actually eats all the seeds. Often the bird will "fish out" only those that really taste good to it.

Many feed mixes for large parrots also contain dried corn kernels. Almost no parrot will touch them because they are hard as stone and become edible only after they're boiled (for 2 hours). After you've found out which seeds your parrot prefers, you can put together your own mixture. All the seeds are available in separate packages in the pet store. To keep the staple food from becoming unbalanced over the long term, mix in other seeds that your parrot hasn't tried yet. Perhaps it will like them, and you will have made yet another source of vital nutrients available to the bird.

Important: If you give your bird a prepared feed mixture as its basic diet, the portions should never be too meager. Possibly the parrot will take only a few seeds. Depending on the size of the dish, add seeds once or twice daily.

Parrots must be fed quite a varied diet. An unbalanced diet can result in vitamin deficiencies and liver damage. Liver damage is one of the most frequent causes of death in pet parrots.

Top, from left to right: broad-striped sunflower seed, small dark sunflower seed, and rape seed; middle: safflower seed, oats, buck wheat, and hemp; bottom: canary grass seed, pellets, and white millet.

37

How-To:
Fresh Food

Parrots remove hulls from seed grains with the help of their tongue.

Vitamin treatment with sprouted seeds

If your parrot receives sprouted seeds for about two weeks every four to six weeks, vitamin preparations are largely unnecessary (see Important Nutrients, page 42). For sprouting, use not only seeds and grains from the staple mix (see Suitable Seeds, page 40), but also these: hulled oats, sprouted wheat grains, lentils, millet, and seeds of cress, radish, alfalfa, mustard, and flax (linseed) from the pet or health food store, which are also used in nutritious cooking.

Germination test: As soon as grains capable of germinating absorb water, the chemical reaction in the grains that causes sprouting begins. When this happens, available vitamins, minerals, and trace elements are released, thus increasing the value of the swollen and sprouted grains. If about 50% of the seeds germi-

38

nate and if they don't get moldy during the process, the food is good.

Recipe for sprouts
Drawing 1
Depending on the size of your parrot, put 1 to 2 tablespoons of mixed seeds in a dish. Cover the seeds with water and allow to soak in the covered dish for 24 hours.

Drawing 2
Shake the water-swollen seeds into a small-meshed sieve and rinse thoroughly with lukewarm water.
Put the rinsed seeds in a shallow glass dish and cover loosely, for instance with a glass saucer. During the next 48 hours allow the seeds to sprout at room temperature in a bright spot.

Drawing 3
As soon as sprouts develop from the grains or small stems grow, you can give your parrot the fresh food. Before use, rinse the sprouts with lukewarm water and dry them well.
Note: Sprouts rot quickly. Therefore—especially in summer—remove the leftovers after two hours and clean the dish.

Presenting fresh food properly
Fruits, vegetables, and plants are indispensable for parrot nutrition. Even a large parrot, however, cannot hold a whole apple with its foot and then eat it. The apple must be cut into "parrot-sized" pieces. The drawings at the right show you how to present the fresh food properly.

Drawings 4 and 5
Some parrots are induced to try fruit and vegetables only by means of a little trick. For instance, tie a piece of green pepper firmly to the climbing tree or in the cage with a sturdy, short string. While pull-

1 |Place seed kernels in a glass bowl and cover with water. Cover the glass bowl. A wooden skewer used as a prop will allow air to get into the dish.

2 |After 24 hours the seed kernels are swollen. They must now be rinsed in a small-meshed sieve under lukewarm running water.

3 |Replace the thoroughly rinsed seed grains in the glass dish. Cover the dish and provide for ventilation with the wooden skewer. Allow the seed grains to sit in the dish at room temperature for 48 hours.

ing on the pepper, the parrot eats a little and then develops a taste for it. Fresh weeds or herbs, wild plants, and leafy vegetables can be bundled and fastened to the cage roof, for instance with a wooden clothespin.

My tip: A parrot is curious. Taste fruits and vegetables in front of it with obvious enjoyment. Perhaps this way it can be encouraged to try some fresh foods that are unfamiliar.

Drawings 6 and 7
Large parrots hold their food with one foot. Cut vegetables and fruit in pieces measuring about 1 × 1 inches (2 × 2 cm). It's best to place them already mixed in a small dish or a little basket. For small parrots—which don't hold their food, but work at it with their beaks—fasten fruit and vegetable slices between the bars of the cage. You can also grate both coarsely, mix them with finely chopped lettuce, leafy vegetables, peas, and cubed fruit, and present them in as shallow a dish as possible.

Individual habits
You can't force a parrot to do anything. What it doesn't like, it won't touch. On the other hand, it also happens that a parrot just won't eat a food the way it's offered to him. In this case the bird often develops its own eating habits. For example, many parrots soak their grains in the water dish before they hull and eat them. For this reason alone, you should always make a bowl of water and a water dispenser available to the bird.

4|Hang half a well-washed pepper pod on a short, stout string from the climbing tree or in the cage.

How-To:
Fresh Food

5|Using a wooden clothespin, you can fasten bundles of fresh weeds to the cage roof.

6|This is how to fasten a carrot between the bars of the cage.

7|Poke only one peeled wedge of apple between the cage bars at a time.

Having eaten enough, the blue-and-yellow macaw finds the plate makes a good toy.

Suitable Seeds and Grains for Parrots

All the seeds listed should be offered to the bird when ripe or semiripe, on bundles of plants or as panicles.

Large parrots: Sunflower seeds, wheat, corn, safflower seeds, canary grass seeds, niger seeds, linseed, a little hemp, as well as walnuts, peanuts, pine and cedar nuts, pumpkin seeds, hulled oats, various types of millets, fresh wood, bark, buds, and young shoots.

Note: Offer nuts with "easy-to-crack" shells. Thus the parrot can free the nut from the shell entirely with its beak and tongue. Never give a parrot salted nuts! Watch out with peanuts and cedar nuts; they are very suscep-
tible to mold (see Monitoring Quality, right), which then spreads as dust when they're broken open. Cedar nuts should be dark and glossy once out of their shells. If they're dull, it could be because of a moldy deposit.

Medium-sized parrots: Small sunflower seeds, a little pumpkin seed and hemp, some niger seeds, a little linseed (flax), wheat, hulled oats, canary grass seed, millets, spray millets, safflower, fresh wood, buds, young shoots.

Small parrots: About 80% different types of millet, spray millet, canary grass, a little niger seed, hemp, and poppyseed, fresh branches, buds, young shoots.

My tip: Use primarily unhulled sunflower seeds. Cracking out the kernels keeps the bird busy and also prevents it from overeating out of boredom and getting too fat.

Monitoring Quality

Seeds that are destined to be eaten by parrots should not be stored, because vitamins and nutrients are lost during storage. This deterioration is not visible, hence the quality of the seeds must be determined by means of the sprouting test (see page 38).

Signs of spoilage
- Rot: Rotten grains smell musty, good ones are odorless.
- Mildew: A whitish-gray deposit can be seen.

Caution: Any mildew can cause fatal illness!
- Bugs: Indicated by clumped seeds and fine cobwebby threads.
- Rancid oil seeds: Unfortunately cannot be determined with the naked eye. Try tasting some of each portion purchased. If they taste rancid, they're spoiled and harmful.
- Poisonous ergot: Search the grain for the poisonous ergot. Ergot is black and has a triangular shape.
- Contaminated grain: Seeds and oil seeds should not be dirty and the grains not damaged. Dirt contains infectious agents. Damage reduces quality.

Proper storage: Anyone with only one or two parrots can get by for several weeks with one package of mixed grains. During this period store the seeds as you do grain, in a dry, airy, dark place or in your refrigerator. It's best to hang the mixture up in a small sack made of natural fibers.

Gathering Wild Plants

Seeds, flowers, and leaves are valuable as fresh foodstuff and provide occupation for the parrot when it removes the seeds from their hulls.

Grass seeds: Of dwarf meadow grass (*Poa annua*), Kentucky bluegrass (*Poa pratensis*), perennial ryegrass (*Lolium perenne*), velvet grass (*Holcus lanatus*).

Flowers and seeds: Of chickweed (*Stellaria media*), sour dock (*Rumex acetosa*), dandeloin (*Taraxacum officinale*), shepherd's purse (*Capsella bursa-pastoris*).

Millet and knotgrass species: Barnyard grass (*Echinochloa crusgalli*), red millet (*Panicum sanguinale*), green bristle grass (*Setaria viridis*), broomcorn (*Panicum milaceum*), bird grass (*Polygonum aviculare*).

Berries and wild fruits: Mountain ash berries, pyracantha berries and rose hips are beloved by many parrots. These can also be frozen in portions for winter.

Note: Chickweed and other weeds can be grown year-round on the window sill in cartons or flower pots. You can freeze many seed clusters of wild plants and thus have a winter supply.

Caution: Don't gather wild plants along the road or edges of fields. They are poisoned by exhaust gases or insecticides. All wild plants should be washed with lukewarm water and shaken dry before being used as food.

Fruits and Vegetables

If your parrot gets fresh fruit and vegetables daily, it will stay healthy, not get too fat, and retain the beauty of its plumage.

Raw vegetables: Eggplant, chicory, green peas and pea pods, pieces of corn cob or cut-off kernels, beet greens, spinach leaves, leaves of iceberg lettuce, torn small, Chinese cabbage, endive, radicchio, lamb's lettuce, carrots, zucchini, tomatoes, celery stalks, fennel bulbs, peppers, watercress.

Fruits and vegetables are indispensable for feeding a parrot. They give the bird essential vitamins, keep it from getting fat, and give its feathers their glossy sheen.

41

Indigestible vegetables: The entire cabbage family, raw and green potatoes, green beans, sprayed leaf lettuce.

Fruit: Fresh pineapple, apricots, peeled apple, banana, peeled pear, blackberries, fresh dates, fresh figs, raspberries, cherries, peeled kiwi, peeled cactus fig, peeled mango, mandarins, oranges, melons, peaches, grapes, papaya, rowan, berries, Japanese persimmon.

Indigestible fruit: Grapefruit, lemon, plums, rhubarb, and avocado.

Important Nutrients

Certain situations, for example, molting (see page 44), lack of sunshine, or a change of environment, can create stress for your parrot and increase its need for important nutrients. To be sure that your parrot gets them all, place a limestone or mineral block of the appropriate size (available in pet shops) in its cage or on its climbing tree. Please take note of the following line on the package: "Limestone contains all the materials necessary for maintaining the skeleton and for feather development." The parrot will also find minerals in bird sand and pigeon grit, if the cage floor is spread with them. If papers are used to cover the cage floor, you must provide a dish of oyster grit.

During the winter, during molting, or during any indisposition of the parrot, it's advisable to sprinkle a powdered multivitamin preparation (obtainable from pet stores or drugstores) over the parrot's fruit and vegetables. Be sure that it contains vitamin A, the B-complex vitamins, and vitamins C and E.

Important: Check expiration dates on all vitamin preparations—vitamins that have been kept too long are worthless.

Food from the Family Table

Parrots are sometimes very keen on having some of the food the family is eating. A few foods are thoroughly recommended for your parrot.

It can have:
- Once or twice a week, ½ to 1 tablespoon of skim milk cottage cheese, enriched with chopped weeds and chopped hard-boiled egg yolk.
- A small ½ inch × ½ inch (1 × 1 cm) cube of hard cheese.
- 1 tablespoon of fresh shredded wheat soaked in a half-milk/half-water solution; also very rich in vitamins are wheat sprouts from a health-food store.
- Unseasoned, boiled noodles, preferably whole-wheat noodles, or a piece of boiled potato (both well cooled).
- A little piece of bread crust, a dry cookie, cornflakes, or some hard white

These macaws are feeding each other. This so-called mate feeding is part of pair formation for many parrot species and is mainly to be seen during courtship.

- bread, softened in a half-milk/half-water mixture.
- Parrots that can hold their food with a foot will gnaw on a chop bone or a chicken leg. They eat the small bits of meat still left on the bone and chew on the cartilage.

These are harmful:
- Cold food that comes directly from the refrigerator.
- Hot food.
- Spoiled, moldy food, even if the bad spots have been removed, because rot and mold can continue to live undetected in the interior of the food.
- Salty, spicy foods, and especially straight salt, spices, or sugar.
- Chocolate, sweet creams, whipped cream, cakes, sweets.
- Pure fat and very fatty foods.
- Alcoholic drinks, including beer; coffee; Coca-Cola; and other carbonated drinks.

Large parrots use their foot to carry big pieces of food to their beak. The foot nervously raised to the beak without food is often an expression of unhappiness or excitement.

Warning: Anyone who allows his parrot to be present at the table must be very watchful. The parrot can scald itself on hot food, burn its tongue, or get hold of something that can be harmful for it.

Drinking Water
Fresh drinking water—as clean as possible—should always be within your parrot's reach. Some species have to let the water run down their extended throats, so they need enough freedom of movement to be able to stretch their heads up and back. Consequently, a partly covered drinking bowl is not suitable for them. Highly recommended is noncarbonated mineral water; its valuable ingredients are listed on the label. Only a sick bird gets boiled water, weak black tea, or herb tea to drink when it is advised by your avian veterinarian.

When Your Parrot Is Sick

Altered Behavior

If one day your parrot's behavior is different from what you are used to, observe the bird carefully. Parrots sometimes are simply in a bad mood, tired, or morose, but such moods don't last long. Usually, bad moods or tiredness are forgotten with scratching or are overcome when you play a little game with the parrot. It is alarming, however, if the bird sits passively on its perch for hours at a time, resting on both legs, with its head buried in its back feathers, and if it takes scarcely any notice of its food or picks listlessly at it. These signs indicate the beginning of an illness.

With parrots, many diseases reach their most critical stage within 24 hours. Therefore don't hesitate to take the bird to the avian veterinarian quickly. Treating a sick parrot is always difficult, especially when the veterinarian has been brought in too late (see How-To, pages 46/47).

My Tip: When you buy your parrot, find out the name of an avian veterinarian with experience in treating parrots. A pet store or bird club will certainly be glad to advise you. Alternatively, you can contact parrot breeders or animal shelter representatives, who usually work with experienced avian veterinarians.

Molting

This isn't a disease, but a natural process for renewal of the plumage. A captive parrot usually molts once a year, but if it is forced to put up with drastic temperature changes, more frequent molting may result. Young, healthy birds usually withstand molting without any particular damage to their general health, but once in a while a somewhat older parrot may seem sick during molting. First-aid treatment with infrared irradiation (see page 46) is then appropriate for the bird, because during molting it requires warmth, rest, and, above all, a diet very rich in vitamins. During molting the parrot loses a considerable number of feathers. Small feathers grow back in a few days, larger ones take a few weeks. Rarely, inability to fly may be caused by molting. When unable to fly, the parrot may need additional footholds to go from the climbing tree to the cage.

*P*arrot diseases, feather plucking, malformed feathers, and molting upset many parrot owners. You will find more details in the following pages.

Contour feathers (bottom), filoplume feathers (top), and down feathers (left). Contour feathers form the main plumage of the body, wing, and tail. Each contour feather consists of a long stem or rachis, which carries the vane with many barbs (see enlargement). Each barb has interlocking hooks and barbules.

Red-and-yellow or scarlet macaws.

How-To:
First Aid

1\Sick parrot. Illness is often detectable by a bird's dull, lifeless eyes.

What's wrong?

If you notice one or more of the following symptoms, take your parrot to the avian veterinarian at once:

• Have the droppings of the bird changed? Watery feces can be a transitory phenomenon, which may result from psychological causes, eating too much fruit, or temperature swings. The droppings should become normal again in several hours. If in addition to watery consistency there is discoloration, if the feces foam, or if there is blood mixed in, place a piece of plastic wrap under the bird's perch. Take the stool sample to the veterinarian so that a fecal examination can be made.

• Are there no signs of any droppings for hours?

• Is the bird sneezing a lot or does its nose run?

• Does the bird yawn often and breathe noisily when it does so?

• Is the bird bleeding from a wound or from the anus?

• Is the cere or are the toes changed in a notable way?

• Does the bird let one leg or one wing hang?

• Is the upper beak too long or pushed to one side?

• Does the bird constantly fidget with its feathers and scratch itself nervously?

First measures

Sometimes it isn't possible—for whatever reasons—to take the sick parrot to the veterinarian immediately. In this case the correct first-aid measures can be crucial to your parrot's survival.

Eyes indicate illness
Drawing 1
Along with changed behavior (see page 44), the eyes will indicate illness. A sick parrot often has strikingly dull, lusterless eyes.

Provide constant warmth
Drawing 2
A sick parrot needs a cage all to itself, rest, and constant warmth. Place an infrared lamp about 12 inches (30 cm) from the cage so that the bird can sit either inside the warmed area or outside it. Since humid air provides relief in some diseases, to be on the safe side, put a dish of hot water between the lamp and the cage to increase the humidity. If no serious illness develops, this heat treatment often helps. The lamp

2\Infrared irradiation. A sick parrot needs constant warmth. Place the infrared lamp about 12 inches (30 cm) from the cage. If it becomes too warm for the bird, it must be able to move into a cooler area of the cage.

may be used for 48 hours. The temperature in the cage area should be about 84° to 86° F (29–30° C). After the patient has improved, before you turn the lamp off again, increase the distance of the light from the cage gradually so that the temperature drops only slowly. Sudden temperature changes can cause chills, which produce a relapse.

Important: With convulsions, irradiation is harmful. In this case, you must go to the veterinarian without delay.

How to grasp the parrot
Drawing 3
If your parrot can't be put into the cage on the stick or on your arm, you must take hold of it. It's best to darken the room somewhat, lay a terrycloth towel around the bird's back and shoulders, and grasp it from behind with both hands so that you immobilize both head and wings. Hold the parrot close, take it to the cage, and position it in front of the open door in such a way that it can only go inside.
Important: When taking hold of the parrot, always hold its head firmly so that the bird can't bite you.

The trip to the veterinarian
If you have the transport container in which the parrot first came to your house, use it for the trip to the veterinarian. Otherwise, the bird must be transported in a cage, which is only possible in a car. In many cities it is also possible to reach an emergency veterinarian at night

and on holidays. For instance, emergency physicians are or should be listed in the membership bulletins of animal rescue groups or in your bird club's newsletter.

Please remember
• Take along the stool sample and instead of sand put clean paper on the cage floor, so that the doctor can examine the most recent droppings too.
• Take along a sample of the seed mix that the bird has been receiving.
• During the trip, protect the bird from cold, dampness, and great heat. Wrap the cage or transport box with a wool blanket, but make sure enough air can get in.

When medications are necessary
If the veterinarian orders medications, follow the dosage and length of treatment exactly. Liquid medicines must be added to the drinking water. In this case, keep the bird from satisfying its thirst with fruit or vegetables or from reaching a dripping water faucet, or it might avoid taking the medication. Powdered substances are best strewn on your bird's favorite fruit or on a particularly beloved treat that it is also most likely to eat. Crush medications in tablet form to a fine powder. If you have to administer drops directly, the veterinarian will offer help and advice. Here there are no general rules, because every parrot reacts differently when you try to open its beak.

How-To:
First Aid

3 | *Holding a parrot. Darken the room. Lay a terry cloth towel around the bird's back and shoulders and grasp it from behind with both hands.*

A compatible pair of bare-eyed cockatoos in front of their brooding hole.

Malformation and Shedding of Feathers

With old, poorly nourished, or not entirely healthy parrots, malformed feathers can be produced after molting. This may be the result of deficiency symptoms, hormonal disturbances, or cysts in the feather follicles. The bird must be examined and treated by an avian veterinarian. Psittacine beak and feather disease (PBFD) however, is almost incurable; it has been found among cockatoos and many other small and large hookbills, and often appears after a molt. The new feathers growing in are weak and soon fall out again with preening. They grow in with gaps, so that by degrees the bird becomes bald. Frequently this is also accompanied by softening and excessive growth of the beak and claws. The virus responsible has been named Diminuvirus, due to its extraordinarily small size.

Feather Plucking

Many parrots begin to pull out their own feathers. Finally only the head area still has feathers on it. Some continue this self-destructive behavior to the point of biting their skin until it bleeds. Many ornithologists relate this dangerous addition to emotional disturbances, brought on by the parrot's loss of its significant human or of its mate, or by lack of a mate at the onset of sexual maturity. Others attribute responsibility to stress from crowded aviaries, lack of exercise, dietary deficiencies, lack of opportunity to bathe, or parasites. Unfortunately, there is no effective remedy for all parrots that have this addiction. I know that in some parrots that began plucking their feathers during their favorite person's vacation or after an illness, this tendency disappeared because the birds received immediate treatment by a doctor and an extraordinary amount of attention. You should never rule out the possibility that it is a symptom of a serious deficiency. One reader wrote me that her plucking Amazon, which was already in bad condition, gave up plucking after it was given drinking water with sea salt added. In every case the feather-plucking parrot has to be taken to the veterinarian.

Psittacosis

This disease, once so dreaded, is difficult to diagnose because it doesn't manifest itself in clear-cut symptoms. Sick birds are apathetic, excrete droppings that are too soft, often with traces of blood in them, have sniffles, have difficulty breathing, or have conjunctivitis, with mucous secretions on the lower eyelids. All these symptoms can appear singly or together. Therefore, it's necessary to treat a bird with such indispositions with infrared light and—if the difficulties don't disappear within 24 hours—to go to the veterinarian. Parrot fever is also transmissible to human beings. Certainly it occurs more rarely today, but it can be very dangerous, especially for older people or those with poor circulation.

Now it is possible to have healthy birds examined for the presence of the organism causing the disease. Parrots can be carriers of psittacosis without visible signs of sickness and without themselves becoming ill. In acute cases, human and birds can be healed by prompt treatment. Psittacosis must be reported to health authorities, and if the occasion arises the veterinarian will tell you what to do.

How to correctly cut claws that are too long. Be careful not to injure the blood vessels, which are palely visible in the claw horn, while you're doing it! If you hold the claws in front of a light, you'll see the blood vessels more clearly.

Breeding Your Parrots

Mating

You must succeed in bringing together two sexually mature, mutually compatible parrots of different sexes of the same species. I've already described to you in the chapter "Life With a Parrot" (see page 22) how two strange birds become used to each other. Parrots that are to breed are housed in either a spacious indoor aviary or an outdoor aviary with a house shelter (see Books for Further Help, page 95). Offer the pair a suitable nesting box in which the female can lay her eggs. Some species even sleep in the

The macaw extends its rump to its partner to allow it to preen the feathers in the tail region. Social preening is important for strong pair bonding.

nesting box all year-round. They feel comfortable and safe in it, but they don't necessarily breed.

The Nesting Box

The size and the construction of the nesting box (see drawings pages 52 and 54) depend on the size of your parrots.

Rules of thumb:

- The length of the sides of the nest box should correspond to the body length of the bird without its tail, and the floor surface should have a nest depression.
- For large parrots, the height of the box should be three times the length of the sides of the floor surface.
- The entry hole must be exactly the diameter of the measurement around the birds' shoulders.
- Climbing aids inside the box should lead from the entry hole to the nest hollow. For this purpose, place short perches to form a ladder and fasten them securely. Below the entry hole, outside, fasten a sufficiently long, sturdy branch. (Don't use metal mesh as a climbing aid inside the box; the birds can get caught in it!)
- The inspection flap (see How-To, page 54) must be able to be fastened from the outside, must be securable when open, and must be big enough to allow a hand to reach in. It should be located in the lower third of the box above the nesting hollow.
- For large species the nesting box must be of hardwood; for small species soft wood (¾ to 1 inch [20–25mm] thick) is adequate.
- For nesting material, let the female

gnaw some soft wood that has been fastened to the inner walls of the box. You can also put a mixture of peat and hamster bedding (pine, for example) in the nesting cavity. (Don't use sawdust, it might come from chemically treated wood.)

My tip: Experienced parrot breeders attach a movable mesh gate over the entry hole of the nesting box so that they can close the hole temporarily by means of a chain. This proves useful when later you need to renew the bedding in the box or inspect the nestlings. The often very aggressive female can thus be kept away from the box.

The proper place: Hang the nest box on the aviary wall so that you can comfortably open the inspection flap and see into the interior of the box. All the arrangements in the aviary should be altered to make it possible for you to accomplish the important maneuvers from the outside, especially filling the water and feed dishes, so that the birds will be disturbed as little as possible.

Entering the Nesting Box
After some possible hesitation at first, the nesting box will surely be inspected carefully by both birds. If the female often busies herself inside the box, she could be getting ready to brood. If the male is also stimulated by this, he will immediately begin wooing his female with the courtship rituals (see Courtship and Mating, page 61). However, you shouldn't expect this to happen in the first weeks after putting up the nesting box. It can be some months before the birds begin to take advantage of their new opportunities.

Note: If the parrots accept the nesting box and make preparations to breed, it's a sign that they feel comfortable living with you.

Getting Used to Rearing Foods
As soon as you notice that the birds are in the mood to mate, give them rearing foods in anticipation, so that they get used to the taste and will later feed it to their young in case of emergency.

Here two birds of different species have bonded into a pair, but there can be no offspring.

Suitable rearing foods are:
• White bread or dark bread softened in a little milk and slightly sweetened with honey or nectar (special food for loris, available in pet stores).
• Baby food for the first few weeks, mixed with a little softened bread and some hard-boiled egg yolk.
• Rice pudding slightly sweetened with honey or nectar.
• Minced boiled chicken.
• Canary-rearing food (Cé Dé, L/M's Universal-Plus).
• Lucerne pellets, a prepared rearing food for farm animals. Soak this feed in water for 2 hours, then mix it with some bread softened in milk.

51

My tip: Enrich each mixture with a calcium preparation and traces of a multivitamin preparation (see page 42). These are available from pet stores. Use the dosage recommended on the package.

Brooding
While your parrots are brooding in an indoor aviary, adhere to the following conditions so as not to interrupt the successful course of brooding:
• The birds need plenty of quiet now. Every unnecessary disturbance should be avoided.
• The room temperature must be constant. If your birds have been comfortable at temperatures of 68° to 72° F (20–22° C) until now, maintain these temperatures without fail.
• The humidity must always range between 60 and 70%. If necessary, use a humidifier.
• The person most familiar to the birds should take care of them. Only for exceptional reasons should anyone else have access to the "parrot room."
• Even if you know that eggs have already been laid, contain your curiosity and don't look in the nesting box. In the first few days the female is extremely sensitive and can respond to a disturbance by abandoning the clutch.

Important: If one day you find the female, her feathers fluffed out, outside the nest on the cage floor, whereas she had been mostly staying in the box, she could be suffering from egg binding. Grasp her carefully, but firmly, with a towel (see How-To, page 47) and place her in the small single cage outside the aviary. Irradiate her there with infrared light. The temperature in the cage should reach 91° F (33° C) so that the cramping eases and the egg can be laid. If this doesn't happen within 2 to 3 hours, the bird must be transported to the veterinarian at as close to the same temperature as possible, because this situation is life-threatening.

What to Do with the Young?
As long as the chicks are still in the nesting box, you have time to consider what to do with the young parrots after they leave the nest. Perhaps you already know parrot fanciers who would love to have a pair. You can also get in touch with the breeder. Perhaps he'd like to take the birds to breed himself or knows other breeders who would be interested in them.

Observe carefully how the parents respond to their young once the birds have left the nesting box. In some species a kind of competitive battle begins quite soon after the young are able to fly. The males of some species chase their sons and drive them away from the food dishes. In other species the females are jealous of their daughters. This must be stopped immediately in any case. Take the young parrots away from their parents and house them in a separate aviary, making sure it's big enough.

This nest box with dimensions of 18 × 10 × 15 inches (46 × 26 × 38 cm) is suitable for small parrot species.

Red-and-yellow or scarlet macaw female feeding her nestlings.

How-To:
Young Birds

Inspect the eggs

Once the female has laid two or three eggs in the nest hollow, you may check about five days after her continuous brooding has begun to see if the eggs are fertile. Wait until the female has left the clutch for a short time.

Open the inspection door
Drawing 1
Open the inspection door in the nest box. Ideally the nesting box will be so placed that you need not enter the aviary to inspect the eggs.
Remove one egg at a time and quickly hold it in front of a source of strong light. Fertile eggs show a dark interior, whereas infertile eggs are light, almost translucent. Even if only one egg is fertile, put them all back in the nest hollow so as not to irritate the female. The chick that will later hatch will get some support from the other eggs and will have a slight source of warmth whenever the mother leaves the nest. If all the eggs are infertile, remove them from the nest one at a time at intervals of about a day. The female will begin a new clutch either quite soon or much later. After this inspection you need do nothing more until the chicks hatch—in 22 to 30 days, depending on the species.

The hatching of the chicks

The male parrot will make you aware at once of the imminent hatching of the first chick. He will act nervous shortly beforehand. The male hurriedly climbs the perch in front of the entrance hole whenever the female leaves the nest. Again and again he looks into the box. Don't be affected by his nervousness. You must not interfere now under any circumstances. Provide for a somewhat higher temperature in the nesting box by turning on the infrared lamp (see How-To, page 47). The ideal temperature at hatching is 98.6° F (37° C); the humidity should now range between 70 and 80%. The chicks will hatch at intervals of two to three days. Their cries stimulating their parents—their mother in particular—to feed them are heard immediately. These begging cries also have an effect on the father: They stimulate him to provide his female with abundant food, which he pokes into her beak at the entry hole.

After the chicks hatch, their survival depends greatly on whether the mother feeds them enough and prevents hypothermia by continually taking them under her wings. Unfortunately there is no way you can influence the behavior of a female that refuses to provide enough food and warmth.

1 | *Ideal nesting trunk for large parrots. Important are the removable "roof" and the* low-placed *inspection door.*

My tip: To increase the humidity inside the nesting box, lightly spray the wood outside once or twice daily with water. Use a flower mister to do this.

The nestling phase

Depending on the species, it takes between 30 and 90 days (see Popular Parrot Species, page 64) until the chicks leave the nest box in the order in which they are hatched. The example of the red-and-yellow macaw demonstrates the different developmental stages of a parrot chick.

8 days old
Drawing 2
The eyes are still closed. They open between the tenth and

twelfth days of life. The young bird weighs barely 3½ ounces (100 g).

32 days old
Drawing 3
The quills are visible on wings, tail, and head.

38 days old
Drawing 4
The plumage on the head, wings, and tail is now clearly recognizable. The young bird weighs almost 28 ounces (800 g).

Even after leaving the nest, the young birds are still fed mostly by the father for several weeks before they are able to eat completely independently. At first they lose weight, because until they learn to remove the husks from seeds they get to their food correspondingly slowly. Besides grain, young birds must receive sufficient fruit, greens, and, in addition, a good commercial (hand-) rearing diet, (see page 52).

Daily inspection

After the chicks are hatched, inspect the nesting box. For one thing, a young bird may die, and then you must remove it quickly so that its decay does not endanger the other siblings. For another thing, the bedding in the nesting cavity has to be renewed from time to time.

• Carry out the inspection at the same time every day. This way the parent birds will get used to it most easily.

• Observe the condition of the nestlings. Freshly hatched chicks raise their heads only when they are fed. As a rule the head lies on the floor or on the body of another nestling. The eyes are still closed. They open between the tenth day and the third week of life, depending on the species.

• With the progressive development of the chicks the excrement in the nesting hollow increases. About every two days, renew the bedding in the nesting cavity. Prepare a small basket or dish that is lined with soft, absorbent, slightly warmed paper. Set the young birds in the dish while the bedding is replaced.

Unfortunately, parrot chicks give no signals when something is not right about their development. Should you get the impression that one of the chicks is no longer gaining weight and seems apathetic or otherwise out of the ordinary, it's best to get in touch with a breeder, who will advise you about possible supplementary feeding.

My tip: Feeding chicks is difficult. You must first watch to see how an experienced keeper does it and try it yourself under his or her direction. Breeders will provide you with the necessary feeding syringe and give you the recipe for the feeding supplement that they have developed through experience. Various excellent handfeeding-rearing diets (with detailed instructions) are commercially availal le.

How-To:
Young Birds

2 | *Red-and-yellow macaw, eight days old. The eyes are still closed. They don't open until between the tenth and twelfth days. The chick weighs around 3½ ounces (100 g).*

3 | *Red-and-yellow macaw, 32 days old. The quills on the wings, tail, and head have begun to sprout.*

4 | *Red-and-yellow macaw, 38 days old. The young bird has come to weigh almost 28 ounces (800 g). The plumage colors are already recognizable on the wings and tail.*

Understanding Parrots

All parrot species show great similarity in their capabilities and behavior patterns. Proper interpretation of behavioral patterns is the key to a good understanding between you and your parrot.

Typical Movements

Flying and climbing: Inhabitants of plains and open country usually have extraordinary flight capability. Forest dwellers, on the other hand, are often particularly adept climbers. Their food consists primarily of tree fruit, which they harvest by climbing. Not only the "forest dwellers," but also the "plains dwellers," are masterful climbers, however. After all, every parrot species explores the trees for suitable nesting holes this way.

Running on the ground: This is an adaptation by all species that in nature find their food primarily on the ground, like some cockatoo species, for example. They are skillful runners and often even advance by means of hops. "Climber" parrots give the effect of being quite clumsy when moving on the ground (see drawing, page 58) because the position of their feet is so strongly adapted for traversing branches.

Leg stretching: From time to time, especially after pausing to rest, the parrot extends one leg and the wing on the same side downward and to the back. This behavior is like a stretch. While withdrawing the leg, some parrots frequently ball the foot into a "fist" and then usually draw it into the feathers of the belly. Resting on one leg implies great relaxation and is also very often part of the sleeping posture.

Beak in back feathers: This behavior is also a facet of the sleeping position of many parrots. During the day, too, they sometimes burrow their beak into slightly fluffed-out back feathers during a rest period.

Warning: This position is also that of sick or indisposed birds, but they usually rest on both legs. Resting on both legs, however, is not necessarily an indication of indisposition.

Shoulder shrugging: The folded wings are flexed sideways. This behavior usually occurs when there is too little exercise, but when it is accompanied by certain other gestures, it can also be display behavior or, with simultaneous loss of weight and biting at the air, indicate fear or pain.

Raising the wings: The wings are lifted up if the bird is too warm, so that way it can give off body heat. Some species also lift their wings when something pleasant happens to them.

Frequent Behaviors

Preening: This is one of the parrot's most important activities. It devotes several hours to this task daily, workings its beak over and over through all the feathers (see drawing, page 50). Adeptly it draws them through its beak to smoothe them, usually beginning with the wing and tail feathers. The head feathers are the only ones the bird can't reach with its beak. It will work its toes through these or rub them on a branch. In the wild, social preening, particularly of the head plumage, is part of the court-

Some parrot species love to sleep hanging head down from a branch or from the cage bars. If your parrot belongs to one of these species, make it possible for the bird to practice this sleeping habit. This is easy to accomplish: Provide a natural branch in which diameter corresponds to the size of the bird's feet.

The little Senegal parrot is native to Africa.

ship behavior of many species (see page 60) and serves to bond the pair.

Shaking out the plumage: Preening is usually concluded by shaking the entire plumage. This serves to return all the preened feathers to their proper locations again and to remove dust particles. Often you can also see this feather shaking when the parrot has overcome stress. For instance, if it was frightened, insecure, or embarrassed and the situation is now stable again, it shakes out its feathers in relief.

Fluttering the wings: Young birds often flutter their wings before the first flight, holding firmly to a branch with their feet, in order to exercise the flight muscles. Grown parrots that have no opportunities to fly, or only limited ones, also flutter because of too little exercise. Birds of the large species will also hold firmly to a branch with their beak when they flutter, in order to counteract the force of their wings.

Beak grooming: After almost every meal the parrot cleans its beak by rubbing it vigorously on a branch. You can also observe this rubbing when it hasn't just eaten, for the parrot also maintains the horny substance of the beak this way. Some parrots also rub their beak on a branch as a greeting to a fellow parrot or a favorite human. I've observed this in African gray parrots and Amazons.

Foot grooming: Like the plumage, the parrot's feet and toes are groomed with the beak, with which the bird picks out scales and foreign matter. Like a pair of pliers, the beak works over the claws, probably to prevent excess length.

Yawning: All parrots yawn from time to time. This is comparable to our yawning, for it often results from oxygen deficiency. If the parrot yawns a number of times in succession during the day, ventilate the room; perhaps the air in the room is stale and you haven't noticed. Sometimes parrots also yawn with heads lifted; the stretching of the neck and beak area is the reason for this.

Sneezing: If occasional sneezing is not accompanied by discharge of nasal secretions, you needn't worry about a cold. Parrots sneeze to keep their respiratory tract free or with abrupt changes in temperature.

Your Parrot's Senses

Sight: Parrots see the world even more colorfully than we humans do. This ability facilitates their search for

The foot configuration of the African gray parrot is better suited for crossing branches than for walking across the floor.

food. Moreover, they can recognize members of the same species by their plumage colors. Because of the side positioning of their eyes, parrots have almost complete peripheral vision, which allows them to detect enemies as soon as possible and flee quickly. The area that both eyes see at the same time is somewhat smaller than that for humans. We can perceive only about 16 images in a second, whereas the parrot can perceive up to 100 times more. The lightning-quick perception of all details while flying fast is of vital importance for a bird.

Hearing: It's obvious that parrots hear well when you consider that they warn each other and communicate with screams or calls across wide distances and that, by using different tone sequences, they ensure frictionless communal life in the flock. In pairs, one bird even recognizes the voice of its partner. During brooding in many species, the first sounds uttered by the chick in the egg affect the behavior of the mother.

Taste: Parrots are primarily seed eaters and have a less developed taste sense than birds that live on fruits and nectar. In captivity parrots develop very considerable likes and dislikes, which allows us to infer their ability to perceive differences in taste.

Touch: The parrot's sense of touch is not essentially different from that of other living creatures. Certainly there are areas especially sensitive to touch. In brooding, for example, the sense of touch has an important function in keeping the mother from crushing the eggs when she is sitting on the clutch. In addition, many birds have a special vibrational sense that allows them to perceive slight vibratory motions and interpret them correctly.

Monogamy

It is known that most parrots choose a partner of the opposite sex in adolescence and remain true to that partner for the rest of their lives. Many species need one to several years before they are sexually mature and actually mate. The loss of a partner produces grief, which impairs the bird. In the wild, a new bond may be formed after some time, but if a pet parrot loses its partner, be it through thoughtless separation of a bonded bird pair or by separation from the human mate substitute, the grief can change the bird's character or even spell its death.

Pair Formation

In a parrot flock, an unpaired bird seeks to win a mate by first drawing near the bird of its choice. If the chosen one does not warn the suitor to keep its distance by slashing indicatively with its beak, the suitor slides closer and closer until it dares to touch the wing or the beak of the other bird. If there is no rejection over several days, a pair has been formed, as is shown by the fact that from now on both birds do everything together in the closest possible proximity. Close together they search for food, sit during a resting period, sleep with body contact, even catch each other's moods. For instance, if a bird needs to stretch, to eat, or to preen, and begins to do so, its partner will follow with the same action at almost the same time.

In the wild, a parrot is almost always fortunate enough to be courted by a member of the opposite sex. In captivity, however, it frequently happens that parrots can only choose from birds of the same sex. Therefore, if two parrots of the same sex form a bond, one of them in time assumes the role of the absent sex by assuming its behavior. The birds can main-

When a parrot slightly fluffs up its feathers while being scratched, it is trustingly giving itself up to pleasure.

Deftly the yellow-fronted Amazon dangles its way along a branch.   *It calmly eats its find.*

tain this partnership serenely until a member of the opposite sex comes along. Then, however, there is an unlucky loser.

Pair Bonding

Mutual preening: For many species this is an important link in strong pair bonding. The head region, especially, is mostly preened by the mate, since the parrot can't reach this region with its own beak. Mutual scratching, however, not only promotes good hygiene but also provides a feeling of well-being for the bird! Your pet parrot will demand that you scratch its head often and repeatedly. It will come either to you with head bent and nodding or sit on a branch with head lowered, its feathers slightly laid back. As

the parrot's substitute mate, you should indulge it as often as possible in providing the sensation it so eagerly longs for.

Mate feeding: Mate feeding also is part of pair bonding in some species, although it is to be observed mainly during courtship. Until a parrot can feed a female satisfactorily, she will not be willing to mate. Moreover, for brooding to be successful, it is important that the mother and nestlings be adequately fed by the father. In most parrot species the female broods alone and later also feeds the young. She receives the food for the nestlings and for herself from the male. The cockatoo family is an exception. Among cockatoos, the female shares the tasks of brooding and feeding the

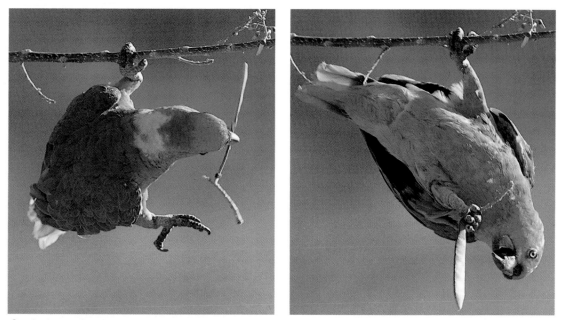

Continuing to dangle, it removes stems that are in the way. . .   *until it reaches the next fruit.*

young birds with the male, and mate feeding is not necessary. If your parrot isn't a cockatoo, it may one day try to feed you. Some parrots attempt to poke the love offering unerringly into their human partner's mouth, others aim for the ear. My Moses likes to press his feed mash between two of my fingers.

Courtship and Mating

In the wild, if a parrot pair has found a nesting hole, the male usually begins courtship. With pet birds, courtship can also occur without a nesting box, but then no offspring appear. The display behavior of the male is striking. More and more often he struts back and forth along a perch, his legs stiff, his posture erect. As he does so he spreads his tail, sometimes also flexes his wings—cockatoos spread their wings and crests—thus showing his colored plumage to full effect. This arouses the female. Some males also circle their females with mincing steps and rap their beaks loudly on wood to show their strength. Some parrots accompany these rituals with vocalization. Ever more frequently the male feeds his female, and preening becomes intensified.

Copulation: Females ready to mate sit on a branch in a horizontal position with their tail slightly raised, some with their wings slightly raised and trembling. They are circled by the excited male. After several nudges with his beak he then mounts his female's back and, in a difficult contortion, lays

About the pictures:
Parrots are master climbers. Their food consists partly of tree fruit, which they can reach only by climbing. The exploration of the trees for suitable nesting holes also demands great skill.

A pair that is very compatible often reacts with synchronized movements, as this pair does with stretching.

haps attack. To a large degree, the threatening posture of the male resembles the display behavior during courtship. A parrot can also threaten another by raising a foot. If neither of them will give in, dueling with beaks may ensue. These battles mostly end without bloodshed, however, unless the two adversaries can't get out of each other's way.

"Reading" Behavior Patterns
Not only the voice, but the body language, too, is important in communication with a fellow parrot or human mate substitute.

Fear and Fright
If your bird is afraid for any reason or if it is frightened, it sits up straight, holding its feathers very close to its body so that it appears very slender and staring fixedly in one direction. Only when the reason for its fear proves to be harmless does it relax, usually shaking its feathers, and turn to some occupation.

Comfortable Relaxation
When your parrot feels secure and comfortable, it fluffs out its feathers slightly. Its bearing is relaxed, not erect at all, and it often makes soft little crunching sounds with its beak.

his cloaca on that of the female. In this manner the copulation takes place.

Disagreements
A pair of parrots that are used to each other scarcely ever have serious disagreements, but conflicts can occur among the birds of a flock, in the wild as well as in the aviary. In the aviary, a pair that is ready to breed may become extremely aggressive toward their fellows because the space is too constricted. The pair must then be housed in its own aviary. In the wild, the breeding pair can withdraw from the flock and maintain the desired distance.

Threatening: In conflicts arise between two rival parrots, the birds threaten each other before they per-

Urgent Requests

If your parrot sits in front of you in a low, almost horizontal position with slightly raised, trembling wings, it wants to ask you for something, Young birds also use this position to beg for food from their parents. A friend's Senegal parrot lets her know every evening by fluttering its wings that it hasn't yet received its usual bedtime snack, a treat.

Attack Caused by Agitation

Even the gentlest parrot can become raving mad when it is handled unreasonably or sometimes when things don't go the way it wants them to. Someone I know has had a red-and-blue macaw for a long time. Toward humans it trusts, the bird is very loving, but if it is disappointed, it acts downright vicious. If you make a move to follow its clear invitation to scratch, but at the last moment don't quite dare to, the macaw will reward your timidity by pecking at you with its full strength. On the other hand, it has never so much as scratched the two small girls in the family, although at times they have handled the parrot clumsily.

Confusion

For a variety of reasons a parrot can become confused: It would like to achieve something but doesn't dare. For example, it knows in a certain situation that it's going to be left alone for a long time, but from agitation and grief it is unable to react. Such a conflict of feelings generates confusion. The parrot first tries spontaneously to satisfy its need, but it becomes uncertain and switches to a substitute action. Each time my Moses notices that I'm going away for a long time, he displays a moving gesture of confusion: He looks at me steadily and nervously lifts a foot to his beak as if he intended to nibble it, but doesn't really touch it. All the while he repeatedly makes a timid little sound, which is probably supposed to get me to stay. . . .

Yawning usually indicates oxygen deficiency, but it can be as contagious with parrots as with humans.

Popular Parrot Species

T*he notes on care that follow always refer to the particular parrot species discussed. Each individual parrot develops its own special peculiarities, however, which you must always take into consideration.*

Threatened with Extinction

The primary reason that many parrots now are threatened with extinction in their native regions is the destruction of their habitats. Whether in the pursuit of profit or to obtain economically useful areas, large forest regions are being cleared. The parrots' sleeping and nesting trees are being sacrificed to the power saw.

The second most important reason for the disappearance of the parrots, however, is still the great demand for these birds. Although the Washington Endangered Species Convention (see page 14) has placed especially endangered species under the strictest protection, poachers today are still capturing wild parrots in their native environments. The risk of legal prosecution for the poachers is small.

Responsible bird lovers can, however, help ensure that poaching will no longer be allowed without further consequences. Refuse to buy any parrot whose origin is not above suspicion. Buy only a parrot that is wearing an official leg band (see page 16) and that is furnished with the legally required CITES certificate. It's best to try to get captive-bred birds. Fortunately, in the last few years growing numbers of parrot fanciers have provided their parrots with such good living conditions that the breeding of some species has been increasingly successful. Perhaps in a few years the entire demand can be satisfied with captive-bred birds.

My tip: If you too want to succeed with breeding, offer your charges optimal living conditions: Only then can you count on healthy parrot offspring.

Should you wish to keep only one parrot and not breed, don't be selfish. Lend your bird to a breeder whose parrot lacks a suitable mate.

Notes on the Profiles

In the previous chapters you've learned in general about parrots' character, maintenance and care, and correct diet. On the following pages you will find pictures and descriptions of popular parrot species with details of their appearance, size, geographic range, and keeping, and special tips on care.

In selecting the parrots, primary consideration was given to species that are covered in Appendix II of the Washington Endangered Species Convention (see page 14) and also can in large part be bred successfully in captivity.

A rose-breasted, galah, or roseate cockatoo on its breeding tree. Frequently seen in zoos, the rose-breasted is one of the commonest cockatoos in captivity.

Many parrot species are threatened with extinction in their native habitat. Although some are under strict protection, illegal trade continues to thrive. True parrot lovers should buy only parrots that have the official leg band and the required papers.

Amazons

A blue-fronted Amazon.

Amazons live in Central and South America and on some nearby islands. All have green plumage. The green varies from light, yellowish green to dark olive green. Frequently the feathers are iridescent all over or only in spots. The individual species differ mainly in their prominent coloration of particular body areas, such as the head, cheeks, shoulder, wing patch (speculum), or primary feathers.

All Amazons live in humid climates and as house or aviary birds also need enough moisture, from spray baths or warm rain, to keep their plumage from becoming

dull and brittle. They have a strong voice, which is heard frequently, even when the bird is well acclimated.

Young Amazons quickly get used to their new environment and to the society of human beings. They become tame and affectionate. With too little attention and boredom they decline, sometimes even wasting away to death.

Even very tame Amazons can become aggressive with humans and destructive when they come into breeding season and have no mate of their species. The only remedy is relocation to a roomy avi- ary with a compatible partner.

Blue-fronted Amazon
Amazona aestiva

Appearance: The breast feathers are lightly edged with black; crown and eye region, sometimes also throat and thighs, yellow; bend of wing and speculum red; yellow band at the end of the tail feathers; ends of the primaries deep blue and blue-black; unfeathered, light eye ring; forehead and lore light blue. Male and female look the same.

Total length: 14 inches (36 cm).
Young birds: Blue and yellow shades in plumage noticeably duller, or one of the two colors is predominant.

66

Amazons

Range: Brazil, Bolivia, northern Argentina.

Keeping: Common and popular pet bird; intelligent and friendly; especially adaptable; the best at speaking of all the Amazons.

Spectacled Amazon

White-fronted or white-browed Amazon
Amazona albifrons

Appearance: The feathers on the back, neck, and breast are dark-edged; white forehead; blue crown; gray eye ring encircled with red. The border of the upper wing converts and the wing patch are red, the primary feathers are black and green-blue; the beak is yellow, light horn-colored in the center.

The borders of the upper wing coverts in the female are usually green, the red wreath around the eye ring is less developed, the red wing patch is missing. The female is often noticeably smaller than the male.

Total length: 9¾ inches (25 cm).

Young birds: The red wreath around the eye ring is incomplete, yellow is "dusted over" the white forehead or only hinted at.

Range: Western Mexico, Guatemala, Honduras, El Salvador, western Costa Rica.

Keeping: Kept as a pet, the dainty spectacled Amazon quickly becomes tame; it is considered a very good talker, friendly and affectionate.

Scarlet-lored parrot.

Spectacled Amazon

Scarlet-lored Parrot

Yellow-, primrose-, or orange-cheeked Amazon
Amazona autumnalis

Appearance: This splendidly colored Amazon has a brilliant red forehead, besides yellow cheeks, which become red around the beak. The lore, front of the crown, and wing patches are also brilliant red. The top of the head is pale blue with dark-edged feathers; white eye rings and black lashes; primaries blue-black and green; tail yellow-banded. Male and female look alike.

Total length: 13 inches (34 cm).

Young birds: Iris dark-brown, forehead and lore paler in color.

Range: Eastern mountain slopes of Mexico, Guatemala to Nicaragua.

Keeping: Popular pet because of gentle nature; affectionate; loves to learn and enjoys contact; intelligent; good talker. Can get its own way with use of powerful voice.

Orange-winged Amazon

Amazona amazonica

Appearance: The plumage is iridescent light blue on the back of the head and nape; lore blue, chin pale blue; forehead and crown flecked blue-yellow; yellow cheeks; orange-red wing patches; orange-red inner tail feathers; deep blue and green flight feathers; unfeathered gray-blue eye ring. Male and female look the same.

Total length: 11¾ to 12½ inches (30 to 32 cm).

Young birds: Resemble their parents.

Range: Northern South America, except for Andes and eastern Brazilian coastal region; islands of Trinidad and Tobago.

Keeping: Charming, alert pet bird with powerful voice; especially adept speaker and easy to tame.

Mealy Amazon

Orange-winged Amazon.

Mealy Amazon
Amazona farinosa

Appearance: The deep-green plumage has a touch of light gray, especially on the back. The bird gets its name from this "mealy" appearance. Contrasting red wing patches and wing edges; striking yellow spot on forehead, which varies in size and arrangement depending on the individual. Feathers on back edged with dark green; tail banded with greenish yellow. Slightly oval white eye ring. Male and female look alike.

Total length: 14¾ to 15½ inches (38 to 40 cm).

Young birds: Yellow spot on forehead only suggested by individual yellow feathers.

Range: Southern Mexico, northern South America to southern Bolivia and central eastern Brazil.

Keeping: Young birds quickly become tame and astound with their extraordinary gift for mimicry. Tremendously strong voice!

Yellow-naped Amazon
Golden-naped Amazon
Amazona ochrocephala auropalliata

The species *A. ochrocephala* contains several subspecies that are not easy to differentiate. Very different descriptions often appear in the literature.

Appearance: Yellow nape spot and yellow forehead; light-gray eye ring; gray beak and dark-gray, slightly feathered cere. Male and female look alike.

Total length: 13½ inches (35 cm).

Young birds: Instead of the yellow nape spot, usually only a few yellow feathers on the nape.

Range: South America, northwestern Costa Rica, northern Honduras.

Keeping: Popular pet bird because of its gentle nature; very intelligent and quick to learn; good talker; uses foot skillfully for grasping objects.

Yellow-fronted Amazon
Amazona ochrocephala

Appearance: Green plumage with iridescent areas; bend of wing and wing patch red; undertail covert yellowish green with red dots at the base of each tail feather; upper beak sometimes partially pink; unfeathered white eye ring; forehead and top of head yellow, feathers on the forehead shot through with green. Male and female look alike.

Total length: 13½ inches (35 cm).

Young birds: Incomplete yellow coloration to the age of about four years; dark iris.

Amazons

Yellow-fronted Amazon

Yellow-naped Amazon.

Mexican red-head.

Range: Surinam, eastern Venezuela, Andes, Colombia, island of Trinidad.

Keeping: Popular pet bird because of its talent for imitation; very intelligent and quick to learn; uses its foot for grasping food or objects. Its vocal utterances are among the loudest of the Amazon genus. Yellow-crowned Amazons constantly need branches to gnaw on. Young birds are especially friendly, playful, and amusing.

Mexican Red-head

Red-crowned parrot, green-cheeked Amazon

Amazona viridigenalis

Appearance: Dark-green plumage; forehead, crown, and lore scarlet red; brilliant green cheeks, which are surrounded by a semicircle of blue-violet featherlets. Primary feathers blue-black with red wing patch; unfeathered white eye ring. In the female the extent of the red feathers on the crown is smaller.

Total length: 13 inches (33 cm).

Young birds: The red appears only on the forehead; the crown is predominantly green.

Range: Northeastern Mexico.

Keeping: Singly kept birds demand a great deal of attention and exciting occupation. They behave very quietly in human captivity and with neglect tend to become indifferent. Mexican red-heads should be kept only in pairs. In the morning and evening the birds love to utter piercing screams.

Macaws

Hahn's macaw.

Green-winged macaw.

Chestnut-fronted macaw.

Macaws are native to Central and South America. The genus is divided into three groups: blue macaws (*Anodorhynchus*), Spix's blue macaws, and the true macaws.

Hahn's Macaw
Diopsittaca or *Ara nobilis*

Appearance: Green plumage that lightens to yellowish on breast and abdomen. Forehead and crown gray-blue; gray beak with gray cere. Brilliant scarlet carpal edge, bend of wing, and greater underwing coverts; smooth, white facial skin that covers the lore and broadens into the eye ring. Male and female look alike.

Total length: 11¾ inches (30 cm).

Young birds: Red plumage color lacking; head region dull bluish.

Range: In east of Venezuela and Guyana to southern Brazil, in woods and grasslands.

Keeping: Keep in pairs. Pleasant voice, which is seldom very loud. The birds need flying space and plenty of opportunities to climb and gnaw.

Green-winged Macaw
Maroon macaw, red-and-blue macaw, red-and-green macaw
Ara chloroptera

Appearance: Dark-red plumage up to the cere. Median wing coverts dark green, secondary coverts rich, dark blue; primaries and secondaries as well as upper tail feathers dark blue; under tail feathers dark red. Upper beak horn-colored with dark edges; lower beak black. Skin of the cheeks marked with fine red feather striping. Male and female look alike.

Total length: 35 inches (90 cm).

Young birds: Upper beak darker; tail feathers shorter.

Range: All tropical South America.

Keeping: It is essential to provide this large bird with adequate

70

Macaws

Blue-and-yellow macaw

living space when it is kept as a pet. Even a short-term cage existence is unreasonable for it. It demands a great deal of care, attention, and contact. Its loud voice can annoy neighbors. Young macaws are roguish and become very tame.

Important: Nesting boxes needed for sleeping.

Chestnut-fronted Macaw
Severe macaw
Ara severa

Appearance: The green plumage is interrupted only on the head by the bright blue-green crown, the blackish brown forehead, and by the red bends of the wings and wing patches; outer vanes of feathers on the primaries are medium blue to greenish blue, as well as the tips of the tail feathers. Upper side of the tail is olive brown; underside of tail reddish. Male and female look alike.

Total length: 18 inches (48 cm).
Young birds: The iris is black.
Range: Panama, southern Bolivia, western Ecuador, western Colombia, northern Brazil.
Keeping: Less difficult than large macaws. Keep in pairs, since single birds pine for a companion.
Important: Needs large indoor aviary with many things to do; nesting boxes for sleeping.

Blue-and-yellow Macaw
Ara ararauna

Appearance: Nape, back, wing coverts, and upper side of tail blue. Primaries and outer tail feathers dark blue. Ear areas, breast, abdomen, thighs, and undertail coverts light to golden yellow; forehead to crown green; throat dark green; white cheeks with dark-green feather striping. Male and female look alike.

Total length: 33 to 35 inches (85 to 90 cm).
Young birds: Dark iris.
Range: Northern South America.
Keeping: See green-winged macaw.

Parrotlets

Caiques

Spectacled parrotlet.

Celestial parrotlet.

Black-headed caique.

For nearly 300 years, South American parrotlets have also been kept in aviaries, where they frequently breed. They are charming pets when allowed to live in pairs or groups. Single birds waste away and die. Isolate breeding pairs, because they become quarrelsome. Separate full-fledged young birds from the parents as soon as they begin to eat on their own. When a cage is too small, murder of a partner can occur. The smallest possible size of cage for breeding pairs and small groups is 79 × 40 × 59 inches (2 × 1 × 1.5 m).

Spectacled Parrotlet
Forpus conspicillatus

Appearance: Light-green plumage, yellowish green in places; the breast is delicate blue-green or blue-gray. Very bright blue feathered eye ring. The male has a blue rump as well as blue back feathers. The feather portion around the eye, the rump, and the lower back of the female are brilliant cobalt.

Total length: 4½ inches (12 cm).

Young birds: Blue coloration not developed, only suggested or shot through with green feathers.

Range: Eastern Panama, western Venezuela, Colombia.

Keeping: See Parrotlets.

Celestial Parrotlet
Lesson's parrotlet, Pacific parrotlet
Forpus coelestis

Appearance: Basic plumage green, in differing shades: Upper head, cheeks, and throat linden green, back and shoulder coverts olive-green. Upper tail feathers strong blue-green; nape and a stripe behind the eye light blue. Rump, wings, and underside of tail cobalt blue. Females display a pale blue color only behind the eyes and on the rump; green shades less vivid than in the males.

Total length: 5 inches (13 cm).

Young birds: Similar to parents; tail noticeably shorter.

Range: Dry regions of Ecuador and Peru.

Keeping: See Parrotlets.

Caiques
All caiques are said to be fearless, friendly, and playful. Their voice is loud, but not monotonous. They constantly need branches for gnawing, because their beak has a tendency to excessive growth.

Black-headed Caique
Pionites melanocephala

Appearance: Lore and fine stripes under the eyes green; throat, neck, and nape yellow; nape down to back feathers orange; breast and abdomen whitish to light gray; wings and upper tail surface green; thighs and underside of tail yellow-orange; primaries dark blue; upper head dark green; cere and eye rings gray. Male and female look alike.

Total length: 9 inches (23 cm).

Young birds: Beak light horn-color, iris dark brown, plumage paler all over.

Range: Guayana, Brazil, southern Colombia, eastern Ecuador, and northeastern Peru

Keeping: See Caiques.

Caiques

Pionus Parrots

Blue-headed parrot.

Maximilian's parrot.

White-bellied caique

White-bellied Caique
White-breasted caique
Pionites leucogaster
Appearance: Yellowish orange head; flesh-colored beak; pink eye rings. The yellow becomes orange on the nape. Back and wings dark green; breast and belly white; lower belly green. Male and female look alike.

Total length: 9 inches (23 cm).

Young birds: Gray-black feathers here and there on the crown; the wings have a bluish effect.

Range: Northern Brazil, northern Bolivia, eastern Peru, eastern Ecuador.

Keeping: See Caiques.

Pionus Parrots
Blue-headed parrots and Maximilian's parrots belong to the genus *Pionus* and are from South America.

Blue-headed Parrot
Red-vented parrot
Pionus menstruus
Appearance: Green basic plumage; head, neck, and breast strong blue. In the ear region there is a round, black spot on a blue ground; gray eye ring; cere and beak black; on both sides of the upper beak a pink triangle.

Throat region old rose to violet; breast dark green with blue-edged feathers. Outer tail feathers blue, under tail feathers red. Male and female look alike.

Total length: 11 inches (28 cm).

Young birds: Up to age of one year they bear a red or orange band on the forehead; blue appears only in a small area on the head.

Range: Costa Rica, Venezuela, northern Bolivia, central Brazil, Trinidad.

Keeping: Gentle pets that suffer when kept singly. Lively and friendly in pairs.

Maximilian's Parrot
Scaly-headed parrot
Pionus maximiliani
Appearance: Olive-green plumage, here and there with a bronzy sheen; bordered with dark-gray on head and nape. Nape feathers striped with white. Chin, throat, and top of breast shimmer violet blue; forehead and lore very dark green; eye rings white. Male and female look alike.

Total length: 11 inches (28 cm).

Young birds: Many have a red band on the forehead until the first molt; violet-blue coloration on the throat region only sparsely developed.

Range: Eastern and southeastern Brazil, northern Argentina.

Keeping: Acquire young and in pairs; provide for plenty of exercise and activity as well as facilities for hanging head down from slender branches when sleeping.

73

Lovebirds

The home of the lovebirds, the Aga-pornidae, is Africa. They are among the best known of the small parrots. Because they can survive in human captivity only as pairs, certain species among them have also bred frequently. Do not keep lovebirds with other species of small parrots. Lovebirds are often quarrelsome and very aggressive during mating season.

All species of lovebirds are best kept in pairs.

Lovebirds seldom imitate words or sounds; they are completely preoccupied with their own lives. For housing them, an indoor aviary measuring 31 × 39 × 78 inches (80 × 100 × 200 cm) is ideal. Two or three well-established pairs can also live in larger areas.

Nevertheless, when a pair is ready to breed, it must be isolated. Lovebirds always need a chance to bathe. When nest building, some breeding birds soften the nesting material in the bath water. Pairs always use nesting boxes for sleeping.

Peach-faced Lovebird
Rosy-faced lovebird
Agapornis roseicollis

Appearance: Emerald-green plumage; blue rump and upper tail feathers as well as rose-red to salmon-pink face.

The red shades extend from the forehead over the cheeks to the top of the breast. Male and female look alike.

Total length: 6 inches (15 cm).

Young birds: The upper half of the upper beak is darkly colored, the red shades are very pale.

Range: Plains and grasslands with water holes up to elevations of 5249 feet (1600 m) in Namibia and southwestern Angola.

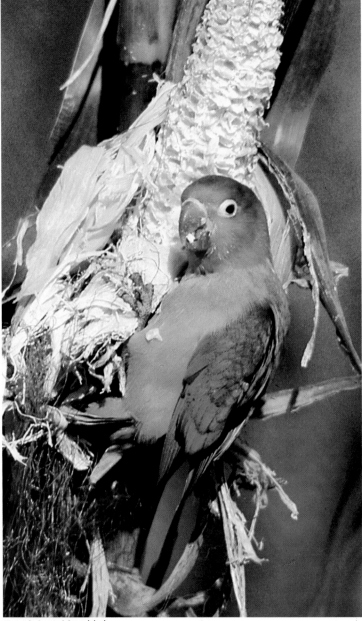

Peach-faced lovebird.

Lovebirds

Fischer's lovebirds.

Black-masked lovebirds

Keeping: Peach-faced lovebirds usually get along among themselves but are very aggressive with birds of other species. Therefore, in aviaries in rows, double-mesh separating walls are recommended. The females carry the nest-building material in the feathers of their lower back or rump and stuff it into the nest box. For nest-building material they use leaves or paper that they shred, sometimes even softening it in their bath water. Males do not take part in this operation.

Fischer's Lovebird
Agapornis fischeri

Appearance: This bird resembles the peach-faced lovebird, except that the forehead, cheeks, and throat are orange-red; breast golden yellow; belly light green. Back, scapulars, and wing coverts, as well as the exterior vanes of the primaries, lush green; inner vanes of the primary feathers black; rump and upper tail feathers blue. The face is rendered very impressive by the distinct white unfeathered eye rings and cere.

Total length: 6 inches (15 cm).

Young birds: The plumage colors are noticeably duller, especially in the face; the upper beak is dark gray at the base.

Range: In the highlands of northern Tanzania.

Keeping: See Peach-faced Lovebird. The female brings the nesting material in with her beak.

Black-masked Lovebird
Agapornis personata

Appearance: Resembles the other species of lovebirds but impressively distinguished from them by the dark brown face with white, unfeathered eye rings; brilliant red beak; breast, neck, and nape sunflower yellow; wing coverts dark green; underwing coverts blue-gray and green; upper tail feathers pale blue. A black band with dark-yellow markings extends across the upper tail covert.

Total length: 6 inches (15 cm).

Young birds: The plumage colors are considerably duller; the upper half of the upper beak is dark gray.

Range: Central Tanzania at elevations up to 5577 feet (1700 m). Naturalized in Nairobi and Dar es Salaam.

Keeping: Pairs only, not compatible in larger groups. For nesting material, shredded bark is carried in the beak.

Long-winged Parrots

Senegal parrots.

Meyer's parrot.

The genus of long-winged parrots, *Poicephalus,* comprises birds of different sizes and colors. All look attractive and have a nice voice and a gentle temperament.

Senegal Parrot

Yellow-bellied Senegal parrot
Poicephalus senegalus

Appearance: Forehead and top of head darker gray than throat and cheeks. The light-green nape feathers encircle the neck and form a sharp triangle on the breast, which is repeated on the thighs. Lateral breast, belly, and undertail coverts golden-yellow to orange-yellow; primary and tail feathers olive-green to olive-brown; shoulders and wing coverts green. Male and female look alike.

Total length: 9 inches (24 cm).

Young birds: The beak is gray and pink, the yellow of the belly feathers is largely missing.

Range: Central Africa.

Keeping: Young birds become trusting pets, sometimes even hand tame. If a Senegal parrot does not bond closely to its keeper, it should be kept in an indoor aviary with a companion of the same species. The birds need a great deal of free flight, however.

Meyer's Parrot

Appearance: Head, throat, nape, upper surface, primaries, and tail gray-brown; rump and belly feathers bluish green with some gray-brown edges; crown, thighs, underwing and undertail coverts and the bends of the wings brilliant yellow to golden yellow. Male and female look alike.

Total length:
8½ inches (22 cm).

Young birds: Predominantly gray. Yellow is missing or only moderately developed.

Range: Central Africa from the Sudan to Zambia.

Keeping: Young birds adapt well to human society and become tame and trusting. Keeping a pair is advisable, however, because single birds easily become lonely.

The African gray parrot is probably

African Gray Parrot

African gray parrot nibbling on a linden seed.

the best known parrot because it is kept in thousands of households. Successful breeding surely will make it possible for the many people who would like one of these especially clever and crafty birds as a companion to have their wish.

Although most representatives of this species look like the one pictured, there are also African gray parrots whose gray plumage is shot through with relatively large numbers of pink feathers. The cause of this phenomenon has not yet been clearly explained.

African Gray Parrot
Psittacus erithacus

Appearance: Gray plumage shading from light to dark gray; feathers on nape, neck, and throat finely bordered with white; unfeathered white facial skin; strikingly brilliant red tail feathers. The Timneh gray parrot—*P. erithacus timneh*—differs from the African gray parrot in that its tail feathers are rust brown and its upper beak, flesh-colored with a dark tip, is somewhat smaller. Male and female look alike.

Total length: 14 inches (36 cm).

Young birds: The red of the tail feathers appears somewhat darker.

Range: From the Ivory Coast to northwestern Tanzania.

Keeping: Hand-raised birds quickly become tame and bond closely to their keeper. Birds that have been raised in a breeding hole are often shy and anxious with humans for months, even years. African gray parrots are among the most skillful speakers and mimics. Their feats of intelligence are remarkable. During the acclimation period, they often will let you hear the sounds of their loud voice. Underoccupied, neglected birds often begin pulling out their feathers.

77

Cockatoos

Greater sulphur-crested cockatoo.

The habitats of the cockatoo are Australia, Indonesia, Oceania, and the Philippines. Cockatoos are classified as either black or white. The white cockatoos are further subdivided into species with black beaks and those with white. Cockatoos are to a large extent restricted to well-wooded environments. Because of the continuing destruction of the forests in their native areas, many species are severely endangered, some even threatened with extinction.

Cockatoos are extremely intelligent and produce remarkable achievements in human captivity. Still, they are suitable as house birds only under certain conditions, because their instinctive need to gnaw and their powerful beaks reduce any wood to sawdust. Shut up in a cage, the bird will become a feather plucker, with fatal results. Only roomy flight cages furnished with many sturdy branches for gnawing can provide an appropriate environment for a cockatoo pair. The floor of this flight must be cemented, for cockatoos constantly dig in the earth with their beaks and can easily escape under the edges of the wire mesh. You should always give cockatoos the chance to dig by shoveling earth onto the floor of the flight, however.

A single cockatoo needs almost uninterrupted contact with its primary person if it is not to suffer and cause trouble with its beak or its voice. Feeding cockatoos is difficult because they are very hesitant to accept unfamiliar foods, yet they need large quantities of fresh food and also additional protein, as well as seeds. Keep trying patiently to get them to learn to enjoy things that are unfamiliar.

Cockatoos

Lesser sulphur-crested cockatoo.

Citron-crested cockatoo.

Lesser sulphur-crested cockatoo.

Greater Sulphur-crested Cockatoo

Cacatua galerita

Appearance: White plumage, yellow crest; slightly yellowish coloring of throat feathers; undersides of wings and tail bright yellow; white, unfeathered eye ring. Males have a dark-brown iris, females a reddish brown one.

Total length: 19½ inches (50 cm.)

Young birds: The iris is brown.

Range: In northern, eastern, and southern Australia.

Keeping: See Cockatoos.

Lesser Sulphur-crested Cockatoo

Cacatua sulphurea

Appearance: Resembles the greater sulphur-crested cockatoo, but with yellow cheek spots. The female has a red-brown iris; that of the male is dark brown.

Total length: 13 inches (33 cm.)

Young birds: They have a gray iris. The iris of young females becomes yellow in the second year of life, then red-brown.

Range: Indonesia, Sunda Islands, small islands of the Flores and Java Seas.

Keeping: Caught young, singly kept cockatoos become extremely tame and affectionate, but they are almost an all-day job for their keeper. Left to themselves, they protest with ear-splitting shrieks or become feather-pullers.

Citron-crested Cockatoo

Cacatua sulphurea citrinocristata

Appearance: It resembles the lesser sulphur-crested cockatoo, except that all the yellow shades of the plumage are a clear, bright orange-red. Males are usually some-

Cockatoos

Rose-breasted cockatoo.

Goffin's cockatoo.

Bare-eyed cockatoo.

what larger than females and have a stronger beak.

Total length: 13 inches (33 cm).

Young birds: Like parents.

Range: Island of Sumba in the Lesser Sunda Islands.

Keeping: Rare as a pet, because almost priceless. Well acclimated, the citron-crested cockatoo is extremely devoted and as a single bird needs constant contact with its keeper. For this reason, it is advisable to keep a pair. Loud voice, which over time can be a strain on the nerves.

Bare-eyed Cockatoo

Cacatua sanguinea, recently
Cacatua pastinator
Little corella

Appearance: White plumage with a few orange-red spots on lore as well as reddish spots on the base of the head, nape, back, and breast feathers; underside of the tail and primary feathers bright yellow; blue-gray eye ring, which broadens to an oval on the lower part; long,

narrow upper beak. Females are slightly smaller than males.

Total length: 15 inches (38 cm).

Young birds: They have a shorter beak; the eye ring is gray, not blue-gray.

Range: North, northwestern, and eastern Australia and Southern New Guinea.

Keeping: See Cockatoos. Talented speaker, gentle, peaceful nature.

Goffin's Cockatoo

Cacatua goffini

Appearance: Basic plumage color white: round, white eye rings; lore and crest salmon pink; light gray beak. Males have a black iris, females a reddish one.

Total length: 12½ inches (32 cm).

Young birds: Like parents.

Range: Tanimar (Tenimber) Islands of Indonesia, mainly in forests.

Keeping: See Cockatoos. Goffin's cockatoos are quite unproble-

matic, undemanding charges when kept as pairs. They have a powerful need to gnaw and a loud voice.

Rose-breasted Cockatoo

Roseate cockatoo, Galah cockatoo
Eolophus roseicapillus, recently
Cacatua roseicapilla

Appearance: Top of head pinkish white; crest feathers rose-red with pinkish white edges; cheeks, throat, breast, and belly bright rose red; back and upper wing and tail surfaces medium gray; under wing and tail surfaces dark gray. The narrow, unfeathered, reddish eye ring can be smooth or wrinkled.

Females have a reddish brown iris, but it is not a dependable identifying mark, because it is variable.

Total length: 13½ inches (35 cm).

Young birds: Up to the age of one year, duller plumage colors; crown and breast are overlaid with a gray veil.

Range: Interior of almost all of Australia.

Keeping: See Cockatoos. Less powerful voices than the previously

Eclectus Parrots

A pair of Halmahera eclectus parrots

Red-sided eclectus parrots.

described species. Should be kept mostly in the aviary.

Electus Parrots
Eclectus parrots are native to Indonesia, the Cape York Peninsula of Australia, the Solomon Islands, and New Guinea.

Halmahera Eclectus Parrot
Eclectus roratus vosmaeri
Appearance of male: All males of the genus have green plumage. Even specialists are uncertain about the assignment of males to a species and base their decision primarily on body size.
Total length: 15 inches (38 cm).

Appearance of female: Red feathers on head and throat, breast and neck blue-violet, bend of wings blue, wing coverts rust-brown. On the tail the ends of the feathers form a broad yellow band; the underside of the tail is dark orange.
Total length: 15 inches (38 cm).
Young birds: The sexes are already recognizable by their plumage colors by the time they leave the nesting hole, although they haven't yet reached their ultimate intensity.
Range: Molucca Islands.
Keeping: When acquired young, single birds become very tame and behave peaceably, but can become sluggish. Keeping pairs

is recommended, especially because eclectus parrots have agreeable voices and a repertoire of melodious sounds at their disposal. Spacious climbing areas are required, with sturdy limbs and branches.

Red-sided Eclectus Parrot
Eclectus roratus polychlorus
Appearance of male: Intense green plumage; red undersides of wings; blue bend of wing; dark-blue external vanes of primaries. Strong, orange-red upper beak with yellow tip.
Total length: 13½ inches (35 cm).
Appearance of female: Plumage on head, neck, throat, and breast red. A blue-violet triangle glows on her back; belly plumage bright blue; wing coverts dark red-brown; finely feathered blue eye rings.
Total length: 13½ inches (35 cm).
Young birds: See Halmahera eclectus.
Range: New Guinea and western Papua Islands.
Keeping: See Halmahera eclectus.

Glossary

How many cockatoo species are there altogether? What is aspergillosis? You'll find the answers to these and other questions when you read through this little parrot glossary. The headings and their short explanations are arranged alphabetically and will expand your knowledge about parrots.

A

Amazon species:
There are approximately 26 Amazon species (opinions vary as to whether some species should be considered species or subspecies). Some are already extinct, others seriously endangered, like the imperial Amazon, for instance, whose habitat is being increasingly destroyed. Today there are only about 80 imperial Amazons left living in the wild.

Active Amazon, all-green Amazon, all-green parrot, Ja-maican black-billed Amazon, *Amazona agilis.* Found in Jamaica, where it is sometimes seen in the company of yellow-billed Amazon. Unfortunately endangered. Rarely kept as a house pet.

Blue-faced Amazon, red-necked, Bouquet's, or lesser Dominican Amazon, *Amazona arausiaca.* Found on the island of Dominica, Lesser Antilles. A very limited habitat, which is increasingly being destroyed by cultivation. Existence of the species severely endangered.

Blue-fronted Amazon, *Amazona aestiva* (see page 66), subspecies: *A.a. xanthopteryx.* Still common regionally, nevertheless endangered by persistent destruction of its habitat. One of the most popular Amazons for a house pet, being a talented imitator. First successful breeding attempts reported.

Cuban Amazon, *Amazona leucocephala;* subspecies: *A. l. bahamensis, A.l. caymenensis.* Found in Cuba, on the Bahamas, Isle of Pines. Threatened species; however, protected in Cuba for several years. Sought after as a pet bird but rare. Breeding has been successful.

Dufresne's or blue-cheeked Amazon, *Amazona dufresniana,* subspecies: *A.d. rhodocorytha.* Found in Guayana, Brazil, Venezuela. Rarely kept as a pet; information about its way of life, endangerment, or keeping is hard to find.

Festive Amazon, *Amazona festiva,* subspecies: Bodin's Amazon, *A.f. bodini.* Found in Brazil, Peru, Ecuador, Colombia, Guayana; mostly in the vicinity of streams; only Am-azon with red rump. Not often a pet.

Finsch's Amazon, lilac-crowned Amazon, *Amazona finschi.* Found in western Mexico; common and widely distributed. Seldom kept as a pet; sometimes seen in parrot collections, where breeding also has been successful.

Imperial Amazon, *Amazona imperialis.* Found exclusively on the island of Dominica, Lesser Antilles. Through destruction of the habitat, threatened with extinction.

Mealy Amazon, *Amazona farinosa* (see page 68), subspecies: *A.f. guatemalae, A.f. virenticeps.* Still common in forested regions. Especially large Amazon, which is not often kept as a house pet, more often seen in zoos.

Mercenary Amazon, *Amazona mercenaria.* Found in the Andes regions of Colombia, Bolivia, and Venezuela; rare species. To a large extent unknown as a house pet.

Mexican red head, green-cheeked Amazon, red-crowned parrot, *Amazona viridigenalis* (see page 69). Endangered by destruction of habitat. Rarely a pet bird; nevertheless, breeding has been successful.

Orange-winged Amazon, *Amazona amazonica* (see page 67). Widely ranging and common species. A popular and often kept pet bird. Reports of breeding have occurred, but only occasionally.

Pretre's Amazon, *Amazona pretrei.*

Occurs in Brazil from Såao Paulo to Rio Grande. Endangered by diminishing habitat. Very seldom kept as a house pet.

Puerto Rico Amazon, *Amazona vittata.*
Found in Puerto Rico, which belongs to the United States. Because only about 40 birds of this species are left, their habitat of some 31 square miles (80 square km) has fortunately been taken under the protection of the U.S. Wildlife Service and is thus strictly protected. Nevertheless, it is one of the most endangered species.

Red-tailed Amazon, *Amazona brasiliensis.*
Found in limited areas of southeastern Brazil; existence endangered because of destruction of habitat. Scarcely known outside Brazil.

Salle's Amazon, blue-crowned Amazon, *Amazona ventralis.*
Found in Haiti; introduced to Puerto Rico. Endangered in Haiti, relatively common in Puerto Rico. Rarely a pet bird; nevertheless, breeding has been successful.

St. Lucia Amazon, *Amazona versicolor.*
Found exclusively on the island of St. Lucia, Lesser Antilles. The existence of the species is severely endangered but strictly protected. Not a house pet.

St. Vincent Amazon, Guilding's Amazon, *Amazona guildingii.*
Found exclusively in the mountain country of the island of St. Vincent, Lesser Antilles. Very rare and endangered.

Tucuman Amazon, *Amazona tucumana.*
Found in Bolivia and northern Argentina; lives primarily on the slopes of the Andes. Popular house pet, which has been successfully bred.

Vinaceous Amazon, *Amazona vinacea.*
Found in southeastern Brazil to northeastern Argentina and southeastern Paraguay. Species endangered through destruction of habitat. Rare as house pet, more apt to be seen in zoos.

White-fronted Amazon, white-browed Amazon, spectacled Amazon parrot, *Amazona albifrons* (see page 67), subspecies: *A.a. nana.*
Not a rare pet bird, nevertheless there is only sparse information about it.

Yellow-billed Amazon, red-throated Amazon, *Amazona collaria.*
Occurs on Jamaica; more common and widespread than the active Amazon, which is also found there. Rarely a pet bird; nevertheless, has been successfully bred.

Yellow-cheeked Amazon, *Amazona autumnalis* (see page 67), subspecies: *A.a. salvini, A.a. lilacina, A.a. diadema.*
In the United States a popular and common pet bird, rare in Europe. Breeding has succeeded under great difficulties, but only to a small extent.

Yellow-faced Amazon, *Amazona xantholora.*
Found in the Yucatán Peninsula in southeastern Mexico, in British Honduras, and on Cozumel and Roatán. Rarely a pet; nevertheless, there have been successful breedings.

Glossary

Yellow-faced or Yellow-bellied Amazon, *Amazona xanthops.*
Occurs in Brazil; common regionally. Very rarely a pet bird; mostly seen in zoos.

Yellow-fronted Amazon, *Amazona ochrocephala* (see page 68),
Subspecies: *A.o. oratrix, A.o. autopalliata, A.o. natteri.*
Often kept as a pet, because it is remarkably intelligent. Breeding frequently successful.

Yellow-shouldered Amazon, *Amazona barabdenis.*
Found only rarely now on the islands off Venezuela, Blanquilla, Margarita, and Bonaire; still relatively common in northern Venezuela. Vary rarely a house pet.

Aspergillosis
Fungus infection arising from mold; for which no cure exists. Life-threatening for parrots. See your veterinarian immediately. Caution: Throw out moldy food, bedding, etc.

B

Brooding temperatures
For most parrots 98.6° F (37° C) is ideal for brooding; with cooler temperatures the hatching of the young may be delayed.

83

Glossary

C

Caiques

This genus has the Latin name of *Pionites* and contains only 2 species, both of which have been bred and can be kept as house pets:

Black-headed caique, *Pionites melanocephala* (see page 72); subspecies: *P.m. pallida* (Pallid Caique)

White-bellied caique, *Pionites leucogaster* (see page 73); subspecies:
P.l. xanthomeri and *P.l. xanthurus* (yellow-thighed and yellow-tailed caique, respectively). Still numerous in areas of their natural habitat.

Cere

This is found at the base of the beak, surrounds the nostrils, and in many species is unfeathered, sometimes strikingly colored, and in other species is covered with fine feathers.

Cockatoo species

Not all cockatoos belong to the same genus. The rare species, which are chiefly to be admired in zoos, like the Banksian red-tailed cockatoo, the glossy black cockatoo, and the funereal or yellow-tailed black cockatoo, belong to the genus *Calyptorhynchus*, while the Gang Gang cockatoo is the only species constituting the genus *Callocephalon* and the great black cockatoo the genus *Prosciger*. In the same way,

the well-known rose-breasted cockatoo by itself formed the genus *Eolophus*, recently changed to *Cacatua*. All other known cockatoos belong to the genus of the black- or white-beaked cockatoos, called *Cacatua* in Latin. Here are the individual species and their subspecies:

Banksian or red-tailed cockatoo, red-tailed black cockatoo, *Calyptorhynchus magnificus;* subspecies: *C.m. naso*. Found throughout Australia.

A hyacinthine macaw, left, and a blue-and-yellow macaw, right. Parrots' powerful, mobile beaks supplement their feet as aids to climbing.

Bare-eyed cockatoo, *Cacatua-sanguinea (pastinator)* (see page 80).
Found in the interior of northwestern and central Australia. (The details given for species and subspecies are somewhat contradictory in different publications.)

Blue-eyed cockatoo, *Cacatua ophthalmica.*
A white cockatoo with brilliant blue eye rings. Found in the Bismarck Archipelago. (In other publications it is also described

as a subspecies of the great sulphur-crested cockatoo.)

Ducorp's cockatoo, *Cacatua ducorpsi.*
Found in the eastern Solomon Islands, where it is still relatively common. One of these charming, dainty cockatoos lives in Loro Park on Tenerife, without a partner, unfortunately. It must once have lived with Spaniards, for it speaks some Spanish phrases. With great skill it induces the visitors to the park to pay attention to it. The bird prefers the male sex. For example, if a brave man puts an outstretched finger into the cage, the cockatoo immediately climbs onto the finger and enjoys its perch, chattering charmingly, but if a woman does the same thing, the little devil attacks and bites the finger and laughs maliciously when its victim screams.

Funereal cockatoo, yellow-tailed black cockatoo, *Calyptorhynchus funereus;* subspecies: *C.f. baudinii.*

Glossy black cockatoo, *Calyptorhynchus lathami.*
Found in eastern and central Australia.

Goffin's cockatoo, *Cacatua goffini* (see page 80).
Known in Europe for only about 20 years, because many birds were deprived of their habitats by extensive clearing and therefore were exported simply as commodities.

Great black cockatoo, *Prosciger atterimus,* subspecies: *P.a. stenolophus; P.a. goliath.*
Found in northeastern Australia and on Cape Horn.

Greater sulphur-crested cockatoo, *Cacatua galerita* (see page 79).
Greater sulphur-crested cockatoos are noted for their gentle temperament and become very devoted in human captivity.

Leadbeater's cockatoo, Major Mitchell or pink cockatoo, *Cacatua leadbeateri.*
Found in interior of western, southern, and southeastern Australia; very uncommon in broad areas of their range of distribution, somewhat more numerous in only a few districts. A sought-after pet bird because of its beautiful, multicolored crest; breeding often successful; mostly to be seen in zoos.

Lesser sulphur-crested cockatoo, *Cacatua sulphurea* (see page 79); subspecies: *C.s. occidentalis; C.s. cintrinocristata,* citron-crested cockatoo (see page 79); *C.s. parvula.* An especially popular pet bird, which bonds to its keeper with devotion; breeding is successful world wide.

Moluccan cockatoo,
salmon-crested, rose-crested, or red-crested cockatoo, *Cacatua moluccensis.*
Found on the southern Molucca Islands of Seran, Saparua, Haruku, and naturalized on Amboina. Sought-after pet because of its particularly outstanding intelligence; virtually unavailable; chiefly to be seen in zoos.

Philippine cockatoo, red-vented cockatoo, *Cacatua haematuropygia.*
Found in the Philippines and in the Palau Islands. Because they inflict damage on wheat fields, they are hunted by farmers. They are still numerous, though extensive clearing of

land is continuing to reduce the population. Successfully bred in Europe and America.

Rose-breasted cockatoo, roseate, or galah cockatoo, *(Eolophus roseicapillus) Cacatua roseicapilla* (see page 80). Since rose-breasted cockatoos are being bred all over the world, they will certainly still be available as pets in the future; frequently to be seen in zoos.

Slender-billed cockatoo or long-billed corella, *Cacatua tenuirostris.*
Found in southeastern and southwestern Australia. Owing to the destruction of their habitats, the number of slender-billed cockatoos has been declining alarmingly for a long time. Today there are only a few still living in their original habitats. With their especially long bills these birds are able to dig up roots, their preferred food.

Umbrella-crested cockatoo, white crested, or great white-crested cockatoo, *Cacatua alba.*
Still commonly found in their natural habitat. Reputed to be particularly intelligent, loveable, and good at speaking.

D

Down
Fine fluffy feathers that cover the bodies of newly hatched young of some parrot species (in some species young also hatch naked). The down falls out later and is replaced by a thicker coat of down.

Glossary

E

Eclectus parrots
There is only one species, the grand eclectus (*Eclectus r. roratus*) from Ceram, which is seen most often in captivity. The six subspecies are differentiated primarily on the basis of geographic origin and size:

Red-sided eclectus, *Eclectus roratus polychlorus* (see page 81), *E.r. cornelia, E.r. riedeli, E.r. vosmaeri, E.r. salomonensis,* and *E.r. macgillivrayi.* The Halmahera eclectus (see page 81), *E.r. vosmaeri,* resembles the nominate form, and is one of the more frequently seen birds in the trade. The subspecies is found on the Molucca Islands and has a bright red head and a black bill.

F

Feed automats
Tube-shaped containers that you fill with the grain mixture. The feed falls down automatically into a small feed pan. Advantage: Theoretically the birds are always provided with food. Disadvantage: The automatic feeder must constantly be checked to see whether it is functioning.

File notch
See parrot's beak, page 90.

Glossary

Floor grating

Many cages are furnished with a floor grating that is supposed to keep the bird from contact with droppings, but it also keeps the parrot from pecking in the sand and taking in the gravel that is necessary for its digestion. Some parrot species like to play on the floor, scratch in the sand, and sometimes also mate there. For these reasons, the floor grating should be removed.

Sex determination. In most parrot species the male and the female are not outwardly different from each other. Experienced breeders and zoologists determine the sex by comparison. The female (right) often sits on the perch with legs wider apart than does the male.

G

Geological age

Fossil finds suggest that parrots were living on the earth 30 to 20 million years ago. The fossils come from strata of the Oligocene, the last third of the Tertiary period. Probably parrots were also living in Europe at that time, for a parrotlike fossil was recently uncovered in these strata near Allier in France.

Gray parrot

= *Psittacus erithacus* (see page 77); subspecies: *P.e. timneh.*
One of the best-known parrots; common, popular house pet, whose breeding has succeeded all over the world.

L

Long-winged parrots

There are nine species with nine subspecies belonging to the genus *Poicephalus.* The best-known are:
   Meyer's parrot, *Poicephalus meyeri* (see page 76); subspecies: *P.m. matschiei; P.m. reichenowi; P.m. damarensis.*
Pleasant to keep; has been bred all over the world.
   Senegal parrot, yellow-bellied Senegal parrot, *Poicephalus senegalus* (see page 76); subspecies: *P.s. versteri.*
Numerous in certain areas of natural habitat. Extremely popular as pet, since young animals quickly become tame, learn to

say something, and are very playful.

Lovebirds

The English name of the bird genus *Agapornis* from Africa points to the fact that only pairs can survive as house pets, which basically is true of all parrots. Some species of the genus have been kept as pets for a long time and can easily be bred; others are so demanding and aggressive that breeding them is only rarely successful.
   Abyssinian lovebird, black-winged lovebird, *Agapornis taranta.*
Found in the highlands of Ethiopia. They eat figs but will also consume berries and other things. Breeding repeatedly successful.
   Black-cheeked lovebird, *Agapornis nigrigenis.*
Found in southwestern Africa, in the Zambezi Valley from the Machili River to Livingstone and bordering regions on the north. (In other publications classified as a subspecies of the black-masked lovebird.)
   Black-masked lovebird, *Agapornis personata* (see page 75).
They eat seeds and can therefore be fed in captivity without any problem. Breeding easy; there are several color mutations known.
   Fischer's lovebird, *Agapornis fischeri* (see page 75). Popular pet bird, which can be bred easily.
   Madagascar lovebird, *Agapornis cana;* subspecies: *A.c. ablectanea.* Originally found only on Madagascar, but natu-

ralized on the Comoros and Seychelles and on Zanzibar and Mafia. They subsist primarily on small seeds and therefore, as pet birds, can be fed easily. Breeding has succeeded a number of times. The female sticks the nesting material into her feathers to transport it to the nesting box.

Nyasa lovebird, Lilian's lovebird, *Agapornis lilianae.*
Found in northeastern Tanzania; naturalized to southern Kenya. Nyasa lovebirds are rarely kept as pets; they can be seen in zoos.

Peach-faced lovebird, rosyfaced lovebird, *Agapornis roseicollis* (see page 74); subspecies: *A.r. catumbella.*
Peach-faced lovebirds are popular pet birds, have been bred all over the world, and are known in many color mutations.

Red-faced lovebird, *Agapornis pullaria*; subspecies: *A.p. ugandae.*
Found in Uganda, in northwestern Tanzania and Angola, and in southwestern Ethiopia. They live in thin forests and on open land in small groups. Their diet is varied, so that they offer hardly any problem as house pets. Red-faced lovebirds can be bred only with difficulty.

Swindern's lovebird or black-collared lovebird, *Agapornis swinderniana*; subspecies: *A.s. zenkeri, A.s. emini.*
Found in Liberia and Ghana, mainly in evergreen forests. They are so very specialized in their diet of figs that keeping them as pets is almost impossible.

M

Macaws
Best-known of all are the large, splendidly colored macaw species, which live in Central and South America. But smaller and often less striking birds also belong to the genera "true macaws," *Ara*; "blue macaws," *Anodorhynchus;* and "Spix's blue ara," *Cyanopsitta spixii.*

Blue-and-yellow macaw, *Ara ararauna* (see page 71).
One of the most familiar macaw species, which is nevertheless gravely endangered by the destruction of its habitat. Not rare as a pet; often in zoos. Breeding frequently successful.

Buffon's or grand military macaw, *Ara ambigua.*
Found in Nicaragua and western Ecuador; commonly seen in zoos; rare as a pet.

Caninde macaw, *Ara caninde.*
Very rare species of macaw, found only in areas of Bolivia; only about 1000 birds still extant. Existence gravely endangered.

Chestnut-fronted macaw, severe macaw, *Ara severa* (see page 71); subspecies: *A.s. castaneifrons.*
Just under 19½ inches (20 cm) long, green basic plumage with blue crown and blue primaries. In natural habitat, common in regions. Primarily seen in zoos. Successfully bred.

Coulon's macaw, mountain macaw, *Ara couloni.*
Found in Peru; less well known; rarely described. Seldom kept as a house pet; seldom seen in zoos.

Glaucous macaw, sea-blue

Glossary

macaw, *Anodorhynchus glaucus.*
Doubtful location in Argentina, Brazil, Uruguay; according to the most recent observations, this species is almost certainly extinct.

Green-winged macaw, maroon, red-and-blue or red-and-green macaw, *Ara chloroptera* (see page 70).
Frequently kept as a pet and seen in zoos. Breeding repeatedly successful.

Hahn's macaw, *diopsittaca* or *Ara nobilis;* subspecies: *D.n. cumanensis "hahni"* (see page 70).
Body length only 12 inches (30 cm). In natural habitat, numerous in regions. Rarely seen as pet but often in zoos. Breeding successful.

Hyacinthine macaw, *Anodorynchus hyacinthinus.*
The largest of the macaw species, with a body length of 39 inches (1 m), with deep-blue plumage and yellow eye rings. Found in Brazil; occurs regionally in uninhabited areas, not yet rare. Strictly protected. Rare as pet bird, because extraordinarily costly and very expensive to keep. Nevertheless, frequently seen in zoos. Breeding has succeeded several times.

Illiger's macaw, *Ara maracana.*
Body length of 17 inches (43 cm); brilliant red forehead, darkgreen plumage. Found in Brazil, Paraguay; endangered through destruction of habitat. Rare as pet and rare in zoos.

A large flock of bare-eyed cockatoos has roosted in the trees in a farm in Australia. In their search for food, bare-eyed cockatoos even dare to invade gardens. In the Australian wheat-growing areas they are unwelcome guests, mercilessly hunted by farmers.

Glossary

Indigo macaw, Lear's macaw, *Anodorhynchus leari*. Found in a very remote region of northeastern Brazil. Species threatened with extinction. It is feared that only about 100 of this species are still alive.

Military macaw, *Ara militaris*; subspecies: *A.m. mexicana*. Found in Mexico, Colombia, Venezuela, Peru, Bolivia, Argentina. Seen often in zoos, but scarcely ever a pet.

Red-and-yellow macaw, scarlet macaw, *Ara macao*. Found in southern Mexico, Bolivia, Brazil; extremely endangered by the destruction of its habitats and by its capture for food by the local population. Nevertheless, commonly seen in zoos and as a pet. Breeding successful world wide.

Red-bellied macaw, *ara manilata*. Found in Colombia, Venezuela, Peru, in the interior of Brazil.

Red-cheeked macaw, *Ara rubrogenys*. Green basic plumage with red crown, red bend of wing, and red ear spot. Found in Bolivia. This species has been known only since 1973 and is very seldom kept.

Spix's macaw, *Cyanopsitta spixii*. Rarest macaw species, which is known only through scanty reports of its small habitat in Brazil. The species is threatened with extinction. There are only a few birds still left. At present there are 17 Spix's macaws alive in zoos and aviaries.

Yellow-collared macaw, gold-naped, yellow-naped or Cassin's macaw, *Ara auricollis*. Found in Bolivia, Paraguay, Argentina; frequently observed regionally. Rarely kept as pets; breeding has been successful in isolated instances.

N

Neotropical
Belonging to the tropics of the New World (North and South American continents).

Nomenclature Set of technical terms of a field of knowledge. For working with the Latin or Greek names of parrots you need to know the following:

The capitalized name of the genus always comes first, for example, *Amazona,* next the lower-cased species name, for example *ochrocephala*. The third term describes the subspecies, for example *panamensis*. Thus the animal under discussion is *Amazona ochrocephala panamensis*, the Panama Amazon.

Nominate form
First described form of an organism.

P

Parrotlets
These constitute the genus *Forpinae* or *Forpus,* belong to the subfamily of the true parrots, and have been popular pet birds for many years. Since they have been bred the world over, they are easily obtained both in pet stores and through breeders. The sexes of these birds are recognizable by color differences in the plumage.

Blue-winged parrotlet, *Forpus xanthopterygius;* subspecies: *F.x. spengeli; F.x. crassirostris, F.x. flavissimus, F. x. olalae, F.x. flavescens, F.x. vividus*. Found in northern Colombia, northeastern Peru, eastern Bolivia, Paraguay, northeastern Argentina, and in the Amazon region of Brazil. They are known to have color mutations when living in the wild.

Celestial parrotlet, Lesson's or Pacific parrotlet, *Forpus coelestis* (see page 72). Found in western Ecuador and western Peru; numerous in dry regions.

Sclater's parrotlet, *Forpus sclateri;* subspecies: *F.s. eidos, F.s. modesta*. Found in eastern Colombia, Venezuela, Guayana, and northern Bolivia.

Spectacled parrotlet, *Forpus conspicillatus* (see page 72); subspecies: *F.c. metae, F.c. caucae*. Found from Panama to Venezuela.

Turquoise-rumped parrotlet, Mexican parrotlet, *Forpus cyanopygius;* subspecies: *F.c. pallidus, F.c. insularis*. Found in northern and western Mexico.

Yellow-faced parrotlet, *Forpus xanthops*. Found in northern Peru.

Parrot's beak

The parrot's upper beak is attached to the bone of the skull by a hinged joint; the lower beak can be shifted between upper and lower jaw by means of a sliding joint. This provides the great mobility of the beak. When a parrot is properly maintained, the horn of the beak (keratin) is constantly worn away; it looks as if the beak scales off. This natural process is balanced by the continued growth of the beak horn. A "file notch" is found on the underside of the tip of the upper beak of almost all large parrot species. This permits the parrot to grasp its food more easily and at the same time promotes the wearing down and sharpening of the lower beak.

Pionus parrots

This genus has the Latin name *Pionus* and includes seven species, all of which have a red undertail covert. The majority of these species are rarely or never seen in zoos, because they are to a large degree unknown. Two species, however, can be bred easily, are also still numerous in their natural habitat, and have become sought-after pets by fanciers because of their gentleness and pleasant voice:

Blue-headed parrot, *Pionus menstruus* (see page 73); subspecies: *P.m. reichenowi.* Lives in forested areas and is still numerous regionally.

Maximilian's parrot, *Pionus maximiliani* (see page 73); subspecies: *P.m. siy.*

S

Sex determination

The surest method to determine the sex of a parrot is endoscopy (see page 16).

Some ornithologists roughly determine sex by a fecal examination in which the proportion of estrogen to testosterone is established.

Experienced breeders and zoologists determine sex by comparison. Because generally the female has a somewhat broader pelvis than the male, the distance between the feet when the bird is sitting is a little wider than that in the male. If there is room for a man's finger between the pelvic bones directly in front of the anal opening of a large parrot, it is probably a female.

The form and size of the beak and head may also provide a clue.

Sexual dimorphism

Clearly recognizable differences between sexes, as for example in the eclectus parrots (see page 81).

An African gray parrot, left, a Goffin's cockatoo, right. Rough perches of various thicknesses and pieces of soft wood should be provided for gnawing so that the constantly growing horn of the parrots' beak is worn down.

Useful Literature and Addresses

United States
American Federation of Aviculture (AFA)
P.O. Box 1568
Redondo Beach, California 90278

Association of Avian Veterinarians
P.O. Box 811720
Boca Raton, Florida 33481

Avicultural Society of America, Inc.
8228 Sulphur Road
Ojai, California 93022

National Parrot Association
8 North Hoffman Lane
Hauppauge, New York 11788

The Society of Parrot Breeders and Exhibitors
P.O. Box 369-CB
Groton, Massachusetts 01450

Great Britain
The Avicultural Society
Warren Hill, Halford's Lane
Hartley, Wintney, Hampshire RG27 8AG

The European Aviculture Council
P.O. Box 74
Bury St. Edmunds, Suffolk IP30 OHS

National Council for Aviculture
87 Winn Road
Lee, London SE12 9EY

Canada
The Canadian Avicultural Society
32 Dronmore Court
Willodale, Ontario M2R 2H5

Canadian Parrot Association
Pine Oaks R.R. #3
St. Catharines, Ontario L2R 6P9

Australia
The Avicultural Society of Australia
52 Harris Road
Elliminyt, Victoria 3249

New Zealand
Avicultural Society of N.Z., Inc.
P.O. Box 21
403 Henderson, Auckland

Books
Cayley, N.W., and Lendon, A. *Australian Parrots in Field and Aviary,* Angus & Robertson, Sydney, Australia, 1973.

Eastman, W.R., and Hunt, A.C. *The Parrots of Australia,* Angus & Robertson, Sydney, Australia, 1966.

Forshaw, J.M. *Australian Parrots*, 2nd edition, Lansdowne Press, Melbourne, Australia, 1981.

——— *Parrots of the World*, 3rd edition, Lansdowne Press, Melbourne, Australia, 1987.

Groen, H.D. *Australian Parakeets*, 5th edition. Audubon Publishing Co., Smithtown, New York, 1987.

Low, Rosemary. *Endangered Parrots*, Blandford Press, Poole, Dorset, England, 1984.

——— *Parrots, Their Care and Breeding,* Blandford Press, Poole, Dorset, England, 1992.

——— *The Complete Book of Macaws,* Barron's Educational Series, Inc., Hauppauge, New York, 1990.

——— *The Complete Book of Parrots,* Barron's Educational Series, Inc., Hauppauge, New York, 1989.

Silva, Tony. *Psittaculture. The Breeding, Rearing & Management of Parrots,* Silvio Mattacchione & Co., Ontario, Canada, 1991.

Sweeney, Roger G. *Macaws,* Barron's Educational Series, Inc., Hauppauge, New York, 1992.

Vriends, M.M. *Lovebirds,* Barron's Educational Series, Inc., Hauppauge, New York, 1986.

——— *The New Australian Parakeet Handbook*, Barron's Educational Series, Inc., Hauppauge, New York, 1992.

——— *The New Bird Handbook,* Barron's Educational Series, Inc., Hauppauge, New York, 1989.

——— *The New Cockatiel Handbook,* Barron's Educational Series, Inc., Hauppauge, New York, 1989.

——— *Simon & Schuster's Guide to Pet Birds,* 6th edition, Simon & Schuster, New York, 1992.

——— *The Macdonald Encyclopedia of Cage and Aviary Birds,* Macdonald & Co., Publishers, Ltd., London and Sydney, 1985.

——— *Popular Parrots,* 2nd edition, Howell Book House, Inc., New York, 1984.

Magazines
American Cage Bird Magazine
One Glamore Court
Smithtown, New York 11787

The A.F.A. Watchbird
P.O. Box 56218
Phoenix, Arizona 85079-6218

Bird Talk
P.O. Box 6050
Mission Viejo, California 92690

Bird World
P.O. Box 70
N. Hollywood, California 91603

Cage and Aviary Birds
Prospect House
9-13 Ewell Road
Cheam, Surrey SM1 499
England

Index

(Pages in **boldface** type indicate color photos.)

94

Important Note:
This book deals with the housing and care of parrots. People who suffer from an allergy to feathers or feather dust should not keep birds. If your are doubtful, check with your doctor before you acquire one.
In working with parrots you can be injured by bites or scratches. Have such injuries treated by a doctor immediately.
"Parrot fever" (psittacosis, ornithosis) very seldom occurs in parrots today (see page 49), but it can produce symptoms that are life-threatening to some degree in both humans and parrots. Therefore, in case of any doubt, take the parrot to the veterinarian (see page 44) and always go to the doctor yourself at any sign of cold or flu; be sure to mention that you are keeping a bird.

The photographs on the cover:
Front cover: Two blue-and-yellow macaws.
Inside front cover: Two African gray parrots.
Inside back cover: Blue-fronted Amazon.
Back cover: African gray parrot.

The photographers:
Angermayer: front cover, page 71; Angermayer/
Ziesler: page 33; Bechtel: page 80 right; de Grahl:
page 69 top left; Hoppe: pages 25, 36, 69 bottom
left, 79 bottom left; Inter-Topics/Rakebrand: pages
20, 21; Jacana/Ferrero: pages 88/89; Jacana/
Labat: page 79 top left; Jacana/Robert: page 57;
Jacana/Visage: page 66; Layer: page 79 right;
Mader: page 68 right; Martin: page 53; Okapia/
Durk: page 74; Okapia/NAS/T. McHugh: page 10;
Oxford Scientific Films/Wells: page 65; Pfeffer: 69
right, 76 right; Reinhard: pages 17, 67, 70 left,
bottom right, 72, 78, inside back cover; Scholtz:
pages 9, 73, 75, 81; Schweiger: pages 2/3;
Silvestris/Bechmann: page 70 top right; Silvestris/
Bertrand: page 68 left; Silvestris/Lane/Hamblin:
page 76 left; Skogstad: pages 24, 48, 80 left,
center; Wegler: pages 6, 7, 13, 29; Wothe: inside
front cover, pages 5, 14, 15, 40, 45, 60, 61, 77,
back cover.

All inquiries should be addressed to:
Barron's Educational Series, Inc.
250 Wireless Boulevard
Hauppauge, NY 11788

Library of Congress Catalog Card No. 92-13619
International Standard Book No. 0-8120-4823-7
Library of Congress Cataloging-in-Publication Data
Wolter, Annette.
    Parrots : how to take care of them and
understand them / Annette Wolter : with color
photographs and drawings by György Jankovics ;
consulting editor, Matthew M. Vriends.
        p.   cm.
    Includes index.
    ISBN 0-8120-4823-7
    1. Parrots.   I. Jankovics, György.   II. Vriends.
Matthew M., 1937–.   III. Title.
    SF473.P3W66   1992
    636.6′865—dc20   92-13619

PRINTED IN HONG KONG
6 7 8 9 0   4900   12 11 10 9 8

Sarah

Jerry Eicher

Book List of Published Novel Titles

A Time To Live
Sarah

Sarah

Fiction/Contemporary

Published by Horizon Books
768 Hardtimes Rd.
Farmville VA 23901

www.readingwithhorizon.com

Editor – Janet D. Miller

This story is fictional. All persons, places, or events are either fiction or, if real, used fictitiously.

Cover design by www.KareenRoss.com

ISBN   978-0-9787987-1-0

DEDICATION

In dedication to the culture I grew up in, for its depth and dedication to values, and for its purpose and passion for life.

CHAPTER ONE

Young Sarah Schwartz was preparing for the day. Standing in front of her cracked mirror on the dresser had to suffice. Not that she was vain. On the contrary, her problem was the opposite. When you are Amish, natural beauty had its disadvantages.

Sarah Schwartz was beautiful. The blond hair she was brushing out flowed down her back. Swinging her head briskly to the side, she began the process of getting it into condition to cover with the weekday Amish head veiling. Few people outside her immediate family had ever seen her hair uncovered. Not that it was entirely necessary to see all of it. What was exposed in the back and front after she was done placing the small scarf told a lot of the story.

Looking into the part of the mirror without any cracks in it, her nose lined up perfectly with her face. Her skin was fair. Spared the youthful ravages of pimples, no blemishes marred her face. Blue eyes, as crystal clear as the spring sky, looked back at her. When her spirit soared, those eyes could sparkle. When her spirit sank, they reflected the clouds. Now as had been the case throughout her school days, she was about five inches taller than her contemporaries. Not too tall to be awkward, her added height supplied that little extra something in her being. She had never felt the need to walk with a stoop.

"*Da Hah* (the Lord) has always smiled on you," her

mother, Deborah, had once told her. "I am just thankful it hasn't gone to your head."

"Why should it, Mother?" Sarah had asked her. "You said yourself it is a gift. How can one be proud of a gift?"

"You are wise beyond your years," Deborah had told her. "It is as if you were a daughter of the One who lives above, and not even mine at all. We were all so concerned with your birth, when you took so long in coming."

"You did good, Mother," Sarah had assured her.

"Are you glad to be Amish?" Deborah had suddenly inquired. Sarah turned that day to see her mother's face. Only fourteen at the time, the concern her mother had shown had moved her heart.

"You know, I am," Sarah told her gently. "What else would I want to be?"

Deborah ignored the question, "See, Sarah, you don't know yet how the world works. I just hope you are spared the worst of it."

"I am sure I will be okay," she had quickly assured her mother.

For some reason, this morning, she was reminded of that conversation. *What was Mom thinking about? She no doubt knows things I don't. What could they be?*

Snapping back to the present, she hurried to finish dressing. There were no buttons, zippers, or snaps on her dress, only pins. With skill born from years of practice, the task was completed quickly.

Running downstairs she passed her brother Mark, the oldest of the siblings. There were three of them, with her sister, Martha, being the youngest. For some reason, unknown to any of the three, there had never been more children. In Amish culture where a dozen children in a family is not uncommon, this curiosity was no doubt satisfactorily resolved. Perhaps this was done by dropping some discrete information that reached the ears of the appropriate church authorities. However, the Schwartz children were not told.

Looking at Sarah blankly as she passed him, Mark commented dryly, "Well, she's up."

"Of course, I am. I'm going to town, and I was up hours ago."

Mark intoned, "She's going to town. The girl is going to town."

"Would you cut it out?"

Mark ventured a little grin, "You are even prettier when you are angry. That's saying a lot for a sister. Now mind you it is."

"Why don't you just use your energies to get my horse ready?"

"Now, why should I do that?" Mark turned toward the front window, rose slightly on his toes, elevated his nose and continued, "A man, he is the man of the house. He is above the strife, above the petty everyday things. He rules. He does not prepare the horse for girls to go to town. How can you think that one such as I would sink to your lowly level? 'Prepare the horse,' she says, 'for I am going to town.'"

"Mom," Sarah shrieked, with a pretend ten-year old voice. "Mark is tormenting me."

Deborah could not help chuckling from the kitchen, "I think he has the horse ready for you."

"I don't need that," Sarah replied quickly, "I just wanted you to tell him to be quiet with all his big talk. I can get the horse ready myself if I have to."

"Okay, children," Deborah spoke up from the kitchen, "Time to grow up. Sarah, off to town, and Mark, you have chores to do in the barn even on a Saturday."

Mark grinned as he headed out the door with one

parting shot. "The boys are going to be falling over each other."

Sarah decided to ignore him, partly because she wanted the conversation to end and partly because she felt fear at the truth behind his words. For a while now she had pondered the situation. It did not take a very bright person to understand the looks she got at the singings on Sunday evening. Yet, no one had asked her for a date. Mark claimed it was because no one dared.

"It will start soon," he had told her just last week. "I am going to start charging a large fee because you know they won't be asking you directly. They will ask me, and I will have to transfer the message. A substantial fee is what I will charge, to be sure."

Heading for the front door, Sarah smiled now at the memory. She knew he would do nothing of the sort, but it brought sobering thoughts and more questions. *How am I going to know? I don't really like any boys that I know. What if they just like me for how I look? How am I ever going to know?*

Shaking her head, she raised her voice enough to be heard in the kitchen, "I'm off, Mom," following Mark out the door once she was sure he had reached the barn.

Their old driving horse was waiting right where Mark had left him. Her father had purchased this horse when he was well past his prime. It did not even take a tie rope to keep him in place when it was time to go to town. Jumping into the buggy, she slapped the reins and slowly the horse began moving forward.

❧

Lamar Wagler had the morning off. A tall, black-haired young man, he was twenty-one years old, and only recently had come of age. Coming of age for the Amish is at twenty-one, not eighteen. His father owned the Wagler Construction Company which had now been in business for twenty years. Known for its quality construction above and beyond even the normal Amish reputation, Wagler Construction reached into South Washington and into Jasper and as far north as Bedford. It ran two crews with hired drivers who also worked as day laborers. Lamar was the foreman of one of the crews. Money was never a problem.

Today he planned on spending a leisurely morning preparing his buggy for Sunday and for tonight's activities. He was dating Malinda, Bloh Jonas's eldest daughter. They had been sweethearts for so long now that marriage was an assumed conclusion. She had her father's dark eyes and good looks. Lamar assumed her eyes twinkled all the time, but he liked to think they only did so for him. Her smile lit up the world, when she was not using her mouth to express disapproval.

She likes me, Lamar thought, pulling his buggy out on to the front lawn. Its black waterproof fabric glittered in the sunlight. *High-spirited, she is, and from a good family. Not that I need the money, but her family has some, I'm sure. You never know when or what you might need that for.*

Walking back into the barn, he climbed up into the hay mow, and dug down between two hay bales. Extracting a jar of car wax, he headed for the buggy. Taking a rag from behind the seat he quickly rubbed the wax on the fabric, cleaning if off with a dry rag. Then going behind the house he got a water hose and proceeded to hose the whole thing down.

Hides some of it, he muttered. *Can't be looking too shiny. Why do I even bother?* He stepped back and looked at the now even shinier black fabric. *Because it helps a little*, he thought to himself. *Now to polish the racing stripes a little.*

Above him, on the back of the buggy were as many lights as would fit, both in a straight and circular designs.

Standing there looking at his buggy through the side door, Lamar's eyes rested on the front seat. It was a dark-brown, plush upholstery. He felt it was a little dubious for regular church rules, but probably okay until he got married. On the left, the English side in automobiles, was where Malinda usually sat. He smiled to himself at the thought, then jerked when he realized where his thoughts had gone. *Where did that come from? Why would I think of her?*

He shook his head in an effort to clear it, but to no avail. Clear as a bell, he saw Sarah Schwartz sitting right where Malinda usually sat. She smiled, just as she had done during the singing last Sunday night. That was when he had first noticed her. It was not that he had not seen her before, but Sunday night was different. For the first time, he really became aware of how beautiful she was. She had been two grades behind him in school, so she was hardly in his immediate circle. Yet, had she really always been like this?

During the closing German song, she had been sitting there with the second row of girls. He sat on the front row completely mesmerized. Even now he blushed when he wondered if someone had seen him. *What was I doing staring at her?* His memory told him why: her blue eyes, her face, her hair, the way she shaped her mouth as she sang the German words.

With effort he had forced his mind to go elsewhere, and he did so again now. I already have a girl, he told himself and got back to cleaning his buggy. When he was satisfied, the dash and the rest of the inside were spotless. Pulling air freshener from a compartment in the buggy, he sprayed a little on the top of the seat.

He sniffed the air: *just right, subtle but to the point. She will like that. Now, I'd better get this done before Jesse stops by.*

On the way to church on Sunday, Sarah rode with Mark in his single seat buggy. Martha still rode with Ben and Deborah on Sunday mornings. "You going home with someone else tonight?" he asked as they drove along in the morning silence.

Sarah looked puzzled, "Are you taking someone home?"

Mark shook his head, "Not me, silly. You."

"So you know something that I don't know?"

"Don't look so anxious," Mark said keeping his face looking straight ahead.

"Has someone asked?" Sarah involuntarily pulled in her breath, "Because no one has come to me."

Mark heard the sound and asked, "Why does my sister want to go home with someone so bad? Is there something going on that I don't know?"

"No, there isn't," Sarah told him shortly. "I just thought you were going to say that a boy had asked me. I guess that has a certain element of, shall we say, suspense to it. That's all. Now, has someone asked you to ask me or not?"

Mark attempted to act as if he knew great news but was not telling. Sarah knew him better. "No one has asked," she said matter-of-factly. "Either me or you."

"No, they haven't," Mark admitted. "Don't you think they should though? It's only normal, like, as good-looking and nice as you are, you know. I am beginning to think you are up to something."

He looked at her questioningly. "Are you up to something? What are you giving them? Icy glances? Frowns maybe? Looking high and mighty? You know you are not supposed to be like that. Smile. That's what you are supposed to do. Look into their eyes. Let your own eyes glaze over with anticipation and longing. That would be about right. You could have a date tonight, I'm sure."

Sarah glared at him, "Are you speaking from experience, Mark, or from some wish you have?" she asked.

"Well, mostly wishing," he admitted. "But that would be nice, wouldn't it? I think it would. Lets a boy know you want him."

"They don't need any encouragement," she commented dryly.

"Well," he said, "you don't have to be so abrupt about it. We just want someone to love us."

Sarah chuckled quietly, reached over and patted his arm, "I'm sure someone will someday."

Mark made a face, "Probably not the right one," he said in a depressed tone of voice and then he shook his head as if to snap out of something. "So what am I to tell them if they ask tonight?"

"Let's see if someone tells you to ask me first and then we will go from there."

"Suit yourself," he said. "Just like a woman. Can't make up her mind until the last minute."

"Of course," she told him, "that's the best way. Now here we are, so no more talk about those things."

"This is where it starts," he said dryly.

She acted as if she had not heard him.

CHAPTER TWO

EIGHTEEN YEARS EARLIER Sarah had been born. A hush had hung over the little, two-storied home of Ben and Deborah Schwartz. Gas lanterns had just been lit in the living room and the kitchen. A small kerosene lamp provided light in the bedroom. Because the birth was imminent, the one-year old Mark had been sent to stay with an aunt. The few people allowed in that night spoke mostly in whispers.

"Niks," the midwife reported to Ben, his lanky frame tense while waiting in the living room. The helper nervously tiptoed past on the way to the kitchen carrying cold towels for reheating. Ben's face was firm and already weather-beaten from years of farming, his head now bowed as he paced the floor. Lost in thought, his hand stroked the beard already reaching the front collar line of his shirt.

"What is the problem?" he demanded.

Pausing again, on her own way to the kitchen door, the midwife shook her head, "I have not seen anything like it for a long time now."

"Is there something wrong with the baby?" he wanted to know. "Should we go to the English hospital for help?"

Again the midwife shook her head, "I am just puzzled. Deborah is worn out, but it seems like the child is waiting for something. Let's see in a little while. If nothing happens soon, we may have to go to the English for help."

"Let me know then if you want me to go call." Ben

stopped pacing and stood in front of the living room window. "Children are best born at home among their own people, but I don't want Deborah or the baby in any danger."

"*Ach, yah*," the midwife agreed, heading back towards the bedroom. "Maybe this baby will come soon?"

A few miles across the fields, as the crow flies, was the little town of Glendale, Indiana. Located on the southern end of Daviess County, it was the home to hundreds of Old Order Amish families. Eight miles north was Washington, home of the Black Buggy Amish Restaurant. Just east of Odon, the area had first been settled by Amish in 1869. While this area was not as well-known as the tourist attractions of Berlin, Ohio, Lancaster, Pennsylvania, or the community in Nappanee, Indiana, things rarely got more Amish than right here.

Within sight of the lily pad-laden northern edge of Dogwood Lake and west of Glendale was the home of Esther. In her mid-twenties, she was Amish, had never married and lived alone. Normally such a situation would hardly have been tolerated but Esther could do the local *brauha* (alternative medicine). Along with that, her herbal garden was well known throughout the Amish community. She usually had a ready concoction for what ailed you.

Esther could have married, but chose not to, again without explanation. She never suffered the scorn and pity usually dispensed to *old maids*.

That night, her dark-brown eyes scrutinized the food she was preparing in the kitchen. She pushed the large head covering she wore over her brown hair farther back on her head. Around here, the Amish had taken to wearing a small work scarf during the week, but Esther preferred the old ways. She made her head covering even larger than those worn by the others on Sundays.

Vass iss lets? (what is wrong?), she asked herself. The answer had nothing to do with food. Setting down the pot of food to simmer on the stove, she moved her already slightly overweight body across the room to the back door. Opening the door, she scanned the horizon and then the skies. A brilliant star hung just over the place the last rays of the sun were biding their good-byes to the day.

"Does this mean anything?" she wondered out loud, looking long and hard at the western sky. "What a beautiful star is in the heavens tonight!"

Letting go of the door, it slammed shut on its spring and she returned to the kitchen and her pot of potato stew.

＊

On the other side of Glendale, *Bloh* (blue) Jonas Yoder was in the barn tending to his sick cow. He was so named not because he was perpetually downhearted, but for other ancestral reasons. Three generations ago, a grandfather had had the same first name as one of his fellow Amish, Jonas Yost. This had resulted in the initials and other things getting mixed up. Since there was a large English-owned lake adjoining the Yoder farm, the solution had been to add blue, *Bloh*, for the color of the lake to his name. So it was that the family name among the Amish still carried *Bloh*.

Although he lived farther west and north, he belonged to the same district as the others. Bloh Jonas Yoder was the youngest minister serving under Bishop Amos. Ordained only the previous fall, church matters were now the least of his concerns. His best cow was sick, the muscles of its neck and legs were slightly swollen. Jonas was sure the cow was also running a high temperature. The vet could not be reached from the phone down the road, and a sleepless night stretched out in front of him.

Confounded, confounded situation. I can't afford this. Why is it always the best one?

The night gave him no answer.

❧

Back at Ben Schwartz's house, in the light of the kerosene lamp the midwife and her helper stood quietly at the bed. Deborah's normally slim but now round body shuddered with each rack of pain. "Thank God, it's not your first one," the midwife said to no one in particular.

"It's worse than the boy," Deborah replied through clenched teeth.

"They usually come easier each time," the midwife said, adding to no one's comfort. "Do you want us to go for help?'

"Where would you go?" Deborah wanted to know.

"There is the English hospital," the midwife paused, waiting expectantly for a reaction.

"But I can't move like this," Deborah said slowly in short breaths as the pain increased.

The midwife nodded, "Ben said he would go call for help. There is, of course, Esther."

Deborah muffled her cry, "I would prefer that. Maybe she could come?"

"Shall I send for her?"

Deborah's only answer was to give up all attempts at hiding the pain. She screamed, filling the bedroom and the whole house with the sound.

"Go tell Ben quick! She wants Esther," the midwife told the assistant. "Tell him to hurry!"

≋

Bloh Jonas, having left his cow in the barn while he ate supper, was now back out with her and beside himself with anxiety. Coming out with his gas lantern, he found the sick cow stretched out on the concrete floor. Worse, when he decided by chance to cast the light of the lantern out into the barnyard, he saw three more cows in the herd with their heads hanging down. When he ran his hand over their bodies the same swelling and fever were evident.

"What is going on?" he said out loud, then in a quieter voice, "Surely it's not Blackleg?" No one could hear him, because no one was around. *This is going too far too fast.* Fear ran through him.

Opening the yard gate he whacked the sick cows to get them moving towards the inside of the barn. Two made it in without any problems, but the third collapsed just inside the door onto the concrete floor. The cow moaned and stretched its neck out straight on the floor.

God help me, he said to himself. *If I don't get help there will be nothing left by morning.*

Quickly hitching up a horse, he headed down to the nearest phone shack and the telephone. Jonas refused to have a phone at the end of his driveway. It would have been allowed, but he just felt better without one right outside his house.

It was still early enough that his trip drew no undue attention from the neighbors. Passing in front of his house on the way to the road, the bright star hung clearly in the sky, but Bloh Jonas did not see it.

Arriving at the phone, he dialed the vet's phone number. There was only an answering machine. In despair, he left a message stating the situation. *Now what do I do? I have to get help.* Then the thought crossed his mind. *Would Esther be of any use in this matter? Of course, she would.* He answered his own question. *I will go and get her.*

⚜

Coming out of the house after his wife's furious scream of pain, Ben ran to the barn. He caught his old horse in the barnyard, took him inside and fairly threw the harness on him. Finding the right moves and partly out of habit, he never paused in his haste as he took the horse to the buggy on a run. Lifting the shafts with his left hand he swung the horse into position. After hooking up the traces Ben jumped in the buggy, nearly slipping on the round step. Once inside he slapped the reins and drove out of the lane in a burst of speed.

He covered the distance to Esther's house in short order. Leaving the horse in the driveway, he headed for the front door. He paused, puzzled by the lack of light in the house since it was dark but still early.

Knocking on the door there was no answer. He banged louder, finally yelling, "Hello!"

Still no answer, he walked around to the back of the house. Finding no one, he headed towards the small barn Esther used for her horses and cows. Opening the door, everything seemed to be in order. The cows looked calmly at him from the back of the barn. Hay hung down from the rafters and a rat scurried between the two horse stanchions. *Where is she?*

CHAPTER THREE

BLOH JONAS PULLED into his driveway in his single-seated buggy. Esther was in the seat beside him. She had grabbed a bucket of something in the barn before they left her place. It now sat in the back of the buggy.

"So tell me again why you pulled me over here in such a rush?" she asked him.

"My cows are sick, four of them when I left. I told you that."

"Ya, you told me, but what was the real reason?"

"Look, Esther, that is the real reason! I can't afford to lose these cows. The vet is out, or at least he won't answer his phone. You were the person who came to mind. Maybe you can help? Isn't that why you agreed to come?"

Esther smiled in the darkness, her features only slightly visible by the dim light coming from the gas lantern in the house. "We will see, Jonas. You and I go way back, you know. It's been awhile, and now you have come to pick me up. Right out front where everyone can see us and in your own buggy, nonetheless. Doesn't that bring back memories from when we were with the young folks?"

"Would you quit talking that nonsense? The past is the past, and the present is the present. Sure we dated a few times, but now my cows are sick and that's plain to see for anyone who wants to see it. I can pick you up now for a reason other than romance, don't you think?"

"So you never liked me just a little?"

Jonas grunted under his breath.

"Now, now Jonas I wish you wouldn't talk like that. *Es macht mich shweah hatsich* (Makes me heavy-hearted). You and I used to have such good times. Of course, we both knew it could never go anywhere. It wasn't meant to be. I knew that. You knew that, but my heart still wants it at times."

"Look, let's just have you look at the cows, and then I'll take you home again."

"Okay, but you'd better tell your wife what we're doing."

Puzzled, he pulled the horse up to the hitching post, got out and tied him. Esther headed towards the barn without looking back. Hesitating, he decided it would be better to comply. Half running towards the house, he jerked open the kitchen door.

Naomi, his wife, looked up from the table where she was cleaning away the last of the supper dishes.

"I couldn't find the vet so I asked Esther to come over. She came," he said. "We will be in the barn working on the cows."

Naomi simply nodded.

After convincing himself that Esther was not home, Ben headed back to his weary horse. Ben turned the buggy around and headed out the driveway.

What am I going to do? Sure, she wants Esther, but I have to do something. Deborah's scream replayed itself in Ben's mind. That helped him conclude that Deborah would surely understand now that Esther was not at home. He would stop and call for help. Pulling up to one of the phone shacks on 600 he fumbled with the phone book. Glendale had no police department or medical aid he knew of. Finally, he found a promising number on the second page. A Montgomery operator answered, took some basic information from him and told him help would be on the way.

He came out of the phone shack with the feeling that a weight had been lifted off him, then he started worrying again. Slapping the lines, he urged the horse back to its top speed. Then the thought occurred to him. *What's the hurry, Ben? There's nothing you can do once you get there anyway. Maybe the midwife has things under control.* At that moment Ben was in sight of his driveway when red and blue lights greeted him with their piercing sequences over the knoll of the road to the north. "The English are coming," he said out loud, and sighed with relief.

When Bloh Jonas got out to the barn he opened the door roughly. This was not a time for pleasantries. All four cows were still lying pretty much where he had left them. He could not have moved them without a horse and traces, and they were obviously much too sick to try to move themselves.

Esther stood in the middle of the best cow and another *milker.* On this night and in the stress of the moment it was hard to tell which cow was which. Her bucket from the barn was sitting over on the side.

"So what can you do for them?" he demanded of Esther.

"I'm thinking," she said.

"Well, do something," he said in a tone of voice that surprised even him. "You brought that bucket along."

Esther looked sharply in his direction. When she said nothing, he was ready to say he was sorry but she told him, "Go check your other cows."

"What do you mean?" he demanded, the sharpness returning to his voice.

"*Gay usht,*" (just go) she told him.

Complying, he took the lantern from the ceiling leaving her temporarily in darkness. Waving its light out over the barnyard he paled at the sight of three more cows down. Despairing, he made no attempt to get the cows inside. Returning inside he numbly put the lantern back on its nail.

"What did you find," Esther asked him.

"Three more are sick," he told her. "What are you going to do about it?"

"I have my own ideas," she said.

"Would you mind using them?" Despair and exasperation were in his voice. His head was throbbing.

She tilted her head to him in thought. "There are a lot of cows down."

Jonas was irritated, "If you want money, I can pay you what the vet would have charged. More than that, I can't afford. We are not rich people."

"What I want is not money."

"What do you want?" he asked, suddenly suspicious of where the conversation was heading.

"You know," she said, a slight smile on her face now, "you might visit the house once in a while."

"Look," he said, "the past is the past. I am married now."

"I know," she said, "but stopping by once in a while to say 'hi' won't hurt."

"Such things ought not to be unless there is a reason," he protested.

"There can be a reason. Remember? You kissed me once," she tilted her head as she looked at him.

Jonas paled even more than he had from the look at more cows down. "Look, this is not right."

"I will take care of that," she told him.

"You know I can't be stopping by your place," he said, drawing out his trump card. "Especially since I'm a minister now."

"You can do your confessions of your failures at next communion," she said with feeling.

"If you don't stop this, I am taking you back home now," he said forcefully.

"Come on, be quiet," she told him. "You know how to do it. Keep the confession in general terms. No one will know. You will know how to do it. How did you say your confessions not that long ago?"

Jonas shook his head. "I have done things in the past that needed confession, but that does not mean I need to do worse things in the future." Images of a just eaten supper and Naomi flooded his mind. "No," he said, shaking his head.

"Then your cows will die."

"Are you sure?"

"I just told you."

Looking long at the four cows on the barn floor, Jonas thought of the three others in the barnyard. It would finish him if something happened to all of them. Even two dying would be a hard blow. Forcefully, with the full weight of what it might cost him, he made up his mind, "I won't do it."

To his surprise she smiled, "*Gut.* That's like the old Jonas. You always were a good man." She paused, "I think I will take care of your cows anyway. What do you think of that?"

"Just do it," he said with clenched teeth.

~

In the flickering light of the kerosene lamp, Deborah was now calm. "One more time. I see what the problem is now, its hand was up beside the head," the midwife told her gently. "Almost."

25

Deborah pulled in her breath and grimaced painfully, "Where is Ben?" she asked through her exhaustion.

"I sent him to get Esther."

"That's what I thought. Shouldn't he be back by now?"

"I would think so but be quiet now. Concentrate. You need all your strength for this. Here," she said turning to her helper. "Take the towels and get the scissors. The baby is coming."

"Is it that close?" Deborah asked.

"Yes, I think it is finally over. Now push."

Shaking violently with her last effort, Deborah's head fell back on the pillow. The midwife deftly held the small baby aloft and then cleared its tiny mouth of any obstructions. A small cry filled the room just as red and blue lights flooded the bedroom windows and bounced off the walls.

"It's a girl," the midwife said with a smile. "Perfect for a second child and a pretty one too from the looks of things. Arrived just ahead of the English. That's very good, Deborah."

The lights became brighter, and then they heard the crunch of gravel in the driveway. "You'd better go open the front door," the midwife told her helper. "We don't want the English tearing down the door. They think nothing is sacred once they have a call for help."

Rushing out the helper arrived in time to hold open the door. She stepped aside as the two attendants came in with their black bags. "Where is the mother?" they asked.

"In the bedroom," the helper said without any emotion in her voice, waving with her hand in the right direction.

Without any further words the two headed in that direction. Finding the bedroom door open they entered. "What's the status?" they asked the midwife who was now wrapping the baby in a blanket.

"Just arrived in the world after a long, hard struggle,"

the midwife smiled broadly. "Some complications, but she's okay now."

"Can we check the mother and baby's condition?" the lead attendant asked, not greatly amused.

"Sure," the midwife told them. "You will find everything in order. She came with the Lord's help. Look how beautiful she is."

Lifting the edge of the blanket the attendants looked for themselves. "Not bad," they both said at the same time. "Looks healthy, too."

"Of course, what else do you expect? This is the Lord's child."

"Well, they all are," the lead attendant said. "Some are just better-looking than others."

"Is that not the truth?" the midwife chuckled. "Now, would you two check out the mother and then be on your way? We have a mother and child to take care of here."

Looking carefully at Deborah the lead attendant said suddenly, "On second thought, that may not be necessary. If we start, we will have to take her in. Let's just leave well enough alone."

"Yes, that is good," the midwife nodded.

Out in the barn surrounded by sick cows, Esther told the relieved Bloh Jonas: "Bring my bag."

He brought it to her, and she opened the cover flap. Producing a jar, she proceeded with a wooden spoon to force some of its content's in the cow's mouth.

"What it is?" Jonas asked her.

"Molasses and horse feed."

"That all?"

She grinned, "Some herbs."

"Will that help?"

"Of course," she said moving to the next cow and then those out in the barn yard. No more then done, truck tires came to a stop outside.

"Who is that?" she asked.

"Don't know," Jonas told her, going to the door and looking out. "It's the vet," he said, making no attempt to hide his gladness.

"Send him home," she told him. "This will work just fine."

"I will not," Jonas replied, waiting at the door of the barn as the vet removed his pouch from his truck.

"Then I'm going," Esther pronounced. "You stay here and take care of the cows with your vet. I will go in and ask Naomi to take me home. The horse is still tied up, and we can manage."

"Sure," Jonas told her. "If Naomi can't, let me know."

She said nothing as she marched past the vet out the door.

The vet grinned at Jonas, "Trying some of your home remedies?"

"I couldn't get a hold of you," Jonas said as explanation.

"Well," he said, "I came as soon as I got back home and listened to the answering machine. Now let's see if we can get these cows well."

⌘

Thirty minutes later the vet was still at work. Jonas jumped up at the sound of Naomi bringing the buggy into the driveway. He ran out and met her when she pulled up. It was not necessary to say he would put the horse away. That was assumed.

"How are the cows?" Naomi wanted to know.

"Seven of them were down, but it doesn't seem to be spreading anymore. The vet is taking care of them."

"Did Esther do any good?"

"I don't know," he said, making no attempt to explain further.

"Well, we'll just have to hope for the best, then. You can't really afford to lose so many cows."

"I know," Jonas said in the darkness.

Early the next morning Ben got up to check on Deborah and the baby.

"How is she?" he asked the midwife's helper who had stayed the night.

"Really getting her strength back."

"And the baby?"

"The prettiest thing I have seen in a long time."

Ben smiled in spite of himself, "That is what they always say."

"Not this one," the helper said without smiling. "She is quite something."

"I'm just glad everything turned out okay."

"We all are," the helper responded. "When is your niece arriving?"

"She should be here by noon."

"Good, and when are they bringing Mark back?"

"This evening, I think."

"Well, I'm sure he will enjoy his little sister."

Ben shrugged his thin shoulders, "I'm just glad everyone is okay."

The helper nodded her head, "This is a special little girl, indeed. What are you calling her?"

"Sarah," he said, liking the sound of the name on his tongue.

In the meantime, Bloh Jonas entered his barn prepared for the worse. Instead the four cows inside the barn where walking around looking hungrily for any pieces of hay they could find. Piles of fresh cow manure were splattered all around. He could hardly control his joy. *The Lord has been good to me,* he thought involuntarily.

Opening the outside door to the barnyard, all the cows in his sight were walking around. *These, too?* Jonas smiled. *Someone helped them. I suppose they both want credit.*

Thus went the story of the birth of Sarah and of the people who surrounded her that night.

CHAPTER FOUR

AFTER THE SINGING that Sunday evening, Sarah walked out of the house with Martha. The singing was always where church was held earlier in the day. Several couples who were dating had already left, their lower buggy lights marking even intervals on the paved road. Girls gathered by the door, acting as if they were only waiting for their rides. In reality, they kept their eyes open for any unusual activity, such as a girl getting into a strange buggy. Neither Sarah nor Martha raised curiosity as it was obvious to all that Mark's buggy was the next in line.

"I'm back," Sarah said as she climbed nimbly into the space Mark had created for them by turning the wheel just slightly.

"Ya," he said, "I see." Half standing in the buggy until both of the girls were seated on either side, he sat back down in the middle. These crowded conditions were the reason Martha usually rode with Ben and Deborah Sunday mornings. However, for the singing there was usually no other choice.

Settling in on the left side, Sarah turned to him, "No one asked, did they?"

Mark shrugged his shoulders, "No. Apparently, neither did you get asked, unless you said 'no'."

"No one asked," she said cheerfully.

In the silence that followed Martha chuckled, then Mark acted as if he were adding an afterthought, "But I thought they were going to."

"Oh," Sarah tried to sound non-committal, "Who was it?"

"Yes, who was it?" Martha echoed.

Slapping the reins as his horse turned on to the black-top, Mark gave him his head. Accented by the low lighting and the darkness, the rhythm of a fast pacer sounded on the pavement as the landscape raced by. "Ah, Jesse Byler. Acted like he wanted to talk to me. He's the kind of boy I would guess could talk to you directly, but likes it the less obvious way. You know, if you say 'no', or something like that, they have a buffer. Anyway, I thought for sure it was coming, but then nothing."

Sarah smiled in the darkness, but Mark could not see it and took her silence for something else. "I still think you are doing something to scare off the boys. If you wouldn't do that, Jesse might be a good catch. He's Lamar Wagler's cousin. Lamar's got lots of money. It might run in the family, you know. Not too bad looking, either. Of course, he doesn't hold a candle to Lamar, but Lamar's already taken."

If they had not been passing under the bright outside lights of a well-lighted English home, Mark would have missed it. As it was he looked over at Sarah's face and caught the red blush that had spread over her face. "Sarah Schwartz," he told her in his best brotherly voice, "I can't believe this!"

"Believe what?" she managed to get out.

"You actually like him. I can't believe this! Whew, is this a surprise!"

Her voice sounded weak as Sarah said, "No, I don't care for Jesse Byler."

"So why are you blushing?"

"I don't know, maybe the weather or something, but I don't like Jesse."

"Don't try this on me, I am not that ignorant."

"I don't like him," she flat-toned convincingly.

In the silence that followed she suddenly wished she had not spoken so clearly, because Mark was obviously thinking. "It wouldn't be something else?" he finally asked.

Her voice trembled in the darkness of the buggy, "I hope not."

"There is," he said matter-of-factly, "and I can't believe it."

When she did not respond he asked point-blank, "It's Lamar, isn't it?"

Her throat caught so that she could not have spoken if she had wanted to. She did not need to, at least not for Mark's benefit. He had already reached his conclusion with or without her words. "I can't believe it," he repeated.

"I can't either," she finally managed to say.

"You know you can't do this," he told her in a quiet voice. "Sure, he's good looking and everything. Has plenty of money, but he's dating already. Has been for years. They must be almost ready for the wedding. If that's not enough, she's Malinda, Bloh Jonas's daughter. The whole family seems close to Esther. You don't want trouble with her. Do you realize what that all means?"

"Yes," she whispered in the darkness.

"Then why are you doing this? Get your heart under control."

"I wish I could," she told her. "It just has a mind of its own."

"Whew," he whistled out of his side of the buggy, pulling in the reins of his horse slightly to make a sharp corner. "Someone will sure have to help us out of this one."

"That's for sure," Martha added, still trying to get over

the shock of the sudden turns of this conversation and what they might mean.

≈

Two buggies ahead of them, Malinda was seated firmly on her side of Lamar's single-seater. The faint smell of the English car refresher still hung in the air. However, the desired effect on Malinda was not materializing.

"You're awful quiet tonight," he commented.

In the darkness he could not tell whether she moved her head or not, but he assumed she did not. He knew her well enough to know that something was wrong, and that it might not be easy to find out what it was.

"Trouble at home?" he ventured.

There was only silence. Trying to break the ice he moved slightly towards her. He felt her body stiffen. "Come now," he said softly. "What is bothering you?"

"You should know," she told him. "You were there."

"What does that mean?" he asked, his voice rising a few octaves.

"You were looking at her," she said.

"What does that mean?" he asked again stuck on one question.

"Sarah, that Sarah Schwartz!"

"What about her? She's been around for a long time."

"I suppose she has, although I don't think you've noticed. Anyway, how do you know? Have you been keeping track?"

"Of course not."

"Then how do you know she has been around for a long time?"

Lamar searched frantically for words. This was rapidly turning into a minefield he had no desire to walk through.

34

"I don't know. How am I supposed to know? You just see things like that."

She moved even farther over to her side of the buggy, pushing in the upholstery. "You were looking at her! That's all I know. With that look in your eyes like some moon-struck kid. Right there in front of everyone at the singing. Don't you think others will notice? What were you really thinking about? How beautiful she is?"

"Look, look," he chuckled quietly. "Sure, she's good looking, but so are you. I, I mean, I may have been out of line, but I don't mean anything by it. It doesn't mean any-thing. It really doesn't."

She did not move in the darkness. Pulling the reins up to slow down for a stop sign, he brought the buggy to a complete halt. Waiting for a passing car, her face was high-lighted briefly by the headlights. Catching a glimpse of her face, he thought the disapproving lines might be softening.

After the car had passed he let out the reins again. She then told him, "You have no business looking at Sarah Schwartz of all people. I mean it. You had better stop!"

"Of course," he said, "that's no problem at all. I don't know why you are worried about it."

"I am and will be until she starts dating. Why she hasn't started already, I don't know. She shouldn't have any problems finding a boy. High-minded creature that she is — maybe that's the problem. But boys usually find some way around those things. This has got to stop. Someone had better ask her out soon!"

"It'll be okay," he told her softly. "After all you and I have been through, you don't have to worry."

"That's why I do," she told him.

Gently he took her hand and pulled her towards him. She responded, slowly snuggling up to him in the darkness. "I don't like her," she said to no one in particular.

"It'll be okay," he said, squeezing her arm between his fingers. In the darkness he couldn't see her face, but he soon would when they arrived at her house. He got ready for the moment. This might not be that pleasant an evening.

In the middle of the week Malinda was in town. She tied her horse securely, while looking at the traffic around her. Over there, she was sure, was Esther's horse and buggy in the parking lot of Wal-Mart. Making sure her horse was comfortable she headed towards the front door. Entering past the checkout counters, she kept a sharp eye out for the familiar form. She soon found it. Rounding the end of the hardware aisle, Malinda saw that Esther was ahead of her. Speeding up her cart she pulled up behind Esther and said softly, *"Goot meiyah."*

Esther turned around slowly, "I thought that was you, Malinda. I wasn't expecting to see you in town today."

"Neither was I," Malinda told her, "Mom wanted some things on short notice. Plus, it gives me a chance to get some of my shopping done if I don't have to get a full load for the house."

"How are you doing?" Esther looked her over carefully. "I see you on Sundays some, but my, you are growing up fast."

"I'm doing okay, I guess," Malinda said hesitantly.

"Something wrong?" Esther asked her.

Malinda was unsure of herself, glancing up and down the aisle. No other Amish were apparent. "I'm not sure," she paused, glancing around again. "It's just that Lamar, well, I don't know how to say it."

"You are about to get married, aren't you?" Esther asked.

"Yes, we have the date pretty much fixed, so maybe I shouldn't be worried, but I am."

"What is he doing?" Esther asked point-blank.

Malinda blushed deeply then paled, "I caught him looking at that Sarah Schwartz on Sunday night. She's only about eighteen, I think. Been around for a while, but Lamar acts like he has just seen her."

"She is a beauty," Esther dead-panned in a low tone.

"I think Lamar is falling for her," Malinda gushed out in one burst. "What am I going to do?"

"You think it's that serious?" Esther asked.

"I don't know. I'm all confused now. Lamar was so nice on Sunday night about it. Said there was nothing to it, but I don't think I believe him. He didn't want to stay late at all, then. What am I going to do if I lose him?"

Esther knitted her brow, "Well, there are many things you can do, I suppose. Maybe I could talk to Deborah. That might do some good."

"No, no, don't do that," Malinda grabbed Esther's arm. "I couldn't stand that. It would be way too humiliating. It would get all over the place that I couldn't keep my boy. No, no, I can't have that."

"You might have to take some strong measures if this gets serious," Esther told her.

"Maybe it won't get serious. Oh, I hope so that it won't. Maybe it's just my nerves. But why do you think it might get serious?"

Esther paused, thinking, "Just my suspicion, I guess."

"What would you do?" Malinda asked breathlessly.

"Well," Esther lowered her voice. "I would see that he is well taken care of."

"Of course, I already do that," Malinda said. "I've let him kiss me a few times. Not that I mind, but it's just something you have to do."

"I know," Esther told her, "I figured you knew that, but just be extra careful when things like this come up. Beyond that, just wait it out, if you can. Boys sometimes go through this kind of thing. Beyond that, just get married," Esther smiled. "Then he's all yours, regardless how he feels. Right?"

Malinda smiled glumly, unconvinced. "Will you help me if I need help?" she asked.

Esther chuckled, "We will have to see, now won't we. We don't want to get something started against one of our own people, do we?"

"I don't like her," Malinda said, starting to push her cart down the aisle as they both saw two Amish ladies come around the corner in front of them.

Esther prepared to head in the other direction. "Let me know if it goes very badly," she said softly, turning to go.

Malinda smiled as she passed the two ladies, *"Goot meiyah"* she said to them. They returned the greeting. Esther had already disappeared into the next aisle.

❧

Jesse Byler came up to stand beside Lamar who was leaning on the edge of some stacked metal gates. Since this afternoon's rain, the clouds had almost cleared. The sun was having no problems peaking through. Its low angle still warmed the backs of young boys gathered here and there to watch.

All around them the sounds of the Friday evening's auction at Dinky's was in high gear. The mostly Amish auctioneers were placed at intervals both inside and outside the two barns. Their helpers were holding up items for sale, while they thundered out the bids with their portable loudspeakers. People milled everywhere, in singles and in groups.

"Quite some auction tonight," Jesse commented.

"Buying anything?" Lamar wanted to know.

"*Nay, usht gukka,*" (No, just looking) Jesse told him.

"Same here," Lamar said although it was not entirely true. If certain household items went for the right price, he would bid on them. It was just that he was not really looking for them. It would not be good to tell his cousin either way, he figured. Even with the wedding coming closer, it was good to keep one's mouth shut.

Jesse cleared his throat, then looked away. "I wonder if you could do something for me, Lamar?"

"Sure," Lamar said quickly. "If I can help, then, of course."

"You don't know what I am going to ask yet, so don't be too sure," Jesse told him.

"Granted," Lamar said, "but let's see what it is."

"I need someone to ask Sarah Schwartz for me."

Lamar was glad he was looking in the other direction at the moment, because Jesse turned around as he said the last few words. He would have seen the startled look in Lamar's eyes. Bringing himself under control, Lamar turned around to look at Jesse, "Why don't you ask her yourself?"

"You know I can't do that," Jesse protested. "What if she says 'no'? I can't have people knowing that. It would ruin me forever. She's the most beautiful girl in Daviess County. Sure I'm afraid to ask her, but so is everyone else. For much the same reason, I suppose. She is just too attractive. What boy has hopes for someone like that? Worse yet, to have it known that you tried and failed on such a big one."

"That makes sense," Lamar acknowledged, "then why not ask her brother to do it?"

"For much the same reason, I suppose," Jesse told him. "People would put two and two together if I talked to him some Sunday, you know, private-like. I certainly am not stopping by the place. Now you, you already have a girl, almost married. No one would think twice about the thing. Even if they did, they could not trace it back to me."

"Sounds like you have it all figured out," Lamar said quietly.

"Are you going to do it or not?" Jesse asked him shortly. "I have thought about this long enough to give me a head-ache. It's about time to have it over with, one way or the other. I doubt if I have much of a chance with her, but I could never stand myself if I didn't try. One does not get such a chance more than once in a lifetime, it seems to me."

"You have that right," Lamar said.

Jesse looked at him sharply. "If I didn't know any better I would think you wanted her."

Lamar chuckled while looking at the ground, "Well, she is good-looking."

"That she is," Jesse said, satisfied with the answer. "Now, will you ask her or not?"

Just inside the barn from where the boys were stand-ing, the auctioneer was just at the point of selling off the main bedroom suite, announcing the fact loud and clear, "Look what we have here, ladies and gentlemen, the best of this household. The finest in cherry, custom-made bedroom suites. Step right up and bid with confidence. This ought to be a good one. That's what I say, a good one. Who will start the bid at $700?"

His voice went into his chant. Lamar at the moment did not care one way or the other. Jesse was waiting for an answer, and he, Lamar, was having chills run up and down his spine at the thought of stopping by and talking with Sarah Schwartz. Did he dare?

"That's the way to go," the auctioneer said, "$900, $950, and now let's see who will give a thousand for this fine piece of furniture."

"I'll do it," he said to Jesse.

"Good, then ask for this Sunday."

"Okay," Lamar told him. "I'll stop by on Saturday afternoon, and let you know what she says on Sunday morning at church. That still leaves you time to get ready by Sunday night."

Standing there beside the fence, Jesse clasped and unclasped his hands. "Please, God," he muttered softly, "let her say 'yes'."

Lamar just leaned on the fence and said nothing. He was having intense feelings of excitement. What surprised him was that he was also feeling just a little bit ashamed, although through it all he kept a straight face.

Chapter Five

PUNCTUALLY AT NINE o'clock, Mrs. Rebecca Florence pulled into the Schwartz driveway. It was a sunny day with a gentle breeze blowing in the tree tops outside the house. Sarah was going to visit for the day. Rebecca was one of Deborah's English friends and recovering from a recent auto accident.

"There's a car coming in. It must be her," Martha announced. "I wish I was going, too."

"It's not my decision," Sarah told her. "She just invited me."

"It makes no difference. You are always the one who gets to do everything. I even have to drive with Mom and Dad to church."

"That's not my fault, either. It's too uncomfortable with three in the buggy."

"You do it on Sunday nights."

"That's because we have to."

Martha made a face, "I wish I were the oldest."

"Girls, girls, let's calm down now. Mrs. Florence is here." Opening the front door, she motioned for Sarah to hurry out. "No use making her walk in. She might still be feeling rough from the accident. Have a good time now and be back before it gets too late."

"I will," Sarah told her as she headed out the door.

Rebecca was wondering whether she should get out of

the car when Sarah came out obviously ready to go. Instead, she simply rolled down her window and waited for Sarah to approach.

"Good morning," she said cheerfully, struck by the Amish girl's radiant beauty.

Sarah returned her greeting with a smile, crossing in front of the vehicle and climbing in.

"You'll have to excuse me this morning," Rebecca said quickly. "I'm not quite used to this vehicle yet. Bill just got it for me."

"I wouldn't know the difference anyway," Sarah assured her. "I don't drive in automobiles that much."

Rebecca chuckled, "You can still tell I'm sure. I just loved the old Caprice. It was so comfortable. One gets used to anything I guess, but this car is so different from my old one. Bill insisted that it had to be an SUV in case I had another accident. He said Toyota was the best on the market. I don't know, so I take his word for it. What do you think?" she asked daring to take her eyes off the road for a moment and glancing towards Sarah.

"You have to remember I know nothing about cars," Sarah reminded her.

"Surely you know something about them?" Rebecca insisted.

"Well, we did study them in school."

"Yes," Rebecca replied, waiting to hear what else Sarah had to say.

"We studied how Henry Ford in America got the concept of the assembly line for making cars going in the 1910's," Sarah told her. "Of course, he was really just copying Ransom Olds' Oldsmobile factory which he had begun in 1902.

"Actually, the first real attempt to build a car is thought by some to have been by Ferdinad Verbiest, a member of a Jesuit mission in China. He did it with steam power in 1672. The first internal combustion engine was fuelled with hydrogen and oxygen and was invented by Francois Isaac de Rivaz, a Swiss inventor. Although the design was not that successful, at least they were trying," Sarah chuckled.

Rebecca was astonished, "You learned all this?"

"Yes," Sarah said innocently. "We never learned much about modern cars, but Teacher Byler taught us the history of them. He said it was interesting information, and good to expand and warn our minds with. That way we could see that man has always been evil and had been attempting to invent maladies for many years."

"Is that so?" Mrs. Florence asked dryly.

"Yes," Sarah said with a smile. "He said the history of man is constant turbulence in which he searches for ways to express his fallen state. Modern inventions are one of the ways this is manifested."

"I see," Mrs. Florence said, "what a vision of the world!"

"Our preachers say much the same thing," Sarah volunteered. "God never changes, so why should we be trying to change all the time? It is our pursuit of pleasure and sensual things that mirrors our sinful nature. This is why they teach us to keep our lives like the forefathers."

"I suppose they never changed either," Mrs. Florence stated quite bluntly.

Sarah shrugged her shoulders, "Well, they did come from the Catholic Church and the Lutherans, but that was good change. Change like that was necessary. Inventions for the flesh are a different category, I guess."

"Well, that's some life," Mrs. Florence stated, deciding quickly that a change of subject was in order. "Tell me more about your years growing up."

"I was born around here," Sarah told her, "in the house where we live now. Mom talks about some trouble that they had at my birth, but I apparently arrived before the English did."

"The English?" Mrs. Florence looked questioningly.

"Oh, I see," Sarah said hastily, "We don't mean that disrespectful like, but that is what our people call Americans who are not Amish."

"I see," Mrs. Florence replied with a slight shake of her head. "That is a different way of looking at things. I never quite thought of myself as English. But you were telling about your birth?"

"Yes," Sarah continued, "because of some problems the midwife was having, Dad called the ambulance. But I was born before it came."

"That wasn't that long ago," commented Mrs. Florence.

"Eighteen years ago," Sarah said. "A little more than that, but not that much. Anyway, things turned out okay. With all the fuss of the ambulance tearing up the driveway with its lights flashing, people talked about it quite a long time afterwards."

"I can see how that would be memorable," allowed Mrs. Florence. "So you were born, and everything was fine from then on?"

"Pretty much," Sarah said. "There was school, of course, till the eighth grade, like we do. I did fairly well and I always liked school. After the eighth grade I helped Mom and Dad at home and on the farm. At sixteen we start going with the young people. That brings in a lot more activities. It also gets you out of the house and off the farm. Kind of makes life more interesting."

"Any boys?" Rebecca asked.

"No," Sarah told her, blushing.

This was not missed on Rebecca who then observed, "I see there is someone. The right one hasn't asked yet, is that what it is?"

Sarah ducked her head, "I don't know. Those things get confusing, at least for me they do."

"They do for everyone, dear," Rebecca told her. "The good Lord will help us sort it all out."

"I hope so," Sarah said although it was clear that she had her doubts.

"How do your people stand on divorce?" Rebecca wanted to know.

"It's not allowed," Sarah said.

"You mean, like it never happens?" Rebecca asked, puzzled.

"Not if you want to stay in the church," Sarah said.

"Does it work? I mean, do the people listen?" Rebecca wondered out loud.

"Sure," Sarah said quickly. "There are no divorced people in church. It's just out of the question."

"But how do you enforce something like that? I mean, everybody is doing it." Rebecca was quite interested in the question.

"I don't know," Sarah said, "The preachers just do it, I guess. No one divorces, or, if they do, they have to leave."

"Are there many of them?" Rebecca wanted to know.

"None that I know of," said Sarah.

"That is the most amazing thing!" Rebecca commented. "You can be thankful for that. Divorce is doing a lot of damage in our world. Thankfully, none of my children have gone through one, but one never knows. It seems like it's everywhere though, even for people my age."

Sarah simply nodded her head. They were fast approaching the South Washington exit. Noticing Sarah looking around, Rebecca announced, "Almost there. We live on the east end of town, just off the 50/150 highway."

A few more turns and they were approaching the house.

Rebecca pointed it out, "We have lived here for years. Raised the whole family in this neighborhood."

Sarah, for reasons of which she was unsure, was expecting a little more upscale area. Instead, it looked much like the rest of Washington with which she was familiar. "Looks like town to me," she said to make conversation.

Rebecca took no offense at the remark. "I suppose it does, much like all the country looks the same to me. It depends on what one is used to, I guess."

Walking towards the house together, Sarah paused to examine the roses planted in the beds on each side of the walk. "You grow these yourself?" she asked.

"Yes, we do." Rebecca said, chuckling, "No gardener or anyone like that. I like to get out and do a little dirt work myself. Bill also likes to when he's home. Helps relax the nerves, I think."

"I suppose it does," Sarah replied, "now that I think about it. Nice roses, though."

"Thank you," replied Rebecca. "Why don't we go on in the house?"

Opening the front door with her key, she showed Sarah inside, then gave her the general tour of the first floor, "This is the living room," she pointed out, "then the dining room, kitchen, and the main bedroom. The rest of the rooms are upstairs."

"It's nice," Sarah commented, feeling the strangeness of being in a modern home with carpet on the floors, paintings on the walls, thick curtains on the windows, electric lights with accessories everywhere, the TV sitting in a dominant place by the fireplace, and a coffee pot sitting on the counter. *No heating up the pot on the stove*, she thought.

Rebecca walked over to the fireplace mantel and pointed out the portraits of her family, "These are the two girls, Claudia and Jenny, when they were younger. Both are married now. Then there is Marcus. He's in school at UC Berkeley, although he's home for the weekend. He and his father are downtown doing something. Over here is Bill and me. Younger of course, but still us." Rebecca laughed softly as if she were recalling fond memories.

"What is this?" Sarah asked Rebecca, motioning towards a large covered piece of furniture.

"That's the piano Bill finally got for me a few years ago. I have played piano for many years, but never owned a Steinway before." Rebecca lifted the covering, sweeping it back slowly. "Built from mahogany wood from South America. Would you like to hear it played?"

"I guess," Sarah said, completely unaware of what happens when one plays a piano.

Rebecca seated herself carefully and placed her hands on the keys, "I play in the church choir," she explained. "This is a number we did last Sunday. It's one of Beethoven's pieces."

With that Rebecca began playing the music, running her fingers lightly over the keys. The sound rose and fell, and, as music can, the player and the listener enveloped in a world too vast for words. Rebecca did not just play the correct notes. Instead, she reached for the soul and meaning of the sound.

Sarah listened with her mouth open. Never had she heard such a thing before. Sunday nights at the singing were not like this. So this was English music? It pulled at her heart. It stirred feelings in her she did not know she had. She felt like a person who has hungered for something all her life, but never known what it was.

Rebecca turned around to look at her, "Oh, do you want me to stop?" she asked, not sure from the look on Sarah's face what it meant.

"No, please go on," stammered Sarah, not realizing

what expression her face revealed. "That was something incredible."

Turning back to the piano, Rebecca continued with another piece. Halfway through the piece the doorway behind them opened. Neither woman noticed. Bill and Marcus entered quietly. Standing there they watched the strange sight of Rebecca playing for an obviously Amish girl.

"She was going to pick up the Amish girl to visit today," Bill whispered to Marcus.

Marcus nodded, vaguely recalling that he had heard something about an Amish girl coming. When the music ended, Rebecca turned around. Sarah was still lost in the music.

"Oh, it's you, Marcus. I didn't know when you would be back. This is Sarah," she said, motioning towards Sarah Schwartz, whose back was still turned to them.

Their voices finally broke through to Sarah's consciousness and she turned around slowly. Marcus could not believe his eyes. Not one normally embarrassed around girls, he was simply astonished that such beauty was possible with those strange clothing.

"Hi, I'm Marcus," he said carefully, not sure whether Amish girls were normal or not. This one sure was not what he had expected.

"Hi," she said demurely, nodding her head, although she kept her eyes on his face. Her blue eyes shone with an intensity he had not before seen. Her eyes did not flirt or flinch, but revealed an expectant air as if this young woman were used to good things happening in life.

Marcus felt completely out of his depth. He decided then and there he would leave beautiful Amish girls to themselves. Who knows what they might be capable of? Excusing himself, he said, "Well, I must be going. Dad and

I just got back from town. See you later, Mom. Nice to meet you, Sarah."

She glanced briefly in his direction. With that he was gone. "He's a nice boy," Rebecca said in a motherly tone.

Sarah was still thinking about the music, not the boy. "That was beautiful music," she said.

"Yes, it is," Rebecca agreed, then decided to make her pitch right then and there. "Maybe you can come up here often, and I can teach you to play like that?"

"No," Sarah said flatly. "That wouldn't work. We are not allowed to play things like that."

Rebecca refrained from further comment on that subject. She felt she was already reaching the limits of what was possible. Instead, she finally asked: "Do you think your mother would allow you to come back just to visit then?"

"Like this?" Sarah wanted to know.

"Yes," Rebecca told her.

"I don't think so," Sarah said. "It wouldn't be allowed to visit with the English that much. One time is okay, with the accident and all, but not more than that."

This response did not please Rebecca and she pondered the situation. Then, hesitantly, "Are there any conditions under which you are allowed to go into English homes?"

Sarah laughed softly, "Yes, as maids."

"Well, then," Rebecca brightened, "that is what we will do. You can come clean once a month. I will pick you up like I did today, and we can visit afterward."

"I will have to actually clean though," Sarah said soberly.

"Don't worry," Rebecca assured her, "you will. This house can use some Amish cleaning, I'm sure."

Thus it was decided, and later when Rebecca dropped Sarah off at her home, she went inside and thanked Deborah for allowing Sarah to come. She then asked about the cleaning arrangement once a month. Deborah readily agreed, and so it was official. Sarah would be going to the Florence residence again.

When Rebecca returned home, Marcus was seated on the couch, engrossed in his schoolbooks. "Aren't you off duty today?" she asked him.

"Not today. Actually, never really if you want good grades," he explained to her. "By the way, Mom, that Amish girl ought to model. She's stunning."

"You interested in her?" she asked, looking closely at him.

"No," he said simply. "She's beautiful. She would make a good model."

"But she's Amish," she told him.

"Yea, I thought of that, too," he said, going back to his books. She shrugged and headed for the kitchen.

CHAPTER SIX

WHILE SARAH WAS still telling Deborah and Martha about the details of her day with Mrs. Florence, a buggy pulled into the driveway. "Who is that?" Deborah asked, already knowing the answer.

"I don't know," both Martha and Sarah replied.

"Don't you girls know the buggies around here?" Deborah asked them. "We used to when we were young."

With that both looked closer at the horse and the buggy now halfway up the driveway. "That's Lamar's horse," Martha said emphatically while Sarah merely looked.

"Lamar who?" Deborah continued, wanting the girls to say it.

"Wagler," Martha said, "the one who's dating Bloh Jonas's Malinda. Got lots of money, they say."

"That's not everything," Deborah told them.

"I know," Martha assured her, already sensing the direction of the conversation. "That's why I'm planning on marrying a poor man."

"No, don't do that," gasped Deborah.

Sarah saw her chance to get into the conversation before they noticed her agitated state. She chuckled softly, "I'm sure she's not serious, Mom."

"She'd better not be," said Deborah with the horror still in her voice.

"What do you think Lamar wants?" Martha wondered

out loud. "He probably wants to talk with Mark, but Mark's not home."

"You'd better go tell him, Mom," Sarah suggested, seeing clearly now that it was Lamar Wagler sitting in the buggy. He made the swing around the driveway and pulled up to the hitching post.

Martha's hand suddenly flew to her mouth, "You don't suppose?" she asked not finishing her thought.

"You don't suppose *what*?" Deborah demanded to know. "Would you girls talk sense for once?"

"Oh, I don't know," she said looking pointedly at Sarah. "It couldn't be."

"This makes absolutely no sense, at all." Deborah was exasperated, "What is the world coming to? We can't just leave him out there."

"You'd better go tell him Mark's not home," Sarah told her mother again.

"Why don't you go?" Deborah asked in Sarah's direction.

"Not me," Sarah said quickly, certain that her face was turning red.

Martha came to her rescue, thinking that she would extract some kind of payback later. "I'll tell him," she said, keeping her voice level lest her mother become suspicious.

With that she opened the front door and headed down the walk. Lamar had gotten out and was now standing beside his buggy. He made no attempt to tie the horse, which meant he was not planning on staying long or coming into the house. His lean body and healthy good looks were framed by the buggy's black vinyl sides. Martha looked at him curiously when she came within speaking distance, but she said nothing.

"Hi," he said, acknowledging her presence. "Is Sarah home?"

"Sarah?" she demanded. "What do you want with her?"

"Now, now," he calmly told her. *"Mach dich naett bays"* (don't make yourself mad).

She glared at him. "Mark's not home, and you have no business speaking to Sarah."

"Oh, so you know all about my business?" he asked her.

"I do this time. You have no business talking with my sister."

"Oh, I don't, miss know-it-all? Now, is that a fact? Indeed, I do have business with your sister."

"And what would that be?" she asked as she planted her feet firmly in front of him.

He paused dramatically, turned his eyes toward the sky, and then grinned, "I am the bearer of a certain question, shall we say? This concerns your sister and a fellow. As to what that is, that is none of your business. As to what she tells me, the same applies. So would you be so kind to tell your sister I need to speak with her?"

"Oh," Martha replied and shifted her weight. "So that's what it is? Why didn't you say so to start with?"

Now Lamar glared at her. She smiled weakly and turned to go. Then, on impulse, she turned back towards him, "And why did this boy send you? I mean, it seems like a strange choice."

"Just get your sister," Lamar admonished her.

"Okay," Martha told him, tilting her head slightly as if pondering the situation. She was not going just yet.

Martha's determined pose finally elicited an exasperated response from Lamar. "I can't believe this. *Gott em himmel*, what are you, her watchdog? Cousin Jesse asked me to come by for reasons you should be able to figure out. Now, is that good enough, Miss Nosey, Busy-body, person, you?"

"I suppose," Martha relented after a moment. "That does make sense. It had better not be for any other reason, though."

"And what other reason would there be?" He threw his hands up in the air.

"Just remember that," she said over her shoulder as she turned to go.

Going back up the walk, Martha opened the door to find her mother waiting there. Sarah was nowhere to be seen. "What is going on?" she demanded. "It took you long enough!"

"He wants to see Sarah," Martha stated flatly.

"Sarah?" Deborah's brow wrinkled. "Now, why would he want to see her?"

"That's exactly what I wanted to know," Martha stated emphatically.

"You asked him that?" Deborah's momentary horror was overcome by her curiosity. "What did he tell you?"

"That he is here to ask Sarah for his cousin, Jesse. That's what he told me."

"You meddled in their business? That's private between the three of them. You had no right interfering, Martha," Deborah looked at her disapprovingly.

"Just making sure," Martha told her. "I don't want him doing something he shouldn't. That's why I asked."

"Doing something he shouldn't?" Deborah looked puzzled. "Lamar wouldn't do that. He's one of the most upstanding young men around. About to be married to Malinda, isn't he? You shouldn't think bad thoughts about him, Martha. Now go tell Sarah to come. You've kept him waiting long enough already." Looking out the front window, she emphasized her words with a shake of her hand. "Quickly, don't keep him waiting any longer."

Martha shrugged and left to find Sarah. She found her

in her bedroom, attempting to clean up an already clean room. "He wants to talk with you," she announced.

"With me?" Sarah could barely speak.

"My, you have got it bad," observed Martha. "You had better get a hold of yourself."

"What does he want?" Sarah croaked, barely getting the words out.

Martha could not help laughing, "Look, don't get all worried. He's here to ask you for someone else, but he needs to see you. It wouldn't do for you to hear it second-hand. You have no choice, you have to talk to him. Although I must say, it does make for a mighty peculiar situation. Maybe you can see some of this boy he is asking about? Might take your mind off of things you obviously shouldn't be thinking about."

"Who is he?" Sarah asked, her state of mind improving somewhat under the barrage of Martha's instructions.

"I don't think I should tell you," Martha said. "Lamar will, then see that you already have your answer ready, and he's already mad enough at me for all the questions I asked."

"Oh, please tell me," Sarah pleaded.

"No, I won't," Martha told her firmly. "Now, go on. He's waiting."

"I can't, I can't. I can't go out there." Sarah was losing her voice again.

Martha took her by her arm and shook it gently. "Listen to me. You have to go out there and hear what he has to say! Hopefully say 'yes'. I would highly recommend that and then you have a date. That's it. There's nothing to it."

Sarah took some deep breaths. "That's a girl," Martha encouraged her. "Now just start walking."

With Martha leading they headed toward the front door. Deborah was waiting impatiently. "What's taking so long? He's waiting." Then glancing at Sarah's pale face she smiled, "Oh, this is sweet. It's so great, Sarah. You will finally have a date. I'm so happy. I can see that you want this boy already. Martha told me who he was. Isn't that wonderful? He's such a good young man. I think he has money, too."

Sarah decided it was much safer to say nothing, so she kept walking, figuring that her mother would excuse any strange behavior at the moment. Watching her go down the walk towards Lamar's buggy, Deborah sighed, "It's so *vunderboah*, isn't it, Martha? I can't believe it's finally happening."

"I hope she says, 'yes'," Martha said quietly.

"Well, of course she will," Deborah stated flatly, "You told her who the boy is, right? What was her reaction?"

"I didn't tell her," Martha replied. "She doesn't know yet who the boy is."

"You didn't tell her?" Deborah asked in exasperation. "Why not?"

"Because Lamar is already upset enough with me, and I wanted her to at least look surprised, like she doesn't know."

"I guess," agreed Deborah reluctantly. "Surely she will say 'yes', though?"

"I hope so," Martha said quietly.

Sarah walked quickly, approaching Lamar with her eyes on the ground and her heart pounding furiously. He watched as she approached and was overcome by her beauty. Never had he been this close to her before. The grace with which she walked and the way she held her hands caused him to draw in his breath and to chastise himself for how he felt. *She's not your girl.*

Finally he said, "Hi. Sorry to bother you."

"That's okay," she said, cautiously lifting her eyes to

his. Their blueness startled him. He felt like he was seeing something that was absolutely forbidden. Had it been possible, he felt he would have happily entered such a world at that moment.

He took a long breath before speaking. "Jesse asked me to come and ask if you would let him see you Sunday," he said simply.

His discomfort surprised her, and also gave her courage. She no longer felt tempted to cast her eyes to the ground again. "That was nice of him," she said quietly.

"I guess so," he said. Not very convincing, she thought. "What am I supposed to tell him?"

For the first time she smiled at him. "That would be your cousin, Jesse, right?"

He seemed surprised at the question. "Well, yes," he said. I wouldn't come for anyone else."

"I suppose so," she told him, "but I would rather be certain. I wouldn't want to be going home with the wrong boy."

"That is true," he told her, looking at the ground. "So, the answer is 'yes', then?"

"I didn't say that," she replied softly.

"Oh," he stammered. "Is the answer 'no'?"

"What do you think it *should* be?" she asked him, the smile now gone.

"Me?" he asked and pointed to himself. "How should I know?"

She shrugged her shoulders slightly and clasped her hands in front of her. He felt irresistibly drawn to her and cast his eyes down to avoid her intense gaze. He lifted them again as she spoke, "I thought maybe you would have an opinion on it."

His heart raced as he told her, "Well, he is my cousin, but I would rather you didn't."

"Any special reason?" she asked.

Totally befuddled now, he eventually managed to say, "Not really. You know, I guess Jesse is a nice boy."

"Tell him 'no'," she said, and she turned abruptly on her heel and walked towards the house without looking back.

Lamar gathered his thoughts and got slowly into his buggy. Slapping the reins he urged his horse forward. The racing stripes on his spokes whirled as he started off. Cobwebs crowded his brain as a storm of emotions swirled through him. *Gott em himmel, what was that all about?*

When Sarah opened the front door, both her mother and Martha were waiting. Deborah could hardly contain herself, "Oh, it's so wonderful. You really have a date. I was beginning to worry, although heaven knows you should have no problems."

"I said 'no'," Sarah stated without any emotion or explanation.

"You said, 'no'?" Deborah placed her hand over her mouth in astonishment.

"I can't believe this," Martha chimed in. "How dare you?"

"It is my life," Sarah replied. "Don't you think so?"

Martha looked at her with horror, "I can't believe you are taking this chance," she said.

Deborah dissolved into tears. "Your first date. You said 'no'. No one has ever asked you before. Now, they might not ever ask again. How can you do this to us? Oh, I can't believe this!"

"Would both of you just quit?" Sarah insisted. "I couldn't say 'yes' when I don't love him."

"How do know you don't love him?" Deborah wailed. "You talk like the English. How can you know that if you never have gone home with the boy? Love comes in many ways. You know, it just happens sometimes."

"I know," Sarah said simply. With this, Martha realized what she meant, but her mother still did not.

"You have more nerve than a fox in a hen house," Martha announced loudly and threw her hands in the air.

"What has that got to do with anything?" Deborah wanted to know.

"Mother, I hope you never find out," said Martha.

"Would you girls talk sense for once? None of this makes any sense. Here you have a nice chance at a boy and you turn him down. Now, your sister says that takes nerve. I say it doesn't. It just makes no sense at all!" Deborah stopped to catch her breath.

"We'll just see what the new day holds." Sarah took her mother's hand. "For now though, life must go on with or without a date. Right?"

"I guess so," Deborah muttered, clearly not convinced. "To see my daughter with a boy would have been a *vunderboah* thing."

"Maybe God will just have to take care of that," Sarah assured her with a slight smile.

"*Ach*," Deborah responded, "don't blame God for this one. It was your own doing."

"I guess so, Mother," Sarah said gently, "but I just couldn't do it."

Deborah looked at her long and hard, then softened slowly, "You are beautiful, Sarah. It will not be a problem for long. Of this we can be sure."

Sarah was relieved that her mother felt better. As for herself, she could not have felt worse. Her heart went from being thrilled at the memory of Lamar standing there beside his buggy to a sinking feeling that she had done something terribly wrong.

"Let's get supper ready," she said, heading for the kitchen.

❧

Earlier, in New York City, Phillip Ryan left his office on 80 Pine Street. The twenty-two year old was the son of Chester Ryan, founder and majority shareholder of "Maxey Jacobs", a business umbrella for subsidiary companies in both men's and women's designer clothing with their own in-house agencies for models. They had offices in Chicago, Los Angeles, New York, and, of course, Paris. After only two months of trading as a public company on the Standards & Poor, their stock went from an opening of $5.50 to the $25.00-plus range. The day before, MJC had closed at $26.55.

Fresh out of Yale, Phillip's degree was in business management. He was restless, hungry for adventure, and confident of advancement. Of medium height, his blue eyes, straight nose, and designer hair caused feminine heads to turn.

"Where are you going for the weekend?" his secretary asked him. That she was working on a weekend did not surprise him, considering the overtime she made and her ambition. She worked hard and knew the business. Her biggest fault was that she had designs on him, although he figured he could handle that.

"Does it matter?" he asked.

"How do I know? It isn't as if you tell me everything," she tried to sound offended.

"I'm going back home for the weekend," he admitted. "Mom rarely gets out much anymore. She doesn't like the business, I think, especially since it has gotten as big as it has. Dad has begun spending more time at home with her. Just thought I ought to follow his example, at least for a weekend."

"Oh, a virtuous young man," she said, admiration playing in the edges of her voice.

"Oh, don't say the 'V'-word!" responded Phillip in mock horror. "After all, I am a Yale man. There is a certain repudiation to uphold."

"Are things really like that at Yale," she asked inquisitively.

"I guess," he ventured, "if those are the things you're after. I was more interested in studying."

"You were not. You're too handsome for that."

He recoiled in fake shock, "Oh really? Now, I'm confused. Which is it? Am I virtuous or reprobate? You can't have it both ways. You don't believe one or the other, do you, Ms. Camellia? Is this how it goes?"

Camellia smiled her most saccharin smile. "I think you are both. Now tell me where you're really going."

"I really am going to Indianapolis, to see my mother and, I assume, my father, if he is there. He was in New York part of the week. I think he was going home for the weekend, unless a problem at the Paris office needed his urgent attention. Either way, my Mom will be glad if I am home, too.

"Ah, that is sweet. Do tell her 'hi' for me."

"I'll see," he hedged.

"What time is your flight?" she then asked him.

"One o'clock out of LaGuardia."

"Why not use Newark or JFK? Either would be cheaper, and I could do the scheduling for you either way," she explained.

He pondered that. "I'll see. Maybe, next time. I don't like Newark because of the distance. Although it has nicer facilities, time is important, too, and I don't think the price for the airport usage is that much different."

"Let me see," she then said. "If you don't need the money, you can put the savings in my paycheck."

"Oh, so that's what it's all about?" he replied quizzically.

At that, she merely smiled. "Have a good weekend," she told him as he headed out the door. "Give my regards to 'Mommy'."

Late on Saturday evening Jesse stopped by Lamar's. He found it impossible to wait till Sunday morning. After tying up his horse, he found Lamar alone in the barn doing the last of his chores. Jesse asked without any introductions, "What did she say?"

"Sorry, she said 'no'," Lamar informed him.

"Are you sure?" Jesse asked, crestfallen.

"I was there. That's what she said," Lamar assured him.

"Any explanation?" Jesse wanted to know.

Lamar shook his head. "No, she didn't offer any explanation."

"Any ideas yourself?" Jesse asked.

"Look," Lamar informed him. "She said 'no,' and I'd leave it as that and move on. There are other girls in the world. Someone will be there for you. Don't take it too hard."

"Not as beautiful as Sarah," said Jesse sadly.

"That may be true in one way, but other girls are beautiful in other ways. The right one will come along for you," Lamar told him firmly. "I wouldn't worry about it."

"You'll keep this quiet, right?" Jesse asked him.

"Sure, why not? I don't want to see any harm come to you."

"Thanks," Jesse told him, taking his leave. Dusk was just falling as he drove out the driveway. Lamar stood listening for a long time in the evening stillness as the horse's hooves faded into the distance.

≈

Next morning in South Washington, Marcus got up early. Rebecca was already up and quietly playing on the piano. "Are you going to church with us?" she wanted to know.

"I would, Mom, but don't you remember I promised to be with Phillip Ryan this afternoon? If I want to be back at a decent time this evening, I have to leave before too long."

Rebecca sighed, "It's just that when the time comes for you to leave, it always comes too soon."

"I'll be back," Marcus assured her. "I don't have to fly out until Monday. I'll still have this evening at home."

"Just a minute. I have a better idea," she suddenly interjected.

"And what could that be?" he asked, suddenly suspicious.

"Now," she admonished, "listen to my idea first. We haven't seen much of the Ryan's lately. Why don't your father and I follow you up there? We could visit with the Ryan's this afternoon, and perhaps even spend the evening. It would give us all more time together, and we could catch up with old friends. You could get a motel room for the evening and we could drive back. That way you would already be there for your flight tomorrow morning."

He cocked his head and thought for a moment. "I think that would be just great, Mom," he finally said. "When Phillip called, he mentioned that his father might be home too. If he is, this would work out great."

"Let's find out, then," Rebecca said.

"Why don't you call Corrine?" he asked.

Rebecca responded by getting her cell phone, finding Corrine's phone number, and dialing it. A brief but pleasant conversation between her and Corrine followed during which details of their plans were arranged. They would have lunch with the Ryan's on Morse Lake in the North Harbor Subdivision.

"Sounds good," Marcus said, when she got off the phone. "When do we leave?"

"As soon as I find your father and we get ready," she said. "Of course, we'll have some breakfast first."

After breakfast they were on their way. They arrived just as the Ryan's were returning home from attending church. After the usual pleasantries had been exchanged, and lunch had been eaten, the two boys headed for the boat sitting in the lawn dock.

"Wow!" Marcus exclaimed when he saw the new speedboat.

"Nice, isn't it?" Phillip stroked the shiny sides carefully.

"Really awesome," Marcus said admiringly as he walked around to the other side,

"Around forty feet long, twin engines. Seats nine, sleeps four," Phillip explained to him.

"Ever take a girl out in it?" Marcus wanted to know.

"Not yet," Phillip told him. "One has to have a girl first."

"No one?" Marcus asked.

"Dated a few times, but nothing serious."

"Same here."

"I figured you would have plenty of them at Berkeley."

Marcus chuckled, "Lots of girls, but I have stuck with my Christian roots. Kind of cuts down on the options, it seems."

"I know what you mean," commented Phillip dryly. "Well, let's get this beauty out on the water, shall we?"

Slowly they cranked the boat into the water. It bobbed lightly and almost seemed anxious to get going. Climbing in, Marcus seated himself in the front as Phillip reversed the propeller until he could turn around. A hundred feet from the shore, he let out the throttle. Almost bouncing out of the water, the 405 Baja took off. They went the length of lake before they slowed down and turned around.

"Nice boat," Marcus commented. "I could use something like that myself."

Phillip smiled, "You could always come up here more often."

"Like we all have time for that," Marcus replied.

"Time does seem to go faster lately, doesn't it?" Phillip acknowledged. "Less of it too, it seems."

Marcus nodded his head, looking off to the horizon where the water met the sky. "Do you know what I saw this week?"

"Of course not," Phillip replied.

"An Amish girl Mom has working for her. Now there is a life that has slowed down."

"I suppose so," Phillip said. "But who wants to live like that?"

"Wasn't saying that," Marcus kept his gaze on the horizon. "What surprised me was that this type of girl would be found among those people. You know, slow paced and all. I didn't figure it would produce such a good-looking girl."

Phillip grinned, "Are you sure you're not seeing things through romantic eyes, maybe? You are that type of guy."

"No." Marcus was unflustered. "I see plenty of girls. This one did not do anything for me romantically, but she was beautiful. Extraordinarily so, I would say. She would be as good as any of your models, I would think."

"Really?" Phillip was unconvinced. "You seem to think I ought to see this girl someday."

"I think you should," replied Marcus with his eyes still fixed on the horizon. "She is quite something. I never thought I would ever trust a beautiful girl, but this is one I think someone could trust."

"I thought you said there was nothing romantic?" Phillip looked at him sharply.

"There isn't," Marcus shook his head. "Not for me at least. I thought maybe for you."

Phillip laughed out loud, "An Amish girl? You really are dreaming."

Marcus shrugged his shoulders slightly. "Think about it. A truly wholesome, good-looking girl would do you good. Might even do something for the modeling business."

Phillip shook his head in disbelief. "You really are something, Marcus. But because you and I go way back, I'll tell you what I'll do: if you can bring this girl, Amish or whatever she is, to New York, or even here, I will have a look myself."

"Is that a promise?" Marcus asked him.

"Yes," Phillip assured him, "but you have to get her here first. That seems like a big job, don't you think? Will you use an ox cart?"

Marcus grinned, "Maybe that would work."

Later the two families spent a pleasant evening together and caught up with what had been going in each other's lives. Phillip insisted that Marcus use his room for the night and he agreed. Then around eight, the Florence's said their good-byes and left for South Washington. Phillip and his father left for the airport a few minutes later. Marcus would fly out early the next morning.

CHAPTER SEVEN

As CHURCH TIME approached Sunday morning, Sarah was sure Malinda was watching her closely. As the girls filed in to sit down, Sarah's neck burned when she noticed that her line of sight was open to the boys' section. Not that this was unusual, it was just that Lamar was in plain view from her vantage point on the third bench. Sarah also knew that Malinda noticed. She kept her eyes lowered, but this would only be a temporary solution. No one, not even an Amish girl, could look at the floor for more than three hours. That would be more noticeable than not looking. *What if she thinks I'm looking at Lamar?*

Taking a deep breath, Sarah raised her eyes to the direction of the preacher's bench. They sat up front of the men's section. From there the preaching would take place later. No one would find it out of the ordinary to look in that direction. As her eyes came up, she could not help seeing Lamar. He was looking at the floor, too. *Poor guy. Oh, no, I shouldn't be thinking that.* Sarah scrambled to master her runaway thoughts before they got completely out of control. She did not dare look in the direction of Malinda.

After the ministers filed out for their council meeting after the commencement of the first song, the singing continued. Sarah kept her eyes on the songbook, only bringing her head up slightly when it seemed clearly appropriate to do so.

She's watching him, Malinda was beside herself. *What am I going to do?* Slowly she kept raising her head to check on Sarah and on Lamar. The girl seated beside her finally looked at her with a puzzled expression as if she wanted to ask her what was the problem.

A wave of panic went through Malinda as she struggled to control her feelings. *I'm making a spectacle of myself, and then there really will be something to talk about.* Dropping her eyes to the songbook as the singing continued, she could only stand it for so long and then had to look again. Lamar had a slight smile on his face although his eyes looked straight ahead. Malinda paled almost to the color of her white head covering. *He's smiling at her.* Lamar, his smile lingering, dropped his eyes to the pages of his songbook. The boy beside Lamar, Joe Mast, gave him a slight nudge with his elbow.

Malinda could see it all clearly. *Joe already knows.* She overcame the instinctual urge to move her hand rapidly to her face, to hide her feelings. The girl seated beside her looked again. Malinda's hand holding her side of the songbook quivered slightly. To cover up, she slowly turned her head away and raised her hand to rub her face. It seemed to satisfy the girl beside her as a kind of explanation, which was the desired effect.

She must be having a dizzy spell, the girl thought. Malinda knew the next time would not be overcome by such a simple explanation. There had better not be a next time, if she wanted to avoid questions from this girl after church. With great resolution Malinda held still, until she could not stand it again, and looked in Lamar's direction. Both he and Joe still had slight smiles on their faces.

Malinda had no way of knowing that Joe had told Lamar a story that morning of how his dog chased several rats in the barn that week. Afterwards a rat fell from the rafters when it was trying to make its escape and landed

on the dog's back. The resulting ruckus with the dog running and shaking, and the rat hanging on, had only grown
with the telling. When Joe told the story, he had no way
of knowing that Lamar would sit beside him in church.
Now he was seated next to Lamar, and both of them were
recalling bits and pieces of the tale in their minds. Under
the circumstances, they both felt like they were exercising
remarkable self-control. It would simply not do to create a
scene in church.

As Malinda studied their smiles over the top of the
shoulder of the person in front of her, Sarah just happened
to decide at that moment to raise her head. There was really
no way of doing that without looking at the place Lamar
sat. She could have turned her head sideways while raising
it, but that would have looked strange. Looking strange was
one thing Sarah did not wish to do right then.

Now Malinda was sure. *She's looking at him. They have
something going on. Even Joe knows and is making fun of me.*

The service continued without anything happening to
cause Malinda to change her mind. The subjects of the sermons were lost on Malinda that day. All she could see was
Lamar smiling at Sarah, and Sarah nodding back ever so
slightly with what looked to Malinda like glee on her face.
The fact that she could not see Sarah's face did not persuade
her that this was not the case.

Sarah sighed in relief when the service came to a conclusion. *Maybe it will get better,* she thought. *I would hate to
have to go through this every Sunday.*

As older girls, both Malinda and Sarah were responsible for helping to prepare the Sunday meal. Tables needed
to be laid out, after the men folk made them out of benches
put together with special foot holders. Sarah rolled out the
white cloth, stretching from one end to the other of the long
bench tables. Silverware and coffee cups came next for the

first batch of men in one room and women in another. Older people went first, with the order strictly observed. Sarah made a point of avoiding Malinda when she could. *No sense asking for trouble. Although, I didn't do anything wrong. Then why am I getting defensive? What a confused world it is!* She gave up and started pouring the coffee.

Malinda was too depressed to try anything like glaring at Sarah, so Sarah needed not to be concerned at that moment. *Lamar won't be at the first table,* Malinda told herself, carrying out two bowls of peanut butter in each hand. Long practice had perfected the skill. It would not do to have peanut butter all over the floor.

After prayer had been offered by the Bishop, Malinda came out of the kitchen without noticing that Lamar had made it to the first set of tables. Sitting with his back turned toward her, she was passing him when he turned towards her and nodded. Startled she kept going without nodding her head. Several of the boys who saw this commented to Lamar, "Already playing hard to get."

He shrugged his shoulders, "They get that way."

"Only when they're almost married, right?"

Lamar declined to comment further and reached for his first piece of bread.

"Anyone ask Sarah Schwartz yet?" One of them asked the other.

"Not that I know of," was the response.

"Why don't you?" the questioner asked.

A chuckle and a shake of his head was all that was given as an answer. Lamar finished spreading his bread and decided it would be safer if he said nothing.

❦

During the singing that evening, the seating between Sarah and Lamar was different so that the situation from the morning was not repeated. She was on the third bench all the way on the left side. Lamar and Malinda, as a senior couple, made the front bench toward the right side. The girls were on one side and the boys on the other. Malinda refused to look at Lamar during the singing. He noticed. There was nothing to be done about it as conversation was not really allowed across the aisle, until after the last song. Where the eyes went was not so easily subject to such rules. He glanced at Malinda often, but to no avail.

When the singing ended, Malinda occupied herself by talking with the girls on either side of her, but made no attempt to acknowledge his presence. *I guess she'll come if I go,* Lamar finally concluded. Getting up from his place on the bench, he followed the second wave of boys now starting to leave.

Finding his horse in the barn proved less of a problem, now that several were already leaving. Once horses were packed in tightly into the available barn space, it could be hard to find one's horse and extract it from such close quarters. Lamar untied his horse, got him backed out and hitched up. Turning on the low beams of his buggy, he got in line to pick up Malinda. It never crossed his mind that she might not come until he was next in line. The walk leading to the house was empty. The girl walking toward the buggy in front of him already was nearly there.

Next was his turn. He let the reins out to move forward slowly. The walk was still empty. With a jerk his horse stopped. *She'd better not stay inside,* Lamar was beginning to steam in the darkness.

As the door at the house suddenly opened, he heard a burst of laughter from some girls. Malinda came out and walked down the path at a brisk pace. *Good, at least it looks like she was keeping me waiting for some sound reason.* Lamar began to breathe easier.

Malinda got her foot on the buggy step and climbed up expertly. She sat down briskly on her side of the buggy without saying a word. "Good evening," Lamar offered her his first words of the day.

"Good evening," she said without any emotion in her voice, as if she were addressing the cows or something.

"Anything wrong?" he asked her, reaching down to his dashboard to throw the switch for his full lights. In the back of the buggy, lights blazed in three different colors.

"No," she said, "just that Sarah Schwartz."

"What about her?"

"That's what I should be asking you. You were watching her all day in church."

"I was not."

"Then what were you smiling at with Joe Mast?"

Lamar thought for a moment, then chuckled, "That was a long time ago, to start with, but we were still laughing about a story he told in line this morning."

"And what would that be?" Malinda demanded to know.

"You wouldn't want to know. Just a story about his dog chasing rats." Lamar looked over at her dimly lit form in the darkness.

"Is that all?" she looked back at him. "You weren't laughing at me?"

"Of course not," Lamar chuckled again, reaching over for her hand, "I wouldn't laugh at you."

Malinda was hesitant, making a slight effort to draw her hand back, but then relaxed. "Well, that's good to hear. That Sarah is just the biggest trouble to everyone right now. It makes us dating girls all nervous the way she is just hanging around and not dating. Makes you really wonder what she's up to."

"Oh, so that's what had you uptight today." A sharp

curve was coming up and Lamar had to let go of her hand so he could devote his attention to the road at that moment.

"So you noticed?" she asked dryly.

"I did," he admitted, his hands tightly gripping the lines, "but if it's Sarah you're worried about, you can relax."

"How would you know anything about this?" She was looking fully at his side of the buggy.

"Boys have started asking her out now. One just asked this week," he informed her.

"How do you know this?"

"I just do," he told her.

It was not enough. "You had better start talking Lamar Wagler. If it concerns Sarah Schwartz and you have information, I had better be told everything."

"It was really nothing," he said. "I just happened to know about the asking."

"Lamar Wagler, tell me," she demanded.

"Okay, okay, but it's top secret. You can't tell anyone a word. Understand?"

"Understood," she told him, settling back into her side of the seat.

"It was like this," he began. "Cousin Jesse came to me at the auction on Thursday. He wanted me to ask Sarah for him."

"He wanted you to ask Sarah for him?" Malinda fairly shrieked the words.

"Well, yes," Lamar said, puzzled at her outburst. "That way no one would find out if she said 'no'. Save him a lot of embarrassment, he thought."

"And you did?" she asked in the same tone of voice.

"Well, yes," he repeated, "it sounded like a good plan on Jesse's part, and I wanted to help him out."

"You," she sputtered in furor, "went to her house, talked to her, looked at her? How dare you? You lowdown rat, you!

You skunk, you stinking skunk you, how dare you do this to me!"

"I didn't do anything." He raised his voice slightly trying to calm her down. "Jesse wanted me to do it. It was nothing."

The calming didn't work. "This is just the last straw. How could you? Go and talk to that thing? That mooning, waiting, bright-eyed spider, that girl. Just ready to pounce."

"Would you quiet down?" Lamar was becoming exasperated. "I like you. I was just doing Jesse a favor. That's all it was."

"My little German foot, it was. That was not more nothing than the sun coming up. You went because you wanted to go. Enjoying every moment you had an excuse to be around her. That's what you were up to. Admit it, you little rascal, you."

Lamar said nothing, groping around for words.

"See, I knew it," she pronounced, her voice now down closer to its normal tones. "I will not tolerate this situation anymore."

"What does that mean?" he asked.

"It means that you can keep your own company, until this Sarah gets out of the way. I will not have it."

"That's not fair," he protested. "I wasn't doing anything. You and I have been dating for a long time now. Almost married. You are just going to throw that all away over nothing?"

"It's not nothing," she said flatly. "That Sarah Schwartz is trouble, and I will not have it."

"She's not trouble," he said, then got himself deeper in trouble. "She seems like a nice girl."

"We're home," she said. "Drop me off at the end of the driveway."

"I can't do that," he told her. "You can't just leave like that. When can I come back?"

"Let me out," she said. "When you get over her, then think about coming back."

"I was doing nothing," he protested loudly, at the same time turning the buggy wheel open on her side before she jumped out without it having been turned and hurt herself.

Malinda said nothing more. She nimbly climbed down and marched up her driveway. She was quickly out of range of the light beams on his buggy. Lamar sat there briefly adjusting himself to this sudden turn of events, then backed his horse up and turned around.

A stab of regret went through him as he thought of the fast rush of events of the last few minutes. He had lost her. It hurt. He could not deny it. Yet, as his buggy gathered speed and was moving away from Malinda's place, another emotion entered lightly into his subconscious. There was nothing in the way of him seeing Sarah again.

If she wants me, he thought, then smiled in the darkness. *Of course she wants me.*

Chapter Eight

WHEN NAOMI CALLED upstairs at five-thirty, Malinda stumbled downstairs to help with breakfast. She had hardly slept during the night and her eyes were red and swollen. She was groping for the eggs in the pantry when Naomi first saw her.

"What happened?" Naomi wanted to know, seeing her red eyes.

At that, Malinda burst into tears. "He's gone."

"Who is gone?" Naomi asked tenderly.

"Lamar. He's gone. I don't know if he's coming back or not."

"Why?" Naomi placed her hand on Malinda's back, for she had turned back to search for the eggs.

From inside the pantry came her muffled voice: "I told him to leave."

Naomi looked concerned. "Was he inappropriate?"

"No," she shook her head, but with her back turned, Naomi did not see the slight blush on her face. "Not with me. He doesn't do anything I don't want him to. It's that horrible Sarah Schwartz."

Now Naomi was puzzled. "But how could he be inappropriate with her?"

"Not in that way, Mother, of course not. They don't have the chance. He just likes her," stated Malinda flatly.

"He likes Sarah Schwartz?"

"Yes."

"You know this for sure?"

"I know, Mother. They like each other."

"Well, that is a problem then."

"That's why I asked him to leave. He needs to get her out of his system."

Naomi looked alarmed. "You think this is the way to do it?"

"Of course."

"You just gave him the opportunity he might use," stated Naomi.

"Like what?" asked Malinda whose voice now grew louder.

"Now he can go see her freely."

"He'd better not." Malinda turned around to face her mother while holding the eggs in one hand.

"And you will do what about it?"

"Esther said she would help me."

"Esther? What has Esther got to do with this?"

"I talked with her, and she said she would help me."

Now Naomi was the one who raised her voice. "I wish you and your father would leave that woman's help alone!"

"She does a good job with Dad's animals when the vet can't help sometimes. Why can't she help me?"

"I just don't like it."

"Her ways are accepted among the people," Malinda reminded her mother.

"I know, but I still don't like it."

"That rotten girl," Malinda returned to the subject pressing on her mind. "Beautiful, she thinks she is. She still can't steal my boy."

"We shouldn't hate," Naomi interjected into Malinda's thoughts.

"She's a no-good, low-down, boy stealer, that's what she is! I won't stand for it!"

"You had better calm down," Naomi told her.

Malinda huffed in response and got busy fixing breakfast, heating the pan for the eggs. Naomi dropped the subject when it was obvious she was through talking about it.

⤜⤝

At about the same time, Phillip Ryan had arrived at the offices of "Maxey Jacobs" in New York. The company Cessna Citation with him and his father had landed in Indianapolis before midnight.

Currently, Phillip was personally responsible to oversee the production and marketing of the *Densine Line* of women's wear. When Ms. Camellia, the secretary, arrived at eight, there would be plenty to do.

When she walked through the door, Phillip was ready to go. "Good Morning, we need to get to work on the *Densine Line*," was his opening remark as she settled into her desk.

"How was your weekend?" she asked sweetly.

"It was just great," he told her abruptly, irritated. Pausing for effect, then, "I want to start working in detail on the marketing plan for *Densine*."

"Did you spend some time with your mother?" she asked, still beaming at him.

"Yes, and I had some time on the water," he added, deciding to play along. Maybe that way they could get to work. *One of these days I'll fire the girl.*

"Who was with you?" she asked, looking at him intently.

"Just Marcus, an old friend," he told her.

"Anyone else?" she asked without changing her expression.

"No," he told her, then added, "There is something you ought to know, though."

"Really?" she asked, her voice soft in expectation.

"Marcus," he started in, "has met this lovely Amish girl." Her brow wrinkled as he continued. "He thinks she is quite beautiful. He also seems to think I should fall in love with her. At the very least, I should place her on the modeling line. Maybe *Densine*? That was my contribution. Marcus may be on to something. What do you think?"

She laughed out loud with a lilting sound, "You had me worried there for a minute."

"Really," he raised his eyebrows, "I am serious."

"You might be," she told him, "but this can't be serious. I know a little about the Amish, and no Amish girl will even talk to you, let alone model for you."

"Even a beautiful one?" he asked.

"Especially," she said. "She would have been spoken for and taken long before you could even get close to her. I would say your dreams are just that, dreams." She paused as if thinking whether she should say more or not. She decided to risk it. "I could be a real dream," she said softly.

"You are my secretary, now let's get to work," he told her sternly, turning around. She watched his face as he headed for his desk. *Have I said too much?*

"Let's get to work," she said, turning back to her desk. "*Densine* line it is."

She opened her file and brought it to his desk, while putting on her best secretarial manner. "These are the models we have now," she said as she paged through the photos. "You know them, and then these are the new ones we are looking at. All very expensive, I must say."

Phillip took the photos and studied them. "I do think we could use that Amish girl from the looks of this."

She wisely refrained from comment.

"Now, would you set up appointments for the new girls? I would like to interview them."

"I'll get right on it," she said as she returned to her desk.

Phillip got ready to say something else then decided against it. *Kind of funny,* he thought to himself. *I can't believe how serious I feel about this. An Amish girl?*

⌘

At nine o'clock Mrs. Rebecca Florence pulled into the Schwartz driveway. She was expected and Sarah left the house without comment. It was just another day in Amish housecleaning life.

"Good morning," she told Rebecca, climbing in the car.

"You look as beautiful as ever." Mrs. Florence told her.

"That's nice of you to say," Sarah replied. "So where do I start when we get to your house?"

"Not so quickly," Rebecca stopped her. "Have you had breakfast yet?"

"Sure, the usual."

"Can you handle some more?"

"Not really. I mean, we have to watch our weight, too."

Rebecca laughed at that remark. "So, Amish girls gain weight like other girls do, too? I guess I did not really think they did."

"It works the same way for everyone. Trust me," Sarah assured her.

"Okay, then we will settle for coffee when we get to the house."

"That's okay, but then I must get to work. I won't feel good getting paid if I don't work."

"Fair enough, so it will be," Rebecca pronounced in an exaggerated final tone. They both laughed.

Arriving at the residence, Sarah prepared to start while

Rebecca poured the coffee. Sitting down together at Rebecca's insistence, they caught up with each other's lives since the time Sarah had visited.

"And now, I am your maid," Sarah said at the end of their conversation, preparing to rise and begin working.

"You know what Marcus mentioned after he saw you?" Rebecca said pensively, glancing at Sarah. There was no sign of embarrassment in the girl's face, so she continued, "He's my son, the one who walked in when I was playing the music."

"I'd like to hear some music again," Sarah interjected.

Surprised at her lack of interest in what Marcus had said, Rebecca paused, then continued, "He thought you were good-looking enough to model."

Looking full into Sarah's face, Rebecca found no reaction at all. "Why would I want to model?" Sarah asked her, looking puzzled.

"Oh," Rebecca thought for a moment. All the reasons she had suddenly seemed strange when faced with this girl, but she tried anyway. "Money maybe, fame, recognition, getting your picture in the magazines."

"Money might be nice," Sarah said off-handedly, "but what would you do with the rest of it?"

"I don't know, people just want it," Rebecca said. "Don't you?"

"Never really thought about it," Sarah said. "We can't do those things anyway."

"You mean as Amish people."

"Yes."

"Is there ever a chance?"

"You would probably have to leave the community. If you haven't been baptized, it might not be too bad, but if you have been, it's pretty bad."

"You mean the things that would happen to you?"

"Yes," Sarah shook her head.

"Have you been baptized?" Rebecca wanted to know.

"No," Sarah shook her head again.

"So you could do this then, if you wanted to, without too many bad things happening to you?"

"Are you trying to get me to do this?" Sarah asked point-blank.

"Oh, heavens no!" Rebecca said quickly. "Just curious."

"Maybe I ought to get to work," Sarah said quietly. "I need to get done and get back."

Rebecca quickly tried to make amends. "I'm so sorry. I didn't mean to offend your faith at all. Really I didn't."

"It okay," Sarah told her with a smile. "If I ever want to model I will ask you how it is done."

"Oh, no." Rebecca was not going to get into any deeper trouble than she was already. "Now, you shouldn't do anything that you think is wrong. I certainly wasn't trying to lead you astray."

"I know you weren't," Sarah smiled again. "What about some music before I start cleaning?"

Relieved, Rebecca seated herself in front of the Stein-way. Softly she began playing. "This is Prelude No. 2, by Johann Sebastian Bach in C minor."

That meant nothing to Sarah, but she stood enthralled as Rebecca ran her fingers over the keys. "That is simply beautiful," she said when Rebecca turned away from the piano.

"I'm glad you think so," Rebecca said quickly, not wanting to say more as she was still sensitive about the modeling talk and did not want to cause another tension point.

"How do you do that?" Sarah wanted to know.

"Practice," Rebecca told her, "and some talent I suppose, but anyone can do something with a piano."

"Do you suppose I could learn?"

Rebecca decided to stay on the safe side of things. "Does your faith allow music like this, on a piano?"

Sarah's face fell. "No," she said. "but it is really beautiful music. Well, I guess I should get started cleaning."

"Maybe I can teach you a little bit," Rebecca softened her stance.

"You probably shouldn't," Sarah sighed slightly, looking up at Rebecca. "It is so beautiful, I'll just enjoy it. Probably couldn't ever play like that myself anyway, at this age."

"You never know," Rebecca acknowledged. "Most people do start much younger, but by all means try if you want to."

Sarah's face lighted up. "Maybe sometime, right now this house needs cleaning. Where shall I start?"

"With the bedrooms," Rebecca told her, going on to show her the important things she thought ought to be done, and Sarah got started. When it was time for Sarah to go, she had done the things Rebecca had instructed as well as many others Rebecca had not mentioned.

"You are an angel," Rebecca gushed on the drive home.

"You will see that I am very much from this earth," Sarah assured her. "We are human like everyone else."

"Wonderful people you are," Rebecca said in thanks as Sarah got out of the car. "See you in a month."

Sarah nodded, waved, and then waited until the car moved before she walked across the driveway and up the sidewalk. Coming into the house no one seemed to be around. Not surprised, she started supper for that evening.

CHAPTER NINE

MONDAY NIGHT WAS little better for Malinda. She tossed in bed, and finally cried herself to sleep. Her tormented mind reached no decision on what to do. What little sleep she got was filled with weird and wild dreams, full of running horses in harnesses without drivers, distorted buggy lights and Sarah's grinning face.

During the early morning hours she gave up and sat in front of the bedroom window and watched the stars. This did little to settle her spirits. When the first streaks of dawn were on the horizon, her mother called her to get up. Disheveled and pale, she stumbled downstairs.

"Did you get any sleep?" Naomi looked at her with concern.

"Hardly," was the response.

"You are really taking this hard," Naomi stated the obvious.

"Wouldn't you?" Malinda wanted to know.

"Depends, I guess, on how much I cared about the boy."

"I care a lot," Malinda stated emphatically.

"That's hard then."

"Did you ever go through something like this?"

"No," Naomi smiled, "your father dated some girls before me, but not after me."

"It's terrible." Malinda was close to tears again.

Naomi took her daughter by the hand. "I can only imagine, but God will take care of it if you are to have Lamar."

"I don't trust Him," Malinda said, her face hardening.

"That's a terrible thing to say."

"Well, I don't. He let Lamar leave me for that no good Sarah Schwartz. With her good looks, she really thinks she is something! But will she take care of Lamar like I would?"

"Look, look," Naomi now placed her arm around Malinda's shoulder. "Aren't you going a little too fast? You don't know what Lamar is going to do. He may be back next Saturday."

"He won't be."

"How can you be so sure?"

"Remember? I told him to leave."

"That doesn't usually stop men the first time," Naomi said knowingly. "If he loves you, which I think he does, he just might be back."

"You haven't seen him looking at Sarah, the little creep." Malinda pulled away from her mother.

Naomi, looking worried, moved towards the kitchen. "We really have to get started with breakfast. I wish you wouldn't be so hateful towards either Lamar or Sarah."

"How can you say that, after you know what they're doing?"

"You are not married to him," Naomi told her bluntly. "He has the right to break up with you if he wants. That's what courtship is about, learning whether you are right for each other."

"I already know that," Malinda's sobs filled the kitchen.

"Quiet now," Naomi admonished. "You will wake the younger ones. Now we really have to get breakfast ready before Dad and your brothers come in from chores."

"What am I supposed to do?" Malinda said in a quieter

but still lethal voice. "You won't help me. God won't help me. I don't want to ask Dad. What I am I supposed to do? I want Lamar."

"You have to calm down," Naomi told her flatly. "You have to trust God. He may be the only one who can help you."

"Will He get Lamar back for me?"

"Only if it is His will, of course. We hope so, but who can know His mind? Certainly not us in our human wisdom."

Malinda's face darkened. "That's the problem, see. I don't trust Him. I know what I want, and it's Lamar. If He wants to help, then good, but that's what I want."

Naomi shook her head sadly, "You have so much to learn yet, my *kinnt,* so much. God always knows best."

"Even when it hurts?"

"Especially when it hurts, because then we often know the least."

"I don't like that."

"You must learn to accept it, Child. It is the best way."

"Maybe for you, but not for me." Malinda looked away from her mother.

"It is for you, too," Naomi said confidently. "What else are you going to do? You can just wait and hope for the best."

"We will see about that," Malinda said, loud enough for her mother to hear.

Naomi shrugged her shoulders. "It would just be easier if you didn't fight it like this. Come now, we have to get breakfast ready."

Malinda said nothing in response to that but followed Naomi out of the living room into the kitchen. There was a gleam in her eyes, but she made sure she did not look at her mother until her anger had died down a bit.

Throughout the day she thought about it, and finally

arrived at a firm decision. She would go see Esther before the news of her break-up with Lamar was general knowledge. Today would not suit. There would be a chance tomorrow while her Mom was at the quilting. She would not have to attend the quilting if she did not want to, and she would go to see Esther. There was a good chance Esther would not attend either.

Wednesday morning after breakfast was over, Naomi left with parting instructions for the day. Going over them in her mind, it was as Malinda had expected. There would be time for a quick dash over to Esther's house.

Right after lunch was the chance, and she took it. Harnessing the horse herself, she arrived quickly at Esther's place.

"I was expecting you soon," Esther stated with a smile.

"You were?"

"Sure, you broke up with him Sunday night, didn't you?"

"Well, yes!" Malinda was flabbergasted. "Who told you, Lamar?"

"No, no, don't worry. It wasn't him. You know how information gets around." Esther smiled again. "Now, how shall we get him back? That's the question."

Still perplexed, Malinda decided to leave well enough alone. Who told Esther did not matter that much anyway. "I want him back," she said without any emotion in her voice.

"It's that serious then," Esther smiled again. "What are you willing to do?"

"Anything to get Lamar back."

"Surely not 'anything'," Esther grimaced. "There are some things that just should not be done, you know. We have to go on living afterwards."

Malinda felt anger rise up in her. "That Sarah Schwartz

needs to be taught a lesson, stealing my boy away like that. It's just not right."

"Oh, so you want to work on her, and not him?" Esther looked at her.

Thinking for a minute Malinda decided, "Yes, on her."

Esther chuckled, "Afraid he might get hurt?"

Malinda nodded, "Yes", as a tear rolled down her cheek.

"It's that bad," said Esther as she noticed. "So, let's get started with some advice."

"Yes," Malinda nodded.

As both women stood there, Esther had a slight smile on her face while Malinda looked worriedly out the front window. "I think you should just forget about the whole thing for now. Let it rest. You rest your mind and see what happens. Sometimes that is more helpful than anything."

"What good is that going to do?" Malinda wondered.

"We will see," Esther smiled again. "It just might do the job. If not, let me know. I will, of course, keep tabs on things, too."

With that Malinda left quickly and arrived home in plenty of time to complete her tasks before Naomi arrived. She said nothing of where she had been.

Phillip Ryan, busy with the pressures of running his office at Maxey Jacobs, forgot about the unknown Amish girl Marcus told him about. It was Ms. Camellia who brought the memory back, and with it the strange desire he felt to meet this girl.

"How's your Amish girl doing?" she asked him chirpily.

"What's that?" he looked up from his desk.

"Your Amish girl, the one from the weekend. How is she doing?"

"Oh," he wrinkled his brow. "I forgot about that."

Oops, kick me, she tried to cover up, "Just curious, not that it's important."

"By the way," he stood up from his desk. "Have you tried to contact her?"

"You're not serious?"

"Why not? Now that you brought it up, I would like to meet her."

"You can't just go meeting Amish girls, especially with visits from strange English boys."

"I wasn't planning on going to her house or anything like that."

"So what are you planning?"

"Marcus could bring her here or to Morse Lake some weekend."

"To New York City?"

"Why not?"

"You are dreaming. No Amish girl will come to New York City."

"You don't say," he grinned.

"Who do you think you are anyway, Phillip Ryan? Someone who can just snap his fingers and people jump at your command? Girls don't work like that. Amish people don't either. They move at their own commands, not other people's."

"That could be a point," he acknowledged. "Maybe I need to visit her?"

"Oh!" she said, not succeeding in hiding the surprise in her voice.

"The least we can do is try."

"Okay, when are you trying?"

"No, you try. You are my secretary."

"You don't have to rub it in," she lifted her chin slightly into the air.

He ignored the signals. "Call Marcus's mother. Maybe she knows how to contact this girl. I really want to see her. She fascinates me."

"You haven't even seen her." Camellia was shocked now. "What is this, some fatal attraction? Amish are weird people."

"Just call Mrs. Florence. You have the number from the other week, don't you?"

Camellia looked for the number, finding it easily. *Horrid number, why weren't you lost.* Without looking at him she dialed.

"Hi," she said, when the call was answered. "Mrs. Florence?"

"Yes," she told her, at the other end.

"How are you?

"Fine, thank you."

"This is Camellia, from Phillip Ryan's office.

"Oh, it was good seeing him again."

"Yes, he had a good weekend with you.

"Thanks."

"You are welcome. He was glad you could come with Marcus. Speaking of that, apparently Marcus told him about an Amish girl."

"Oh, the girl who works for me?"

"Yes, yes. That must be the one. He would like to get in touch with her.

"With the Amish girl?"

Camellia glanced at Phillip, "Yes, with the Amish girl.

"Marcus must have told Phillip about her."

"I see." *What is this, a family project?*

"I think Phillip ought to see her, too."

"I see. You want to talk to him?" Camellia pressed the hold button. "She wants to talk with you."

"Hello," Phillip lifted the receiver at his desk. Thereafter, Camellia only heard his side of the conversation.

"Good to speak with you, Mrs. Florence.

"Yes, we were glad to have you.

"She does.

"Worked for you on Monday.

"You did.

"It didn't go over well. They are traditional people.

"Yes, I understand.

"Well, let me know if there is ever an opening and she's willing.

"She's beautiful?

"Yes, Marcus told me.

"Better than our models?

"That's saying a lot, Mrs. Florence.

"Well, I look forward to it." Phillip gently put the receiver back on the hook. "Sounds like some girl," he said more to himself than anyone in his office.

Camellia decided to say nothing.

By late Sunday afternoon the news had spread to all who were interested. Lamar and Malinda had broken up. Rumors about the cause of the break-up ranged from an agreeable parting to a fight over future money problems. Nowhere was Sarah Schwartz mentioned.

Amish couples frequently broke up in their early dating relationships, and only passing interest was shown. However, a couple in the later stages of courtship and only months away from marriage was quite another matter. The issue was discussed at length, out of earshot, of course, of either Lamar or Malinda.

Lamar acted normal at the singing, sitting on the front row as usual. Malinda sat across from him, also as usual. It would not do to show any break from normal routine. It would only cause this to drag out longer than necessary.

With considerable effort, Malinda refrained from tears the entire day. No sign of crying gave her away in public. Sitting on the front bench with her clearly in his line of vision, Lamar did feel pangs of regret.

Yet, he made no move to mend the breach. Other matters occupied his mind. Sarah Schwartz was sitting on the second row, but he continued to take severe measures to not even appear to look in her direction. She was on his mind enough already. Moreover, it was important that no connection be drawn between the break-up and Sarah.

Lamar's memory of the look on Sarah's face soothed the turmoil he felt inside. *I wonder how soon I can ask her?* The very thought of her sent a shot of bravado and masculine confidence through him. She would be a girl to have. *She's going to say 'yes'.* A smile nearly came over his face, but he caught himself just in time. *I want to ask her out now, but it's way too soon.* He breathed deeply to calm himself.

Later a long line of buggies was pulling out of the gravel driveway. Many of them waited to turn on their full lights until they hit the paved road. Seated between Mark and Sarah, Martha leaned over to her right.

"Hold still," Sarah told her. "It's tight enough in here without you moving around."

"I want to see if that's his buggy up front," Martha explained.

"Whose buggy?" Mark asked her.

"Lamar's, of course."

"Why, of course?" he wondered.

"Just seeing if he has all his lights turned on?"

"You are strange," Sarah told her.

"No, I'm not!" protested Martha. "I think it's a good indication of how his spirits are. You did hear that he quit with Malinda."

"Yes," Sarah said in the darkness.

"What has that got to do with anything?" Mark wanted to know. "You're just jealous of his lights. Probably wish I had some."

"No, I don't," Martha assured him. "I like your modest buggy. It would just be nice of him not to turn on so many lights the first night he's without his girl. Might show a little regard of heart, wouldn't you say?"

"Do you think he has any?" Mark asked.

"Of course he does," Sarah answered before she thought about it.

"Whew, are we quick to his defense?" Martha turned toward her sister. "You had better watch yourself."

Sarah resolved to say nothing more, but then just as quickly overcame her resolution and remarked, "He seemed sad enough all day to me."

"Were you looking?" Martha wanted to know.

"Yes," she admitted.

"Do you always look?"

Sarah found her resolution again, and said nothing more.

"What are we going to do with the girl?" Martha asked, obviously turning in Mark's direction.

"She's got it bad, that's all I know," he replied.

"Do you think we can help her?"

"I'm not sure. What do you do with matters of the heart?" he asked with flourish and a dramatic gesture of his hand in the dark.

"Would you two stop talking about me?" Sarah found her voice again. "I'm here, you know."

"She's here," Mark repeated in Martha's direction.

Martha grunted under her breath, "I hope he doesn't start coming around our place."

"What are you going to do if he does?" asked Sarah in a low tone.

"You don't have plans already?" Martha asked, horror in her voice.

"Of course not," Sarah told her. "I don't know anything."

"Do you want him to come?" Mark prodded.

"I don't know."

"Yes, you do," Martha replied sarcastically. "You want him to."

"He's not going to," Sarah said dourly.

"She's gone," Martha said in Mark's direction. "It's a lost case."

"She's gone," he repeated. "My sister's done fell off her rocker, for a no-good run-around rich boy. I thought we raised you better than that?" He finished in a fatherly tone.

Even Sarah had to chuckle as Martha's laughter pealed out of the buggy. "Would you two quit it?" she protested. "Nothing has happened yet, and no one knows whether it will."

"How would you feel dating him so quickly after he quit Malinda?" asked Martha, no longer laughing.

"I don't know," Sarah said in the darkness. "It's all mixed up."

"I think you ought to tell him a big flat 'no' if he comes calling," Martha said in Sarah's direction.

"You don't know if he will," Sarah protested.

"Count on it," Mark assured her, "he's coming. I think you ought to say 'no', too."

"You don't know if he's coming or not." Sarah protested again. "He probably won't."

"Will you tell him 'no'?" Martha asked as Mark pulled into their driveway.

"I don't know, it's all mixed up."

"'No' is easy to say."

"I'll see when it happens," Sarah finally told her, as Mark brought the buggy to a halt. "It has to happen first."

"She's gone, the thing is done," proclaimed Mark as he jumped down.

"I think you're right," Martha agreed, moving over to climb down on Mark's side. Sarah left by the other door and walked rapidly towards the house, leaving them to unhitch the horse alone.

"Were we too hard on her?" Mark asked when she was out of earshot.

"Probably, but I don't like the boy."

"Neither do I."

"It's not like we can do much about it, though. Let's just hope for the best."

"She is our sister, I guess," Mark pretended to sigh, then chuckled. "It would be nice to have a rich brother-in-law."

"There are other things in life," Martha told him. "I'd take a decent boy any day."

"Decent, but poor. That's me," Mark said grimly.

"Don't worry, it could be worse."

"Like how?"

"Rich and bad."

"I want to be both."

"Bad and decent?"

"No, decent and rich."

Martha chuckled. "That doesn't seem to happen very often, for some reason. Just be happy you have the decent part."

"Then, there's hope for me." Mark pretended to whistle merrily as he led the horse into the barn. Martha watched him go before she walked towards the house. Soberly she wondered what would happen to Sarah and what the future held. *Hope he stays away, although I doubt it.* Looking around in the darkness, she perceived no answer or indication she was being heard. *Help us Lord,* she whispered in the darkness. *We could use it.*

Chapter Ten

LAMAR PONDERED THE situation. His intense desire to talk with Sarah was only growing. Yet, how would it look if he went to see her this week? Would she disapprove of an appearance so soon? More importantly, what would be the talk in the community if he dated her this Sunday? The question of whether she wanted to see him did not cross his mind. He was confident of a positive reception, provided the initial approach was handled correctly on his part. However, if he waited too long, that might not give the correct impression either.

Finally, he reached a satisfactory conclusion in his own mind. He cleaned and polished his buggy as usual on Saturday morning. As dusk was just settling on the rolling farmland around him, he set out for Ben Schwartz's place. As a gesture towards disguise, he turned on only the lower two running lights on his buggy. Except for the spinning racing stripes on the wheels, illuminated only if car headlights hit them, he was by all appearances just a decent Amish boy out for the usual Saturday evening pursuits.

Sarah was just getting ready to go upstairs, and Martha and Mark were already in their rooms, when the sound of buggy wheels on gravel could be heard in the driveway. With absolute certainty, she knew who it was. Her heart skipped a beat at the thought. She would have fled if that had been possible. However, that would only necessitate her being called back, which would be even more uncomfortable. She might as well face it.

"I'll see who it is," she said to her parents. Ben and Deborah were still taking turns reading the Budget in the living room.

Her father looked up in surprise, "You don't have to. I'm here."

Sarah paused, a look of uncertainty on her face. Deborah noticed, and knowing the unusualness of Sarah offering to see who was in the driveway at this hour of the night, she did some quick calculations. Her conclusion was close enough to the correct one to suffice. A boy was calling, and Sarah somehow was expecting it.

Before Ben could get up Deborah nudged him with her foot. When he looked at her, she shook her head. Perplexed, he stopped halfway up, *"Vass es letz?"* (What's wrong?)

Deborah gave up any attempt to hide from Sarah any further instructions to her husband. "Let her go."

Relieved by her mother's help, Sarah still waited for her father to decide. Ben did not wait long, signifying his answer by settling back onto the couch. Slowly Sarah moved towards the door. No sounds from outside could be heard. She opened the door and stepped out onto the porch.

Inside, Deborah finished the explanation to Ben, *"Es is un boo."* (It's a boy)

"How do you know?" he wanted to know.

She shrugged her shoulders.

"Did Sarah tell you about something?"

"No."

"How do you know then?"

"I just do."

"Do you know who it is?"

"No, but I do know we had better get out of this living room, so she has a place to go with him."

"I'm not ready for bed yet," he protested.

"Then make yourself ready. You can read in the bedroom."

Knowing that to argue was pointless, he gathered up the scattered pages of the Budget and retired to the bedroom.

Outside on the porch, Sarah was struck with a sudden flood of uncertainty. *What if it's someone else? I'll look like a real dunce coming out alone to meet him. The talk will never stop. They'll say I couldn't wait for the boys to come. Goes out on the porch hoping it is one.* She peered through the now gathering dusk across the lawn to the hitching rail where visiting buggies were usually tied. The dim shape of a horse hitched to a single-seat buggy was outlined against the barn, but she could make out nothing else.

Lamar had climbed down and tied the horse and was trying to decide what to do next. Walking up to the house to announce his presence seemed a little pretentious now that he was actually here. *What if she's not at home? How do I explain all that?* His characteristic brash boldness kept him from simply fleeing, but he still did not know what he should do.

While he was wondering, the front door opened to reveal Sarah herself stepping out. When she shut the door, she was wrapped in darkness except for what light came through the front window from the gas lantern inside. He waited for her to move off the front porch and down the walks, but there was no movement.

Why is she just standing there? Is she having doubts? It was then that it occurred to him, she was unsure who it was. With this revelation he leaned inside his buggy and briefly turned on the dome light. Knowing his back was turned to the waiting girl on the porch, he looked sideways before switching off the dome light. *That ought to show her who it is.*

Sarah did recognize him and the gesture. This consideration made her movement down the walks easier. Approaching the buggy in the darkness, she was grateful her face did not show.

"Good evening," she said, sure that her face was red.

"Hi," he said. "I just had to come over and see you. Is that okay?"

"I guess," she said in the darkness. Then, even though she already knew the answer, she asked, "Aren't you dating Malinda?"

"You must have heard," he said. "We quit."

"Last Sunday?" she asked, both to answer the question and to move the conversation along.

"Yes," he acknowledged, again following her lead.

"Which of you quit," she wanted to know. This question caused him sudden discomfort.

Where she is going with this, he wondered. *Should I tell her the truth? Is she going to like it when she finds out Malinda did the quitting? That won't make me look good.* He decided quickly what he would tell her as she stood in the darkness in front of him. He wished fervently he could see her face but could not.

"I decided it was better that we stop," he told her, keeping his voice calm.

It must have been the right answer, he figured, because from what he could see of her, she seemed to relax.

"Well," she said, her voice cheerful, "now, that you're here, why not come inside? It's not too nice out here in the dark."

"Sure," he said, glad that the hard part seemed to be over.

Following her up the walk, neither of them made any further attempts at conversation. Sarah was wondering how she would explain this to her parents, and Lamar preferred to see people's faces when he talked to them.

Opening the front door, Sarah's first glance revealed an empty living room. *Thank you, Mom. How had she known?* Thrilled, she turned to motion Lamar with her hand. The gas lantern, still hanging on the living room ceiling, fully illuminated her face. Still standing out on the dark front porch, he couldn't believe his good fortune. Never in his wildest dreams had he ever thought of dating such a beautiful girl.

"Have a seat," she told him as they stepped inside, her blue eyes intent on him. "I'll get something from the kitchen for you."

"That's not necessary," he said, laying his Sunday hat causally on the floor.

"Sure it is."

"I'm fine."

"Be back in a minute," she insisted and returned with a plate of pecan tarts and a glass of water for him.

Although his interest was not food at the moment, he took a tart to satisfy her. "Your parents in bed?" he asked, hoping it didn't sound too forward, as if he had wanted them out of the way.

She did not seem offended by the question. "I don't think so, but apparently Mom wanted to leave the coast clear."

"Did you know I was coming," he asked.

"No, I suppose Mom just figured it out. You know, when you drove in."

"Did you know who was driving in?"

"No," she blushed, "but I thought it could be you and I guess Mom picked up on that."

This was even better than Lamar had hoped it would be. Keeping his face as neutral as possible to hide his pleasure, he decided to get the formalities out of the way. "I hope I'm not being too forward coming tonight, but I really wanted to see you." He paused to look at her face.

She nodded, listening.

"I was just hoping to be able to see more of you. I know that it's kind of soon, you know, with Malinda and me breaking up last week." He paused again, then continued, "I thought maybe it would be proper to ask you if I could stop by on Saturday nights. Nothing formal for now — not that I wouldn't want to ask," he smiled, "but you know how people talk."

"That's fine with me," she told him. Surprised by how quickly she felt like letting him come, she continued, "Whatever you think."

He smiled, satisfied with her response. It was all he had hoped for.

"There's a gathering on Thursday at the community center. Are you coming?" he asked.

"I'm not sure." She tilted her head. "It's kind of far up there. We don't go usually, unless the gatherings are closer."

Sarah soon relaxed on the couch beside him and they chatted about other community news, the weather, and the latest couples. They excluded the topic of themselves, which they both knew would cause quite a stir when it came out.

Lamar soon made motions to rise. "I'm glad I got to come," he told her. "I'll see you later, then. Next Saturday. I should be going."

She opened the door for him, but made no attempt to step outside. As he bent to pick up his hat, she was struck by how gracefully he handled himself. His motions were smooth like a well-oiled hinge. Yet at the same time, for some reason it made her uneasy.

Stepping towards the open door, he turned completely towards her. "Goodnight," he said, "see you later."

She let her eyes move across his handsome face, feeling her fears fade away. "Goodnight," she told him. "Have a safe trip home."

With that, he stepped briskly outside, and disappeared quickly into the now complete darkness. She shut the door and waited for the sound of his buggy wheels on the gravel. It came quickly, as she expected, and her impression of his efficiency was confirmed.

No sooner had the sounds of his buggy faded away than Martha stuck her head out of the upstairs door. "Was that who I think it was?"

"Who do you think it was?"

"You know," Martha glared at her.

"Yes," she grinned sheepishly.

"I hope you sent him packing."

"Not exactly. He wants to come on Saturday nights."

"Why on Saturday nights?"

"It might give people reason to talk if we dated this soon after the break-up, you know."

"I would say so. And this won't?"

Sarah shrugged her shoulders, "I guess they won't know."

"Won't know?" Martha laughed, throwing her head back in mock imitation of one in throes of great mirth.

"You're just exaggerating."

"They will know," Martha insisted.

"Well, that's what he wanted, so that's the way it is."

"What did you want?" Martha wanted to know.

"It's fine with me," Sarah insisted a little too emphatically.

Martha made a face at her. "I hope you're careful. I don't trust him."

"He's real nice."

"Ya, and good-looking, too."

"Is there anything wrong with that?"

"No, and I guess money doesn't hurt either."

"I'm not dating him for his money," Sarah's eyes flashed.

"So you are dating him?"

"Well, informally. He's coming over on Saturdays."

"I don't like it," Martha stated.

"Maybe you can learn to like him."

"I doubt it."

"Well, I'm the one dating him, not you."

"You can say that again."

"Okay, enough is enough," Sarah stated flatly, "We will just see what happens."

Martha came out of the stairway door and softened her stance as she looked at Sarah. "I'm sure it will all work out. I'm glad you like the boy."

"No, you aren't," Sarah said with a slight grin. "Isn't it time for bed?"

"If we want to stay awake for church tomorrow, it is."

"Don't you want to sleep in church like Henry Mast does?"

Martha laughed, this time genuinely. "Can't you just see him?" She dropped her head halfway down to her chest, breathed loudly in through her nose, and exhaled softly through her mouth.

Sarah roared at the vision, causing Deborah to come down the hall from their parents' bedroom. "What's going on? Did you chase him off?"

"No, Mom," Sarah assured her. "I was just laughing over Martha. It was Lamar. He wants to stop by on Saturday evenings. I told him he could, Mother."

Deborah's hand flew to her mouth. "I can't believe this. Lamar. He's rich. He's going to date you. Oh, my. *Da Goot Mann gleichdt uns.*" (The Good Man likes us.)

"You know that money's not important," Sarah told her mother, as Martha wisely kept her mouth shut.

"Of course not," Deborah said quickly, "but this is wonderful."

"I guess we will see," Martha broke into the conversation. "Now can we all go to bed?"

"We probably should," Deborah agreed. Sarah nodded and headed for the stairs. Martha followed her upstairs where they parted without any more discussion of the subject.

After getting ready for bed, Sarah stood looking out of her upstairs window. The night was still and pitch dark, with no sign of the moon evident. She stood there, her feelings now mixed. Without succumbing to her doubts, she reviewed the events of the evening. In her mind she heard the buggy wheels on the gravel again and she thought of her tension on the front porch. Lamar's handsome face flashed in her mind, his smile, and the way he deferred to her when he asked questions.

But would she ever be able to drive in his fancy buggy? That thought caused more questions than she wished to deal with right now. *I'd better get some sleep.* She forced her mind to stop thinking and crawled into bed. Sleep came quickly for her.

CHAPTER ELEVEN

D URING THE SUNDAY morning church service the next morning, Lamar was certain Malinda was keeping a watch on him. He ignored her while at the same time was careful to avoid all appearances of looking at Sarah. In his heart he felt there was no need to add insult to injury. Beyond that, however, he was rapidly losing his former feelings of attachment to Malinda.

His mind was completely occupied with Sarah. By taking sideways looks at her, he was careful to give no indication to an observer of what he was doing. Halfway through the service he wished he could stop himself, but soon found his focus on her again. She was simply too beautiful to stay away from, and now he was beginning to feel he had a right to her.

He shifted his weight on the backless bench. *I can't believe she's my girlfriend.* Shaking his head lightly, he smiled to himself. *What a girl!*

Determined to get his mind on something else, he turned his full attention to the preaching. Bloh Jonas was halfway into the main sermon. He was telling the story of David and of how he had returned from battle to find his town had been ransacked and all the women and property stolen.

Poor fellow, Lamar thought. *How awful to have your woman stolen.* However, such thoughts only made him focus his gaze on Sarah again, which in turn increased his sympathies for David. *I've got to stop this*, he resolved firmly.

Lamar again turned his attention back to Jonas, who was continuing the story of how David's men had wanted to kill him as a result of their perception that he had failed to protect the tribe. Lamar kept listening.

"David then sought the Lord," Bloh Jonas said dramatically. "He drew apart and talked with God. The Lord told him to pursue the enemy. We, too, are supposed to pursue the enemy that steals from us." Bloh Jonas paused and looked across his audience. "The enemy wished to steal values, learned from our forefathers, from us. He wants to leave us wasted with nothing left. He steals our morals and we are left with the dress styles and habits of an unholy world. He steals our holiness and we are left with the luxuries and riches of the world which are not Christian."

Lamar decided to tune out, partly because the sermon was beginning to irk him, and partly because Malinda was now in his line of vision whenever Bloh Jonas shifted his preaching position towards the living room. She was staring at him. It was hard to avoid her gaze when he looked at Bloh Jonas. At present, Lamar wanted to deal with neither member of that family.

He made it through until twelve, as well as the church meal afterwards. No one broached the subject of his break-up with Malinda until he was leading his horse out of the stall to leave.

"Sorry to hear about you and Malinda," his cousin Jesse said as he headed towards his own horse. "Is it serious?"

Lamar did some fast thinking. If he acted innocent and told Jesse nothing about Sarah, the news could eventually come out from someone else. His relationship with Jesse might well be jeopardized. He hated the thought of that.

There was no need to cause unnecessary family conflict, even if it was with a cousin.

Having made his decision, Lamar cleared his throat. "Jesse, I need to tell you something." He felt like he was jumping off a cliff, but there seemed no other way.

Jesse stopped and turned expectantly towards Lamar. Lamar knew he needed to continue.

"It's just that, I saw Sarah Saturday night," he said simply, his heart sinking with the full knowledge that now the secret was out.

"You did what?" Jesse was looking straight at him.

"I was over to see Sarah for the first time," he repeated.

"And?"

"She agreed to see more of me."

"You were after her then," Jesse said horrified, "when you asked her for me? So this is who you quit Malinda over?"

"No," Lamar grinned sheepishly, "it was really nothing like that. It really wasn't. When you asked me to go with your request to Sarah, there was nothing going on. This whole thing has happened so fast. Besides, Malinda quit me, not the other way around. I was not expecting it, but now that the chance is there like this, it is hard to pass up."

Jesse relaxed and grinned. "Well, that's different. Good for you. If she likes you, I can understand how you would feel. Hope it works out."

Relieved, Lamar sighed under his breath, "We'll have to see."

"See you tonight then." Jesse headed toward the stall where his horse was.

Lamar nodded as he left the barn with his own horse. Of course, now he was absolutely certain that by tonight the news would be out. There would be no secret. *Why did that have to happen that way?* Lamar could kick himself, but there had seemed no other recourse.

As expected, by the time the singing started that evening the word was everywhere and the rumors flew back and forth: Lamar was seeing Sarah; Malinda dropped Lamar, someone said, and then others claimed that Lamar quit to pursue Sarah. The general consensus soon seemed to be that Lamar had dumped Malinda. When it was repeated in his hearing, he chose only to grin, which was then taken as confirmation of that theory. *It's better that way,* he thought as justification.

With great effort, Malinda managed to keep her composure throughout the evening, but she barely made it home and into the house before dissolving into tears.

Naomi was waiting up for her when Malinda arrived. "Dear me, what's wrong?" she asked.

"He's seeing her," Malinda wailed.

"How do you know?" Naomi wanted to know.

"It's all over the place. People were looking at me with looks of pity all evening. They say he dumped me for her. How can heaven be so cruel? I can't stand it!" she cried.

Naomi got up and put her arms around her distraught daughter. "God will take care of you" she tried to console her.

"How do you know that? He seems to be doing a real poor job of it."

"He will," Naomi assured her.

Malinda only wailed louder on her mother's shoulder until Naomi felt like there had been enough crying. Taking her by the hand she led Malinda into the kitchen. She insisted Malinda have a bite to eat before she sent her up to her own room for the night.

"Life will go on," Naomi told her. "It always does. You'll feel better in the morning."

"I'll never feel well again," Malinda declared now with dry eyes. "That Sarah Schwartz is an evil creature."

"You must not say such things about a Christian person," Naomi told her firmly. "I know you are feeling bad, but that's no excuse for such an outburst. Now go upstairs and tell God you are sorry for saying such a thing."

Malinda said nothing, which Naomi took as assent. However, when she was halfway up the stairs and out of earshot of her mother, Malinda muttered under her breath, *I'll do no such thing!*

When she was in her room she flopped down on the bed and cried some more. Finally, she tired of weeping and got up as she resolved what she should do. *I'll go see Esther as soon as I can. That's what I'll do.* That resolve helped dry her tears but, at the same time, hardened her heart. At least, she felt that it didn't hurt quite as much as before. *That's exactly what I'll do,* she repeated as she fell asleep.

As darkness deepened with the night outside her window, a few bullfrogs croaked in the distance as she tossed and turned in her dreamless, tormented slumber.

❦

True to Naomi's words, morning came and life did continue. Malinda made no more mention of her pressing problem although it penetrated her every thought. While keeping her thoughts from her mother, she waited for an opportunity to arrange her next visit with Esther.

As if on cue, she ran into Esther on Wednesday while driving through Glendale on an errand. When she saw Esther's buggy coming, she pulled over beside the road in front of the AM/FM radio station. After checking to make sure that no traffic was coming, Esther pulled off the road across from her. Since none was in sight, they would have a few moments of time to talk.

Esther looked at Malinda intently.

"It's not working," Malinda stated with emotion.

"Think you could give it some more time?"

Malinda shook her head.

"I was afraid it wouldn't work with her."

"Nothing works on that girl."

"Well, we tried at least."

"What else can we do? You said there was something."

Esther's countenance darkened. "You really want to do this?"

"Of course, I have to get Lamar back."

"Okay, I will let you know in a few days."

"How am I going to get in touch with you? I don't want Mom to know anything about this."

Esther nodded, "I'll come over for something, and we can speak then. Your mother shouldn't mind if I have something to give you."

"What is it?"

Esther chuckled, "You will just have to wait to see."

A faint sound of a distant vehicle became audible. Looking down the road, Malinda saw a car coming. "We'd better get going."

"See you," Esther slapped the reins and drove off. Malinda waited until the car had passed before she continued on home.

I wonder what she can do about this? Probably nothing, like everyone else.

Chapter Twelve

To his own consternation, Phillip Ryan could not get his mind off the thought of this beautiful Amish woman. She held unknown qualities he could not quite identify. He worked with girls all the time, but was usually disappointed the closer he got to know them. That beauty and wholesomeness could possibly be found in the same person tugged at his heart. Whether that was all, he was not sure.

Finally, on Thursday he decided to take action. He went over his work that morning, and finished the most pressing things. He called the company pilot to be ready for an afternoon flight. Telling Camellia only that he would be out for the day, but back tomorrow, he left the office.

Reaching LaGuardia by 1:30 p.m., he landed at Indianapolis International around 5:00 p.m. After checking out and getting to Avis for his rental car, it was almost six before he was on the road. After leaving town on Interstate 70, he switched lanes a couple of time until he was satisfied. The GMC Envoy they had given him was satisfactory, although he preferred the Denali. The Avis attendant had told him that none were available on such short notice.

Being familiar with the general area from the few years spent here in his childhood, he never bothered looking at a map. Dropping south on 231, and then 57, he neared Elnora as dusk was falling. Several times he had thought of calling Mrs. Florence to ask for directions to this Amish girl's house. Always, he had then changed his mind. Although his knowledge of the Amish was meager, he knew a little about human nature. He also knew that a strange boy showing up at any home asking for a girl without some pretty good reason was problematic.

Realizing that he was hungry, he stopped and asked if there were any good restaurants in the area. Two men loitering in front of the gas station in Elnora seemed friendly enough. One of them offered his opinion on local places to eat.

"There's a couple of places in Washington. Amish folks run one of them. They have good cooking."

"Anything closer?" he asked the man. "I'm actually going towards Odon."

"There's an Amish restaurant there. The *Essen Haus*, right off the main road."

"You from around here?" Phillip asked the man in response, in light of his extensive knowledge of local restaurants.

"Actually, Florida," the man told Phillip.

"How do you know so much about the area?"

"I have friends here," pointing towards the other man. "Stop by every chance I get. Plus, this." He patted his rounded stomach. "It keeps track of things like that."

Phillip chuckled, expressed his thanks, and headed west towards Odon.

Following the man's directions, Phillip found the *Essen Haus* in the center of Odon, a block south of the main drag through town. He was greeted by a waitress with a white apron, a tall girl with a strange headdress, who showed him to a table. Used to evaluating girls on their looks, he decided she was definitely not modeling material.

"You Amish?" he asked, as he took his seat.

"No," she told him, with a patient look on her face, as if she got this query all the time. "Mennonite."

"What's the difference," he asked her.

"A big one is one drives cars and the other doesn't, also electricity use and the German language."

"I see," he said. "Are there many Amish around here?"

She grinned, her face lighting up, "All over the place. We are kind of in the center of them. Mostly south of here, though."

The answer went by him, as he was still in awe at what happened before she started talking. That grin had changed her whole countenance, as if the inside had suddenly been illuminated. A quality of warmth for humanity appeared with which he was not familiar. He found no trace of subtlety, or of the deviousness he so often felt lay just beneath the surface of even a girl's smile.

"I'll be back with the menu," she interrupted his thoughts, "or will it be just the bar?"

Glancing over at the peninsula of prepared food, he quickly made up his mind. "The bar's fine."

"Anything to drink?"

"Water," he told her.

"Then help yourself to the food. I'll be right out with the water."

He did that and piled on potatoes, gravy, sliced ham and fried chicken. *This is good food.*

When he had finished eating and she had brought him the bill, he was astonished at the low cost. *It would have cost five times this in New York. Of course, that's New York, but even Indianapolis would have been twice this.* He left a generous tip.

Driving south directly from Odon, dusk was rapidly settling around him but he saw little to indicate it was Amish country. A house here and there had no electric wires or cars in the driveway. He supposed a more knowledgeable viewer would see other signs, but those were the obvious ones from the information he had.

Now how in the world do I find this Sarah Schwartz? More than once, Phillip thought of calling Mrs. Florence but each time the thought arose he decided against it. *I'll just see what the countryside looks like first.*

A few miles south of town he started passing buggies. From what he could see of the interiors, the buggies seemed to carry either single males or couples. This did nothing to enlighten him as to why the buggies might be on the road. Neither businesses nor towns were anywhere to be seen. The rolling countryside contained only houses and open farmland. He passed a church on the right. Its sign said Bethel Mennonite. *No Amish yet.*

As the dusk deepened, he grinned at the multiplicity of the lights on the next buggy he came up behind. His headlights illuminated the multiple painted circles on the buggy wheels. Between the lights and the randomly colored whirling wheels, he was reminded of a Christmas Tree. *Must be some wild ones among this bunch.*

He grinned again, thinking that youth were little different the world over. His own 2001 Porsche Boxster convertible sat home in the garage on Morse Lake. Rarely did he use it now, but this must be an Amish equivalent of the experience. He laughed aloud at the thought. *I guess trying has its own rewards.*

A few miles farther south he noticed a community center on his left, its name, Simon Graber Community Building, in large letters out by the road. Elevated above the main road, the center building was huge and a ball-park could be seen behind it. Tied to the property fence in the side parking lot was a ring of more than sixty buggies with their horses still hitched. Cars took up the center having been arranged in two neat rows. *Must be youth night. Hah, pay dirt! She might even be here.*

Pulling in, he gingerly parked in an available spot, carefully getting out of the Envoy. Would he be welcome? Looking around, he saw a group playing on the basketball court inside the building. Other youth milled around, all of them looking normal to him. No signs of the Amish. Walking towards the ball field where a game was going on, he passed several groups of girls. These looked more like he expected Amish to look, in monochromatic dresses, with wrapped, black head coverings on their heads. They were speaking a language he could not understand. *Where are the boys, though?*

Approaching the group by the field, which contained both males and females, he heard the strange language coming from the boys, too. *Must be Amish then. But they don't look Amish.*

"Good evening," he said approaching the group on the bleachers.

They looked him over, but offered only a few nods in return.

Really friendly folks.

"You from around here?" one of them asked him.

"Used to live in Washington," he offered, hoping that was a better answer than New York City.

The group seemed to accept the answer. "Joe Mast is the name," one of the boys offered his hand.

"You wouldn't know of Sarah Schwartz?" he asked innocently enough as he shook Joe's hand.

The atmosphere stiffened. "Why do you ask that?" Joe wanted to know.

He thought about explaining but changed his mind. This seemed no place to give details. "Just wondered," he said.

This would not suffice, he could tell by their stares. "You know her?" a boy standing beside Joe wanted to know.

"No," he said, deciding again against divulging further information, hoping the interest level would fade.

It did not. "Hey, Lamar, come over here," Joe yelled towards the other end of the bleachers.

Phillip looked around suddenly with the feeling that he might need a fast exit plan. His Envoy was parked just around the other side of the building. Amish, he reminded himself, were harmless people. He hoped the premonition of danger that swept over him was merely over-reaction. *Calm down,* he told himself.

A tall boy detached himself from the distant end of the bleachers and walked over. "Lamar," Joe ignored Phillip, "this fellow says he knows Sarah. Any idea why?"

"I didn't say I know her," Phillip clearly felt the need to protest.

"Why are you asking about her?" Lamar glared at him.

Deciding that an aggressive stand might serve him well, Phillip glared back. "It's none of your business. I am trying to locate her for business reasons." He figured the reason had enough honesty to it to be told without any guilt. Guilt was not something he needed at the moment.

"Business?" Lamar paused, as if thinking. "You ever met her?"

"No."

"Then what need have you got of her?"

"I told you, it's none of your business. Apparently you know her," he added, taking a stab into the unknown.

The look on Lamar's face clearly gave him the upper hand. "Is she your girlfriend or something?" he tried another stab.

The answer was clear on Lamar's face. "I see," he said,

his face falling. *So Camellia was right. Such a girl would long ago be spoken for and unavailable. Securely,* he figured.

"Excuse me," he ventured, "I need to be going." No one seemed disposed to offer any words or actions in opposition.

"So what was that?" Joe mused out loud as Phillip retreated around the corner. "You know him, Lamar?"

"Never seen him before. How do you think he knows of Sarah?"

"Do you think she knows him?"

"What was his name?"

Joe searched the recesses of his mind. "Phillip, I think. Ryan maybe, but that's a strange name to have, isn't it. Maybe I misunderstood."

"Phillip? This is all really strange."

"You sure you know what you're getting into with Sarah?" Joe asked looking at Lamar.

"I thought I did."

"Strange English boy comes walking in, asking for her. You call that knowing her?"

Lamar rubbed his face. "Just forget it, okay. It probably was nothing."

Joe shrugged his shoulders. "Glad you trust her. I'd look into it."

"Just let me handle it."

"As you wish."

Lamar decided it was best if he did not respond further, and nodding his head he moved back to his side of the bleachers. Several of the others looked at each other, shook their heads and went back to watching the game. Whatever the problem was, each was glad it was not his girl who was involved. Indeed, there was no interpretation of the evening's events they could come up that did not represent a troubling scenario.

~

Esther's eyes scanned the Wal-Mart pharmacy shelves. *Where was it?* It was not on the lower shelves, and not on the upper ones. It must be in the middle, but where? Keeping a nervous eye out for any one who knew her, at the same time she figured it wouldn't matter if she were seen. However, it might be worth taking some precautions in case things turned out poorly. What if someone recalled seeing her buying something in this area of Wal-Mart. Worse would be if someone remembered what she had been buying.

With another glance up the aisle in each direction, she continued looking. *Sodium... Sodium ... Sodium... yes, there it is, sodium hydroxide.* Carefully she took a package of pure white, solid sodium hydroxide off the shelf, and placed it in her cart. Next she went over to the paint section and grabbed a package of vinyl gloves.

Now, for the final item. Pushing her cart down a couple of aisles, she stopped in front of the women's section of facial items. She quickly found a jar of Pond's face cream. Choosing the scented version, she placed two in her cart. *That should do it.*

Ten minutes later she was through the checkout with her half-empty cart. When she arrived at her buggy, everything fit nicely beneath the back seat. Untying the horse, she climbed in and took off towards home, plodding slowly through the downtown traffic.

CHAPTER THIRTEEN

PHILLIP WALKED INTO his office at the regular time on Friday morning. He had landed sometime after midnight at LaGuardia, having called ahead to Indianapolis while he was still in Odon, to tell the company pilots to get ready for the flight back.

I've got to put this foolishness out of my mind were his first thoughts when walked in the front door.

Camellia came in fifteen minutes later, right on time.

"Did you find the beautiful Amish girl?" she chirped cheerfully.

He gave her a warning look.

"You shouldn't try to hide things," she told him. Camellia forged ahead, "Dreams are really about the things that lie closest to us. What we can reach with our hands, that is what we should reach for," she pronounced sagely, sitting down at her desk.

He cleared his throat. "The schedule for today, I see, you have me down for a ten o'clock meeting. Move that to 2:30, if you can. I need more time this morning to work on our advertising plan."

She grimaced, nodded, and reached for the phone. *Why doesn't it work?*

"Let me know as soon as you find out."

She nodded again. *What does he see in her that I don't have?*

He hasn't even seen her. Maybe I should disappear. Yeah, right, Ms. Camellia, you have to work.

❧

Lamar came well before dark on Saturday evening. The news was out, and there was no need to hide his dating relationship with Sarah Schwartz. He would rather have waited until Sunday night to take Sarah home in front of everyone. Just the thought of pulling out of the Sunday evening hymn sing with such a beautiful girl beside him made him carry his head a little higher. Now, however, he had no such arrangement with her and would have to settle for the next best thing. *That will soon change though, I hope.*

The thought of Thursday night suddenly darkened his thoughts. *What was that boy, Phillip, doing looking for Sarah? Did she have something in her past he knew nothing of? Surely not?*

That would just be all he needed. Finally having the best-looking girl as his girlfriend, and then to find out she was messing around with an English boy! *Where would she find the opportunity for something like that?* Nowadays, one just never knew what opportunities came one's way. *Surely she wouldn't be dating an English boy on the sly. She didn't seem like the type.*

Pulling in the driveway, he tied his horse. *There's no use unhitching. He can easily stand there for two hours or so.* That was about all the time he figured he would stay on his second date. *Even then I might be pushing things a little.*

Turning around he saw Sarah coming out of the front door. Stepping down from the porch, the setting sun caught her blond hair, sending its rays through them from one side to the other. As she ducked her head, the front hair that was not covered by the head covering glowed with an almost supernatural light. It took his breath away. *This was his girl!* He took a deep breath as she walked towards him.

"Hi," she said shyly approaching him.

"Good evening," he returned, having a hard time keeping a normal tone to his voice. It would not do to show too much emotion.

"We can sit on the front porch," she offered, "or walk down to the park. Whatever you like."

Her willingness to let him make the decisions thrilled him. *This is some girl.* Malinda had always let him do pretty much what he wanted to, but this was giving permission without passivity. It was as if she enjoyed finding out what his choice would be. "The porch will be fine," he said.

"I'll get some chairs then," she smiled at him.

He followed her back up the walk and waited while she went inside. It bothered him that they would be sitting close to the front window. He reckoned that conversations could easily be heard on the inside.

While setting up the lawn chairs, she answered that concern without being asked, "Mom and Dad are gone right now. The others are upstairs."

Gratefully, he settled into the lawn chair. This was one conversation he preferred not to have overheard. As she took the chair beside him, he considered not raising the subject. *Why place this relationship in jeopardy?* Sarah was saying nothing at the moment.

"I was at the community center on Thursday for the ball game," he started.

"Yes. Were lots of people there?"

"The usual crowd."

"Anything interesting happen?" She seemed generally interested.

This was his opening. It was now or never. He cleared his throat. "You know an English boy by the name of Phillip Ryan? It's a funny last name, I know, but that's what he said."

She smiled and shrugged her shoulders slightly, "I don't think so."

Suspiciously he looked at her. This was not the solid answer he was looking for, "Do you or don't you know him?"

Startled, she paused, her face becoming serious. "What is this about anyway?"

He quickly backed down and regained his calm. "Oh, it's nothing, I guess." She looked questioningly. "It's just that an English boy none of us knew stopped in and asked about you. Used your exact name and everything."

"And that's nothing?" her eyebrows were still knitted.

"Well, I guess it is, but maybe it isn't. I just wondered whether you knew him."

"I've never heard his name before."

"Do you know other English boys?"

"Of course, but not one by the name of Phillip Ryan."

"What are their names?"

She looked like she would not answer. "You're not suspicious of me are you?"

"Of course not, it was just a little strange, him walking in and asking about you."

"Really."

Finally he abandoned the effort to go slowly. Beautiful or not, he would have it out with her. "It's like this. A strange English boy walked in and asked for an Amish girl — in front of everyone, to boot. I would say that would be suspicious, unless we knew him. Now do you or do you not know of Phillip Ryan or anyone who might be called by some other name who could be him?"

She laughed heartily. "You are a strange one, Lamar."

"How's that?"

"You should know me better than that."

He would not be put off. "Do you or don't you?"

"I don't," she replied again seriously. "I'm disappointed you should think so."

He breathed deeply. "I'm sorry. I just had to know. Okay? Where would this boy have found out about you?"

"I have no idea." She was not smiling.

"Don't you work for an English woman?" He remembered faintly that she cleaned for someone.

"Yes."

"Have they got a boy?"

"Yes."

"What's his name?"

"Marcus Florence," she said without missing a beat.

He leaned back in his chair, not sure where to go from here. He didn't like how quickly she said that English name. *It just rolled off her tongue.*

"If you are so uncertain of me, you don't have to come here," she told him softly.

Jerking up in his chair, he quickly assured her, "No, no. That's not what I meant at all. Let's just leave it. Okay? I trust you. I just wanted to be sure."

"Are you satisfied?"

"Yes, most certainly." He attempted to smile, and pulled off a good show with how nervous he felt.

"I don't know any English boys called Phillip Ryan or any others that well either. Marcus was only home from college once when I was there."

"It's okay," he assured her. "I'm sorry."

She nodded her head, and they settled into silence as the sun dropped below the horizon. Breezes, undetectable the entire day, stirred, brushing their faces lightly, as they sat there on the front porch. They were two young people lost in their own world and thoughts. However, at this moment, this world was also not the most comfortable one.

Sarah was disappointed by Lamar's questions, and puzzled as to who this Phillip Ryan was who knew her. Lamar was not entirely sure that he knew everything yet. That lack of knowledge bothered him severely. *I'll just keep my eyes open*, he thought, turning towards her, "I'm sorry this evening has gone this way. I really enjoy seeing you."

She smiled grimly, looking at him. His handsome face did things to her, even now when she was still irritated with him. "It's okay," she managed.

Pulling his watch out of his pocket, he glanced at it. "Can I see you again?"

She paused as if thinking, "Sure."

He didn't like that pause, but at least she was saying "yes". "Could I take you home on Sunday evening? I know it's tomorrow night, but maybe things will go better if I keep my big mouth shut."

"You will have to talk," she deadpanned.

"Is that a 'yes' then?"

She tilted her head, "Sunday night?"

"Yes."

Thoughts of riding in his fancy buggy flashed in her mind. "How about next Saturday night again?" She looked at him.

"Oh," he pretended to groan. "That's a long time."

"Saturday night, then?"

"I'll see you then." He rose from the lawn chair, turning on all the charm he had. "I'll be looking forward to it."

She nodded, staying on the front porch until he got in the buggy. When he pulled past the front of the house, the porch was empty. *I wonder what she's up to?*

Inside, her irritation returned. *What was that all about, anyway? Already he's jealous. I can't believe it!* She shook her head, trying to think clearly. She finally concluded that next Saturday would come soon enough. *I'll deal more with it then.*

Glancing at the clock, she noticed it was only nine o'clock. *He sure left early. Not really a good way to start things off.*

Martha stuck her head out from the upstairs door. "He left early. Trouble, have we?"

Sarah made a face, "You hope."

"Yes."

"You should wish me well."

"With that creep?"

"You're just jealous."

Martha grinned, "Maybe I should be, but I'm not. Are you seeing him again?"

"Yes, next Saturday night."

"Not on Sunday evening?"

"No."

Martha looked surprised.

"I'm not comfortable riding in his buggy yet."

"You still have some sense. Maybe there is hope for you after all!"

Sarah grinned, "I hope so."

Esther decided it was time to see if this plan worked. *It ought to.* Taking the solid package of sodium hydroxide and the two jars of Pond's scented face cream, she placed them all on the kitchen table.

Carefully she spread a piece of plastic over one end of the table and transferred the items to the plastic. Pulling on a pair of the vinyl gloves, she opened the jars of Pond's scented face cream. Getting an old bowl out of the cupboard. she next broke a small piece of the solid sodium hydroxide into it. Adding water, the block dissolved, bubbling vigorously, as she expected.

Now, let's see if it works. Pouring a small dash out of the bowl into one of the Pond's scented face cream, she stirred the cream, careful not to let any of it spill out, or even touch the edge of the jar.

Finished to her satisfaction, she leaned over and sniffed the jar. Only the normal scent was perceptible. *Not too spoiled.* She sniffed the other jar, then the one to which she had added the liquid. There was a small dilution of the odor, but not enough to matter.

Now for the test. There was no way she was going to put any of the cream on her own arm. *What can I use? The cows' skin is too thick. The dog?* That produced the same conclusion. *Yes, the cat.*

The cat, Kitty, was basking in the warmth of the midday sunshine just outside the front door. She picked him up and carried him over to the kitchen table, placing him on the piece of plastic that was still unused.

Taking a table knife, she stuck it into the altered jar, bringing out a small amount of the cream. Spreading a little on Kitty's leg, she let him go and waited.

Nothing happened. *It doesn't work.*

Kitty meowed, suddenly looking at his leg. He shook it and then shook it again. Putting his head down to lick the spot, Esther stopped him by putting her vinyl-gloved hand in the way. The result was that he yowled and leapt into the air, shaking his paw violently.

Landing on the kitchen floor, she tried to grab him to wipe off the cream, but he was airborne again. She ran for the front door to open it before he tore up the house. He did not need an invitation and bounded past her, spitting as he went. With his tail in the air, he never slowed down until he disappeared into the open barn door.

I guess it works, she smiled to herself. *Ought to make a nice blister.*

Chapter Fourteen

Rebecca picked Sarah up on Monday morning for house-cleaning at the Florence residence.

"How are you doing, Dear?" she asked.

"Just fine, and you?"

"Fine, I think. Still seems I have after-effects from the accident, but not too bad."

Pulling out of the driveway, Mrs. Florence accelerated the Toyota through Glendale and then drove north on 257.

"So anything interesting going on?" she asked Sarah with a smile.

At first Sarah shook her head and then remembered Lamar. "I'm dating a fellow."

"Oh, that's wonderful," gushed Rebecca. "Is he good-looking?"

Sarah blushed. "Yes, black-haired, tall, a nice guy."

"That's wonderful," stated Rebecca.

"Do you know a Phillip Ryan?" Sarah asked suddenly.

Rebecca was astonished. "How do you know him?"

"I don't."

"Then why do you ask about him?"

"Lamar said he came to the youth gathering on Thursday asking about me."

"That rascal!" Rebecca looked like she wanted to say more, but stopped herself.

"Who is he?"

133

"A good friend of ours. Well, his whole family is. We have known each other for years. Recently we spent a Sunday afternoon with him and his family at their home on Morse Lake."

"How does he know me?"

Rebecca looked at Sarah's concerned face. "I'm so sorry. I hope no harm was done. I suppose it was Marcus who told him about you."

"Why would Marcus tell him about me?"

Rebecca paused, myriad thoughts swirling around in her head, but there seemed no way out but to say it. "Remember when I told you Marcus thinks you could model? He mentioned that to Phillip."

"How can this Phillip have models?"

Rebecca took a deep breath. "Phillip's father owns 'Maxey Jacobs'. The company designs women's clothing, as well as models their own lines. It's quite a large operation. Successful, too."

Sarah waited.

Rebecca plunged ahead, "Phillip really is interested in seeing you. Probably wants to offer you a job. Why he came down here looking for you on his own is beyond me. I am really sorry if he caused any problems."

Sarah was processing the information. "Did you tell him where I lived?"

"No. That's probably why he decided to try on his own. I never would have thought it proper to have him come to your home unless you wanted him to."

"Is that why you were asking about modeling the last time I cleaned for you?"

Rebecca weighed her words carefully again. "We never discussed him coming to your house. He did ask me if you might be willing to work for him. I told him I had hinted at it to you, and you were not interested."

"You discussed all this with a man from New York City?"

"Yes." Rebecca turned into the driveway. The way this conversation was going she might have to turn right around and take the girl home again. "We are good friends," she added quickly, hoping it would help.

"Why is this Ryan fellow so interested in me?"

Rebecca sighed in relief, the girl was not demanding to be taken home. "You are beautiful," she said quietly. "He thinks you might work as a model. It's a business question."

"*That* beautiful?" Sarah sounded baffled.

"Yes."

"That I could be in a magazine?"

"Well, test photos would have to be taken, but, yes, I think so."

Sarah was pensive, sitting there in the car. "I never really thought much about this before. I'm still not sure why a person would want to model, but now that you explain it like that, for a business, it does sound different. Do you think I could really do it?"

"You would be wonderful," Rebecca told her.

"You think so?"

"Sure."

"But I'm Amish."

"I guess that could be a problem."

Sarah chuckled, "I think I had better get your house cleaned before Mom wonders where I am."

"I could take you up to New York some week. Give you a guided tour of the city and then we could stop by and see what you think of this Phillip Ryan project."

"You would do that for me?"

"Sure."

"That costs money, and I don't have the money to pay for the trip."

Rebecca grinned, "I'm sure Maxey Jacobs would pay for both of us. Phillip must want to see you badly to come all the way down here."

"Why would they do something like that?"

"It's part of their business."

Sarah shrugged, "That does make sense, I suppose. Well, I will think about it. I just never thought I would do something like that, but who knows?"

Rebecca nodded, not wanting to press the subject. It just seemed like such a shame that Sarah was not taking this opportunity. "Maybe we should go inside," was all she said as she opened the car door. Sarah followed Rebecca into the house.

Later when the cleaning was done, Rebecca played a piece from Handel's "Messiah" for Sarah, the prelude to "Comfort Ye My People". Sarah was still raving about Handel when Rebecca dropped her off in front of the Schwartz's sidewalk.

"See you next month," Rebecca said as she climbed out of the car.

"See you," Sarah waved and walked up the sidewalk, saying nothing about what Rebecca really wanted to hear. *I guess she has my phone number.*

Rebecca waited until Sarah was inside before she pulled off. *Wouldn't it be wonderful if she would go?* The tires of the car crunched on the gravel driveway as it pulled forward.

❧

Wednesday was the day of the womens' quilting. This morning, Malinda announced that she would attend. Surprised, Naomi was nonetheless glad to see her willing to go. Usually Malinda considered herself beneath the activity of a group of older women of which she was not yet a part.

"We leave right after breakfast, as usual," Naomi told Malinda smiling.

Malinda nodded, already well aware of the schedule, and feeling a little guilty at her mother's delight in her going. *What if she knew the real reason?* There was no doubt in Malinda's mind what the reaction would be.

Together they hitched up the buggy and began the drive. It was a cool morning, the mist still clinging to the upper edges of Dogwood Lake that bordered Route 600. A bullfrog croaked his hunger for morning breakfast. The steady clip-clop of the horse's hooves drew mother and daughter into its gentle embrace, as time seemed to slow.

"How are you feeling now?" Naomi broke the silence.

"About what?"

"About Lamar, of course."

"I want him back."

"You can't make someone like you, if they don't. Don't you think it's time to let him go? After all, he is dating Sarah now. Looks pretty serious to me."

"No."

"You have to submit to the will of God."

"He hasn't told me what that is."

Naomi sighed, "He might be speaking through circumstances. Maybe you ought to listen. It will stop hurting sooner if you just accept it."

"I'm not going to accept it. He's my boyfriend, and Sarah Schwartz is not going to steal him."

"He's not your boyfriend anymore." Naomi looked at Malinda. "You have to stop thinking like that."

"I don't accept it. It's wrong what she did to me."

"How do you know she did anything wrong? This was all as big a surprise to us as to anyone else. Lamar can't be made to do things. He asked her. Don't blame it all on Sarah."

"She doesn't have to be so good looking."

Naomi was exasperated. "The girl can't help how she looks!"

"I don't care. She shouldn't use her looks to steal my boyfriend!"

Naomi gave up, slapping the horse's reins more out of frustration with Malinda than desiring any greater speed from the horse. "I wish you wouldn't take it this way."

Malinda said nothing, sitting in gloomy silence for the rest of the trip. Naomi glanced at her, and would have said something if she was shown signs of anger; instead a tear glided down her cheek. Her heart softened and Naomi reached over and squeezed her hand. "Maybe God will work things out for you."

Malinda's tears dried up as a glint came into her eyes, but she said nothing.

Finding their places around one of the four quilts, the two women got right to work. Malinda could see nothing of Esther, and figured her plans for the day would surely be in vain.

Around ten with her back turned towards the door, she heard Esther's voice as she came in. She was talking with Millie Stoll about the poison ivy her little boy got into last week. Malinda kept her head down, lest her eagerness show. *I will have a chance to talk with her later.*

By lunchtime, considerable work had been completed on the quilts. When the call came that lunch was ready, many of the women straightened their backs trying not to show their fatigue. The afternoon was yet to go, and it would not do to be known as one who could not keep up.

Malinda saw her chance and sat down beside Esther. With plates of food in their laps, the chatter of the women was a free-for-all. Any conversation between Esther and Malinda would seem totally appropriate.

"Have you got it?" Malinda asked, trying to look like she was discussing the pranks of her younger brothers and sisters.

Esther nodded her head and smiled as if she thought something said had been funny, too.

"Where?"

"Under the seat of my buggy."

"What is it?"

"A jar of Pond's facial cream, scented." Esther lowered her voice lest the English sounding words carry to someone's ears. Malinda glanced around nervously, but it must have looked as if they were simply sharing an innocent secret because no one paid any attention. They were all too busy with their own stories.

"What is that for?"

"For you to give it to Sarah."

"I can't give anything to Sarah."

"Of course, not personally," Esther looked at Malinda knowingly, "but you can as an unknown friend. People do that all the time."

"She will know."

"I have figured out a way."

Malinda took some deep breaths, her face turning pale. "Now, now," Esther muttered under her breath, "don't go weak on me. This will really work," she said out loud.

"What will happen if I give her this jar?" Malinda asked, trying hard to muster her courage.

"Just consider that Lamar will no longer be hanging around her. That's all you need to know." Esther was smiling again.

"What if this is wrong?"

"You want Lamar back, don't you?"

"Yes."

"Then go outside, take the jar out from underneath my

buggy seat, walk over to the Schwartz's buggy. I'm sure you know which one that is," said Esther sarcastically. "Lay it on the seat where they will see it, then walk back into the house. If anyone sees you, just act like you were looking for something. It will all look very normal."

"How will she know it is for her?"

"Just do it. You will see."

Malinda took some more deep breaths, now unable to eat the last portion of her meal. "Here, I'll take that," Esther said, taking the plate and rising to carry it to the kitchen table.

This was her cue. Malinda rose, her legs shaking. *What if someone sees them shake.* Quickly convincing herself that it felt worse than it was, she walked around two of the quilts and then out the front door.

Several other women were outside, getting things out of their buggies or putting things into them. Malinda was not quite sure, but in her state of mind did not really care. Finding Esther's buggy without any problem, she reached under the seat. A small package came into the reach of her outstretched fingers.

Pulling it out, she looked at it, puzzled. It did not look like a jar of anything. It was all wrapped up in white wrapping paper. Turning it over, writing came into view. "From a friend to Sarah Schwartz," it said, "Best Wishes."

Now Malinda's legs really shook. *How can I do this?* A voice then sounded in her head, "You want him back, don't you?"

"Yes," she said out loud, looking around embarrassed. *I have to get control of myself.*

Having spotted the Schwartz's buggy on the way to Esther's buggy, she walked over to it, carrying the white package close to her dress. *Look natural. Look natural. Oh, what am I doing? I've got to get him back. What is this thing anyway? Quiet, quiet, just do it.*

Walking up to the side of the Schwartz's buggy, out of view of the house, she opened the door. Carefully placing the package on the seat, writing side up, she shut the buggy door and headed back towards the house.

Halfway there, waves of regret and remorse swept over her. There was no turning back now and she kept walking.

Chapter Fifteen

With the quilting over, Sarah got the horse from the barn while Martha stood ready to raise the shafts to get him hitched up.

"Whoa, there," Sarah spoke to the horse gently. He was getting riled up with all the activity around him.

"Let's get out of here before too many get going," Martha urged.

"We have to keep him calm," Sarah told her.

"He's just an old plodder. He's not going anywhere fast."

"That's true," Sarah chuckled, "maybe he's just feeling his oats from the memory of the good old days."

"Let's just get him hitched up." Martha stood by the now raised shafts holding one side with both hands. Deftly Sarah maneuvered the horse under them.

As the tugs were slipped into place, Deborah came out of the house. After opening the buggy door she commented, "Looks like someone left something for you, Sarah."

Neither of the girls paid much attention. It could be anything from garden vegetables to a forgotten birthday card from three months ago.

Climbing in, Deborah took the reins with a daughter climbing in on either side of her. "The package is back there," she pointed toward the little shelf behind the buggy seat.

Sarah reached around and got the white package and read the writing. Then tearing off the wrapping the jar of facial cream was revealed. "It's face cream," she muttered.

"Who would give you something like that?" Martha wanted to know.

"Maybe they think I need it for my face."

"It's not like you aren't good-looking enough already," Martha made a face.

Sarah shrugged, ignoring the vibe. "It says, 'from a friend'. Who do you think that could be?"

"How would I know?" Martha told her.

"Okay, girls, enough now," Deborah interrupted them. "It was probably someone just being thoughtful. Use it if one of you wants it. It doesn't have to be just for Sarah. Don't get vain, though."

Both girls wrinkled their noses in distaste since neither of them was fond of facial creams. "Should we be thoughtful and use it anyway?" Sarah asked Martha.

"Not me," Martha told her. "I don't like the stuff. Good old hand lotion is all I need."

"Maybe you would like it if you tried it," Sarah stated, slowly unscrewing the top.

Sarah held the jar up for her sister to sniff, before doing so herself. "It's not so bad."

Martha concurred with a nod of her head. Sarah slowly and carefully replaced the cap, roughly wrapped the paper back around it and laid the jar on the shelf behind the seat.

To the clip-clop of the horse's hooves on the pavement, they discussed the day's events and the general gossip. Such a large gathering of Amish women produced a large volume of things that needed to be said. Comparing notes now, the three soon had a pretty good grasp of what was going on in their immediate universe as well as the Amish world in the neighboring states. They were home before they knew it.

Sarah jumped out while Martha took her turn to take the horse to the barn. At the last minute she remembered to grab the Pond's cream in its rumpled, white paper.

Going directly upstairs to her room, she opened the dresser drawer and placed the jar in a bottom drawer after removing the paper. *I'll try it later. I should at least appreciate it enough to do that.*

As she shut the drawer the jar was sent rolling backwards. A pair of socks tumbled from its little pile inside the drawer and landed in front of the jar. The jar stopped rolling and was half hidden by the contents of the drawer.

On the way home, Malinda rode along silently with her mother. Naomi took this to mean that she was still getting over her memories of Lamar, perhaps stirred up by the gathering of the women.

"You okay?" she asked looking at Malinda with concern. *The girl looks really pale.*

Malinda nodded her head silently. *I can't tell her. What if she knew what I have done? Oh, what a mess I have gotten myself into!*

"Maybe you'll feel better after supper."

"Malinda nodded again, keeping her eyes straight ahead. She was sure they revealed all of her wild emotions. *Mom will know for sure something is wrong.*

By the time they were home, Malinda managed to calm down a little, enough to help unhitch the horse and prepare for supper. Now, with the evening over, and most of the family settled down for the night, she was tossing in her bed. All the horror of her deed returned.

What have I done? What's in the package anyway? Esther told me it was a jar a facial cream. I wonder if it's something else.

Maybe it's too terrible to say. Something really awful. Maybe a bomb. Surely not! What if it is? Oh, no, what have I done? She turned again, pulled the pillow over her head lest she scream in sheer terror. *It's going to go off and I'll be a condemned as a murderer! Oh, no, help me! Why did I do it?*

She paused for a moment, almost sure that a distant boom confirmed her fears. *She's already dead, and I did it.* Getting up she walked to the window and looked out. The night was silent except for the sounds of creatures stirring in the woods and on the pond. It was all she could do to keep from racing downstairs and running down the road on foot, in the direction of the Schwartz's home, screaming for Sarah not to open the package.

"I can't do that," she whispered quietly to herself. "Calm down now. Breathe deeply. You have to get Lamar back. Esther knows what she's doing. Trust her, just trust her." A new wave of fear went through her. *Can I really trust her? Stop thinking like that, stop thinking, stop thinking!*

She stuck her head out the window and took deep breaths of the night air. *Control yourself. It had to be done. You want Lamar back, don't you? Yes, then don't do anything reckless. It will be better this way. Esther knows what she's doing.*

But she made you do the dirty work. She pulled her head back in from the window. *Why did she do that? Now you can be blamed. Stop it, stop it, stop thinking like that.* With extreme effort she regained control of herself and climbed back into bed.

It was well past midnight when she finally dozed off. The last thing she heard was the big Ben clock in the living room as it sounded twice.

She awoke with a start at five-thirty. The alarm was just ready to go off at its customary time. She punched the button before the shattering racket could begin. Her window was still open, letting in the chill of the early morning. It also let in the freshness of a new day. No breeze stirred yet, and the world awaited the rising of the sun.

Malinda almost felt free. She swung her legs out of bed, walked over and shut the window and smiled at the new morning. Then the memories flooded back into her conscience. She had given that package to Sarah. *Don't start again.* She held her head. *I have to stop it.* Reaching deep inside herself for resolve, she steeled her nerves and got dressed for the day.

～

That morning, Mrs. Rebecca Florence placed a phone call to the New York offices of Maxey Jacobs, located on Pine Street, in the heart of the financial center of Manhattan.

Camellia answered the phone, "Hello, Maxey Jacobs. Camellia speaking."

"Could I speak with Phillip Ryan?"

"He's not available at the present."

"How would I speak with him?"

"You can leave a message, and he can call you back. May I ask who is calling?"

"Rebecca Florence. I believe you already have my number."

Oh, it's her. "Yes, Mrs. Florence, I will tell him you called."

"Thank you," Rebecca hung up the phone. *He had better call.*

An hour later Phillip walked in, frustration showing on his face, "Why do so many things go wrong?"

"Having trouble with the commercial?"

"Always more money and then they don't cooperate."

"That's models for you. Mrs. Florence just called. She wants you to call back."

"Did she say why?"

"No, but I think you should. Maybe she has that Amish beauty with her ready to come to New York."

Phillip glared at her, "You would look really funny if she did come."

"I suppose I would. An Amish girl, stumbling around New York City, now that would be a sight to see."

Phillip said nothing but picked up the phone and dialed the number Camellia had copied down for him. "Hello, this is Phillip Ryan. You called?"

"Were you here in the area last week?" she asked him.

"Yes, I was."

"Any idea how much trouble that made for the girl?"

"I did? Well, I am sorry. I was just trying to contact her in a normal manner."

"You must not know much about the Amish."

"That's not normal for them?"

"No, it isn't, and it really made problems for Sarah."

"Made trouble. I'm sorry. I suppose that means the end of this deal, doesn't it?"

Rebecca smiled, although Phillip couldn't see her. "I think I might have taken care of it."

"Oh, you covered for me. What did you do?"

"I'll let you know if anything comes of it."

"I see. That sounds interesting."

"We will have to see. She might just be a little inclined to visit New York. On a sightseeing trip, perhaps."

"Yes, well that's good. Keep me posted if anything comes of your plans."

"I will."

"Thank you."

"You have a good day, Phillip."

"Yes, thanks for covering for me. I will do better next time."

Phillip hung up the phone. Camellia was looking at

him expectantly. He said nothing, never looking at her as he walked out the door.

"When will you be back?" she hollered after him.

"I'm not going anywhere," he said, as he shut the door.

Lamar came over early on Saturday evening, as Sarah was expecting he would. She had already changed from her chore clothing and was waiting in the living room. Not very eagerly though, she noted to her own disappointment. *What's wrong with me? He's a nice boy.*

Watching him pull in, she felt some better. It would not do to seem too excited, even if she was. She waited until he was at the front door before answering.

"Good evening," she smiled at him.

With her standing in front of him, he found himself overcome again with her beauty. A few moments too many passed before he could say anything. *What's wrong with you? You're going to look all moon-struck.* "Good evening," he finally managed. "What about that drive to the park tonight?"

"We can walk," she told him quickly.

"Well," his face darkened slightly, "I was thinking of going all the way down to the Wildlife area. It's really nice there. We can tie the horse, and walk down to the lake from there."

"Sure," she said without hesitation. "Whatever you think."

It thrilled him again, her willingness to follow his suggestions. "Let's go then," he told her.

"Just a minute and I'll grab a coat. You can step inside." She looked at him expectantly.

"No, I'll just wait outside." He really had no desire to see her sister, if she happened to be around. *No use taking the chance. We'll deal with her later. The family can always be managed if one likes the girl.* He smiled to himself.

Sarah came out with her coat on her arm. She followed him down the walks, climbed in the buggy and deposited her coat on the shelf behind the seat. They were off.

Finding herself a little uncomfortable sitting this close to him, she smoothed her dress and slid farther over on her side. Lamar seemed not to notice. *He probably wouldn't say anything anyway. I wish he would say something.*

"Awful nice evening," he said as if in answer to her thoughts, and she relaxed, joining him in discussing general farming conditions and the prospects for the winter.

"Going to be a hard one, Grandpa says," Lamar chuckled. "Claims he's been right now for fifty years, but who knows?"

Sarah laughed, "Dad thinks so, too, so maybe between the two of them they will get it right."

Arriving at the park, Lamar turned the wheel, letting her out first before climbing down on his side. Together they walked down to the edge of the lake by the boat dock. No fishermen or sightseers seemed to be out at this time of the day. Lamar nodded toward the park bench and sat down first. Clearing his throat he decided to address the subject most important to him. "Can I take you home from the singing next Sunday night?" he asked, looking at her, he hoped not too eagerly.

She kept her gaze directed to the lake, her head covering slipped slightly back by the lake breeze blowing across their faces. Some of the strands of hair that had escaped fell across her face. He thought she had never looked more beautiful, yet he wondered what she was thinking.

"I don't know," she told him, still not looking at him.

"Why not?" he asked playfully. "You know I like you."

"Well," now she was looking at him, "that's not good enough a reason."

"Is there someone else?" he asked, crestfallen, "That English boy maybe?"

"No," she laughed out loud. Then sobered again, "It's the racing stripes on your wheels."

"The racing stripes?" He stared at her with open mouth.

"Yes," she told him, her fears fading fast.

"Then I will paint them black," he pronounced.

"No, you won't," she said equally emphatic.

"Then I won't," he said, "but you will let me drive you home?"

"Yes."

"Then it's settled?"

"Yes."

"Okay, then." He settled back on the park bench seat as silence settled around them. He felt his arm slightly touch hers, but she pulled away. *That's okay, she'll come around.*

An hour later, just as dusk started to fall, they left the park. Lamar made no effort to come into the house, nor did she ask him to. "See you next Sunday then," he said, as he parked with the buggy wheel pulled back so she could climb out.

"See you," she said, without looking at him.

He let the reins out when she closed the door. *She'll come around. She's too beautiful not to.* When he hit the pavement at the end of the driveway, the sound of his rubber tires humming on the pavement seemed to agree with him. *Not tomorrow, but Sunday after that it will be. I will drive off with her in front of everyone.*

CHAPTER SIXTEEN

MALINDA'S ANXIETY EBBED and flowed all that week but by Wednesday she could no longer stand it. *I have to see Esther.* There was no other way. She would have to ask to go.

"Could I go see Esther today?" she came right out after breakfast and asked Naomi.

Naomi tilted her head. "We're not too busy today, but why do you want to see her?"

"I want to ask her something."

"Seems like the two of you are together a lot lately. I just get that impression. This wouldn't be about Lamar, would it?"

Malinda thought quickly. Lying did not really appeal to her and besides the truth would probably seem the best course in this case. "Yes," she answered.

"I wish you wouldn't ask her advice in this situation. She may not know what is best for you."

Malinda decided to admit the truth, at least partially. "I already asked her, but I need to talk to her again."

Naomi smiled, "Advice not working?"

Shrugging her shoulders, Malinda again answered truthfully, "I don't know."

"Well, just be careful then, but you really don't need her advice."

"Is that a 'yes', then?"

Naomi nodded her head.

Malinda thought she should have been thrilled, but she felt only a dull ache. "I'll go right after lunch then."

"That would be a good time. Be back before three, though. I need help with supper and the chores."

"I will be," Malinda agreed.

Right after lunch she hitched up the horse by herself and was off. On the way a thought suddenly occurred to her. *What if Esther's not home? Oh, no.* But there was no turning back now. She would just have to continue and hope that Esther was home. *If she's not, Mom might let me come back another time.*

Pulling into the driveway, she spotted Esther working in her garden. Sighing in relief, she climbed out, tied the horse, and walked over. "Hi."

"It's you," Esther said in response.

"I couldn't stand it anymore. I have to know what I did. Am I going to kill her?"

Esther laughed heartily. "You worry too much, my dear. You have to learn that life is tough, and get over some of your feelings. Sarah will not be hurt long-term, only learn a little lesson to get Lamar away from her. That's what I have planned."

"But I placed the package in her buggy."

"Don't worry about it. You can always say I told you to do it."

"I would never do that."

"That's what I thought. Then we will all be safe with this nice little plan."

"I don't like it."

"Then why did you do it?"

"Because I wanted Lamar back."

"Then keep thinking about that. You'll be okay."

"What will happen to her? Is it a bomb?"

Esther laughed heartily again, "No, it's not a bomb."

"Then what is it?"

"Look, I'm not going to tell you anything more than what I have already told you. It's a jar of Pond's face cream. You're not in any danger. If someone discovers the little secret, it cannot be traced back to us."

"What about Sarah?"

"Why are you worrying so much about her? Remember, she's the one who stole your boyfriend."

"I guess that's right." Malinda nodded her head and tried to overcome her queasiness with this whole thing. "So nothing really bad will happen?"

"No, it won't!" snapped Esther. "Even if it did, you shouldn't worry about it now. You wanted Lamar back, and that's what I'm trying to do. Be a little thankful for that at least."

"I guess I should be. I'm sorry. Well, I need to get back. See you later."

"Hold your head up, Child. You'll get that boyfriend back yet."

"When is it going to happen?" Malinda gathered the courage to ask.

Esther's face darkened again. "It should already have happened. But don't worry. Just wait. Okay?"

Malinda nodded, and walked towards the buggy. As she drove out the driveway Esther was again bent over the weeds in her garden, pulling vigorously.

Slapping the reins, Malinda hurried to get back home. *Oh, I wish I hadn't done this, but what can I do now?* She paused as if listening for an answer, but there was only silence.

❧

When Sarah was honest with herself, she had to admit she was not looking forward to Sunday. The vision of riding in Lamar's buggy with its racing stripes was simply not that appealing to her. She thought for sure that after her talk with Lamar in the park, it would stop bothering her, but it did not.

Now something else was also bothering her. The idea, planted by Mrs. Rebecca Florence, was bearing fruit. Slowly it began growing in the night hours and during the daytime, it stuck out tiny test leaves. Wouldn't a trip to New York City be wonderful? She would get to see the sights she had only read about so many times in her school books: Queens, Brooklyn, Ellis Island, and the Statue of Liberty. *It would all be so grand, wouldn't it?* Although Sarah would then shove the thought aside, it still returned.

You just want to see that boy. She thought about that a bit. *Yes, a little, but it is a lot more. You ought to be ashamed of yourself. You're dating.*

Well, she was, a little, but still she wanted to see New York City. There might never be another chance like this. Finally, she gathered all of her courage and broached the subject with Deborah that afternoon. "Rebecca has offered me quite an opportunity."

"When was this?" Deborah asked, mildly interested.

"On my cleaning day with her."

"And what is this opportunity? Will it cost you anything?"

"No, it's free."

"Well, that's good. So what is it?"

"She offered me a free trip to New York, to see the City."

"Why did she do that?" Deborah looked at Sarah suspiciously.

Sarah thought for a moment before answering. Deborah waited.

"Well, I want to see the city, and she would show it to me."

"Did you ask her to do this for you?"

"No."

"Why would a woman like Rebecca offer to take you to New York City?"

Sarah was getting ready to tell the whole story and possibly doom her chances of actually going to New York, when Deborah interrupted her.

"It doesn't matter, I guess. One never knows what the English are up to. If she wants to take you, free of charge, of course, by all means take the opportunity."

"Really?" Sarah could barely conceal her delight. "I would really like to see the Statue of Liberty."

This outburst fully satisfied Deborah. "What they teach you children at school is beyond me. We never learned such things in our time."

"I'll call her tomorrow, then," Sarah said, surprised at her own excitement. *Oh, no, what am I getting myself into? Well, I didn't lie about it.* This thought comforted her somewhat.

In the morning, she walked down to the phone shack and called Rebecca. "Hello, this is Sarah," she said into the receiver.

"Sarah?" Rebecca asked on the other end. "I'm surprised to hear from you. Is there something wrong?"

Sarah suddenly had an attack of misgiving. *What if she was not serious?* "Ah," she said into the receiver, "about that trip to New York, were you serious about inviting me to go?"

Rebecca almost dropped the receiver. "Most certainly," she found her voice. "Yes, of course I am. When do you want to go?"

"Anytime would be fine. As soon as you would want to."

Rebecca did some fast thinking. It simply would not do to call the girl back. She might change her mind, not to mention the difficulty of getting in touch with her. A decision would have to be made now. If Phillip didn't like it, she would deal with that later. "What about? Oh my, let's see?"

"You don't have to take me if it's too much trouble," Sarah said, responding to Rebecca's apparent hesitation.

"Oh, no dear, it's not that. My, I think next week would be just great. What about Wednesday, yes, Wednesday morning, and then we can come back on Monday. Would that work for you?"

"Sure."

"Then I will pick you up at your house at our regular time on Wednesday morning."

"Okay," Sarah told her, "I will be ready."

Sarah hung up the phone, faithfully recording the call for charging purposes. Rebecca hung up, wiping her brow with the back of her hand. *Whew. These Amish sure do things fast for how slow they are. Now a call to Phillip. He'd better not back out on this.*

Dialing the number, she waited while the phone rang. Phillip himself picked up the phone.

"Where's your secretary?" she asked without introducing herself.

Phillip chuckled as soon as he recognized her voice. "Just stepped out. What's up?"

"She's coming." Rebecca could hardly control her excitement.

"Who's coming?"

"The Amish girl."

"You're not serious."

"Yes, I am."

"When?"

"I'm picking her up at nine on Wednesday morning."

Phillip did some fast reckoning. "Bring her to Indianapolis International. I'll take care of the rest. How long will you be staying?"

"Until Monday."

"Okay, well done. I will call you with more details later."

"That will be fine. I'll be staying with her all the time, just remember that."

"Don't worry," Phillip chuckled, "you will give me some time to talk with her, won't you?"

"We'll see," Rebecca said wryly, "remember she's Amish."

"I won't forget," Phillip assured her, and then they hung up.

"She's coming," he said out loud. "I can't believe it." *We'll keep this a secret from Camellia for a while.* He smiled to himself as he looked over to her empty chair.

⚈

Sunday night arrived all too quickly for Sarah. For his part, Lamar could hardly wait. All day the thought of driving off in front of everyone with Sarah in his buggy made him nearly giddy. He tried not to show it, or to notice Malinda's face. She was making a valiant effort to hide her hurt, but he knew her well enough to observe the signs of recent tears.

She'll have to get over it. Turning his thoughts from her he let the full impact of his date with Sarah hit him. He was driving her home. *It's doesn't get any better than this!*

After church, Jesse walked by him in the barn. "Looking kind of chipper, are we?"

"Oh, so, so," Lamar commented in as calm a voice as he could muster.

"Ever get that English boy thing straightened out?"

That question was not quite the subject Lamar wished to think about at the moment. "I think so. She claims she doesn't know him."

"You believe her?"

"Of course," Lamar retorted, making an outward show of confidence he wished he felt on the inside.

"Awfully strange, is all I can say."

"She's fine," Lamar insisted.

"You'd better watch your back," Jesse tossed over his shoulder.

Lamar walked back out of the barn wishing Jesse had just kept his mouth shut. This was not what he wanted to be thinking about on this of all Sundays. Repressing the fears in his mind, he concentrated on this evening. *It will be good. She's mine now, and I don't have to worry about it.* So he comforted himself, hoping it was true.

"It is true," he said out loud as if in answer to an unseen questioner. *Why did Jesse have to bring this all up? Confound him.*

The afternoon dragged for him until after supper when they all filed in for the singing. Sarah made the front row, which he took as a good sign, and his spirits lifted considerably. *She's feeling confident. That's good.* In the second row Lamar saw Malinda. *She'll get over it* he told himself firmly.

The singing went well and finished promptly at nine. Lamar filed out immediately with the front row, heading for the barn and his horse. The sooner he got in line, the more attention he would get. Holding back the urge to run, he walked quickly and hitched up. Getting in line his was the seventh buggy out. *This is really good. They will all be looking.* He swelled with feelings of deep accomplishment. *I'm pulling out with the most beautiful girl in the county. In the whole Amish world, maybe.* He took deep breaths to control his increasing excitement. Sarah was coming.

She stood by the kitchen door, waiting. Noticing that Lamar had gone out quickly, she knew he would soon be up. Years of this sort of experiences with fathers, brothers, and boyfriends provided Amish girls with impeccable timing.

Sarah noticed that several of the girls were looking at her out of the corners of their eyes. The looks were not exactly friendly. She should have felt angry with them, she thought. Even by the strictest Amish standards, she was doing nothing wrong. Instead, however, she felt sympathy with them. This surprised her as much as had her sorrow earlier when she had seen Malinda's obviously tear-streaked face. *Something isn't right here. But what is it?*

Sarah's thoughts were then interrupted by the approaching buggies. None of the girls said a word. No words were required. They were experts at identifying buggies, even in the dark.

He's the seventh one. He only has his lower lights on. Sarah was grateful. It was an expression of consideration of her that she appreciated.

The door opened to let each girl out when her ride was even with the walks. Sarah stepped out when it was her turn. In the dim light of the windows lit by lanterns, she looked like any Amish girl. Watching her coming, Lamar knew better. He could not have been happier.

Each buggy turned its wheels slightly to let in the girls. Lamar had done the same. Sarah nimbly jumped in. This was no meager feat in the dark, as a slip off the narrow step could send a girl flying under the buggy in a crumpled mass of clothing.

"Good evening," Lamar greeted her.

"Hi," she returned sweetly. He fairly glowed in the dark as they took off.

On the way home they chatted about the usual Amish

news and events. Sarah's aunt was sick in Pennsylvania. Lamar had heard of rumors of drought before winter set in. It was not until they had reached Sarah's home and were settled on the couch that she broached the subject uppermost on her mind.

"I have something I need to ask you," she cleared her throat.

"Really?" He raised his eyebrows. "Is it that serious?"

"I guess it depends on how you take it."

"Oh," and with that she now had his full attention.

"You remember that boy you asked me about?"

"The English boy?" Lamar said the word with disdain.

"Yes."

"What about him?"

"Well, I asked Mrs. Florence. She knows him. He is a friend of her son. But that's not really what I want to ask you about."

"Why not? That is what's important."

"No, it isn't." Sarah looked at him. "Mrs. Florence has invited me on a trip to New York."

"Is that boy involved in this?"

Sarah blushed a little, to her own discomfort, simply from the look he was giving her, "Not really, although we might meet him."

"I knew it." Lamar felt all his fears descend upon him again like a ton of falling bricks. "You do know this boy."

"I do not. You have nothing to fear, really. It's just a trip she's taking me on next week. We will be back by Monday."

"Leaving that soon? You sure don't wait around, do you?"

"Your jealousy is not becoming," she told him.

Her words hit him like a slap on the face. He glared at her, at which she burst out laughing. "It's not funny," he pronounced, completely disarmed.

"Don't look like that then."

"I'm not looking like anything."

"Yes, you are."

"I am not."

"This is silly of you, arguing with me. You don't even know how you looked."

"Yes, I do. You think I looked jealous."

She looked at him intently. "Are you jealous?"

"Of course I am, and you would be, too, in my position."

"Well, I'm not a boy, but I think you shouldn't be."

His face darkened. "I don't like it. You have no business tripping off to New York with some strange boy hanging around."

"You have seen him?" she asked without embarrassment.

This did not help his frame of mind. "Look, I don't like this conversation. I don't want you going to New York."

"Is he handsome?" she asked teasingly, ignoring his pronouncement.

"I wish you wouldn't go," he was pleading now. "I don't want to lose you."

"It's just a trip to New York. I am coming back, you know."

"It's too dangerous. You might decide to stay."

She laughed heartily. "I don't think so. Don't you have any confidence in me?"

"You shouldn't be going."

"You don't trust me, do you?"

"No," he came right out and said it.

She looked at him for a long time, her blue eyes focused on his face until he squirmed in discomfort. "You should trust me, you know."

"We will see about that when you come back. Since you

are apparently going, even if I don't like it." His lower lip quivered.

Feeling sorry for him, she changed the subject, but neither of them reached any level of comfort for the rest of the evening. A little after eleven she glanced at the clock, and he followed her gaze and got the message. "You ought to be going," she said it anyway.

Unaccustomed to being dismissed by a girl in this manner, he fumbled for his hat which he had left in the buggy. "I guess I should. Can I see you after you come back from New York?"

She nodded her head. "We need to talk some more about this."

"Sunday night?" he asked, hoping for some good news.

"Sunday night," she said, opening the door for him.

He stepped outside and off the porch. Swallowed up by the darkness after she shut the door, he found his way down the walk. *At least she waited to shut the door until I was off the porch. I can't lose her. Just hold on, old boy, she'll come around.*

He found his buggy in the darkness, untied the horse and was off into the night. When he got out of sight of her driveway, he turned on all his lights. Like a living Christmas tree he rode down the road. *That will teach her! Let the whole world see me going home from Sarah Schwartz's house.*

❧

Sarah bustled around the next few days preparing for her trip on Wednesday every spare moment she had. There were still the regular household duties to do. No one thought to excuse her from them just because she was going to New York City. Martha, for her part, was clearly resentful and on the prowl to make trouble for Sarah.

"Why does she get to do this stuff?" she raised the question with Deborah.

"Because she has the chance, I guess."

"It's not fair."

"You weren't invited."

"That's why," Martha insisted, "it's still not fair. Has someone got something against me? Am I to be punished just because I was born second?"

"Of course not." Deborah was rapidly tiring of this conflict.

Martha's campaign against her was beginning to have an effect, Sarah could tell, with her next line of attack. "What if the ministers found out about this? Would they like it? Someone like Bloh Jonas, you know how conservative he is. What would he say, if someone dropped a little word, you know? Besides, he will find out sometime anyway."

Deborah paled, "I hadn't really thought of that."

Martha, seeing her opening, quickly followed up. "I really think Dad should go over and ask Bishop Amos what he thinks. He can still ask the other ministers. If they can't decide so quickly, maybe Sarah should put this off until they can make up their minds."

Deborah did not know what to say, Sarah could tell. She also knew she'd better do something quickly, or the whole trip would unravel. The footing had gotten mighty swampy, mighty fast. "I have an idea," she said, pausing to catch her breath. What the idea was, she was not sure, but it had better be good, whatever it was.

"I have an idea," she started out again. "Why, yes, that's it. Martha can come along, too. I would like that," she added to complete her counterattack.

Deborah looked at her. "Well, that would solve some of the problems, I guess. What do you think, Martha?"

Martha's mouth was open. "Ah, I guess so. I hadn't thought of that."

"What about Mrs. Florence, though?" Deborah's asked. "We can't just plan this without her permission."

"I'll go ask her," Sarah said confidently. "She won't mind."

"Okay," Deborah said, "do it quickly, though, or Martha will have no time to pack. Oh, help us, how are we going to get ready? It's already late in the day, and you are leaving on Wednesday morning."

"Let me find out," Sarah told both of them. Martha was still standing there with her mouth half open. "I'll be right back."

Half running, half walking down to the phone shack, she dialed the number. Rebecca answered, listened, thought for a minute, and declared it a grand idea. "Thanks so much," Sarah told her. "We'll be ready Wednesday morning."

"I'll be there," Rebecca told her handing up the phone. *Strange people these Amish. They change plans at the drop of the hat. Mighty strange.*

Sarah arrived back at the house with her news, and packing took on an added sense of urgency. Martha was going, too. Having gotten over her surprise, she had sense enough to be embarrassed.

"You don't have to take me," she told Sarah when they were alone.

"Hey, I like the idea," Sarah told her, because now she really did. "It will be fun to have you along."

Martha gave her a hug. "You are a great sister, you know. Thanks for taking me along."

"You're welcome. Now let's get our chores done so we can pack."

That evening Sarah opened her drawer looking for clothing to pack. Her eyes settled on the partly covered jar of facial cream from the unknown friend. *Hey, this would be good to take along. Use it in the English world. English product for the English world.* She smiled at her own thoughts and dropped the jar into her suitcase.

CHAPTER SEVENTEEN

THEIR SUITCASES WERE ready and waiting by the front door and Sarah and Martha were listening for car tires on the gravel.

"There she is," Martha heard it first.

"We're off," Sarah announced in the direction of the kitchen.

Deborah hurried out to say goodbye. "Now take good care, girls. The money I gave you is for food and gifts only. Remember not to pay your own way. That was the deal."

"Yes, Mother," Sarah assured her, "we will be taken care of."

"Let's go, let's go, let's go," Martha urged from the open front door. "She's here!"

Deborah stood and watched them go down the walk and load their suitcases into Mrs. Florence's car. *My two girls, heading for the big city. I hope they aren't damaged while they are gone. Surely not, it's just a few days.*

Rebecca made sure she waved before climbing back into the vehicle. "It's awfully nice of your mom to let you go," she told the girls.

"She didn't mind," Martha said confidently.

"Not even a little?" Rebecca wondered.

"I think she did, more than she showed," Sarah spoke up, "but we got to go, so here we are."

"I'm actually going to New York," Martha pronounced, "*Vee en die veld* (how in the world) did that happen?"

Rebecca chuckled, "English girls, English. You can't be talking like that on this trip."

"Oh, I'm sorry," said Martha, "I'll try to be more careful."

Rebecca chuckled again, "Is that hard to do?"

Both girls nodded. "When we are with each other, we just speak our own language without thinking," Sarah explained.

"Especially when we have secrets," Martha added.

"Well, we may have to settle for translations then on this trip, because we will be together till Monday. I will have you back, all safe and sound for your mother, by then."

"By the way," Martha spoke up, "how are we going to get to New York? I never heard anyone say."

"By car, of course," Sarah stated. "How else would we go?"

Rebecca cleared her throat. "Well, we are driving up to Indianapolis and then we will be flying to New York from there." She thought about saying more, but wanted to see how this information was absorbed first. Now, from what she could see of the looks on their faces, she was glad she was breaking the news slowly.

"Flying?" Sarah asked. "We have never flown before. Oh, my, is it too bad?"

Martha, for her part, was on cloud nine. "I can't believe it!" she said, "Not only am I going to New York City, but I am flying on a big plane."

Rebecca almost said something, but changed her mind. Maybe a Cessna Citation 5 was a big plane to an Amish girl. She would wait and see.

A little over two hours later they drove into the long-term airport parking. "We will ride the bus from here, girls," she told them.

Sarah and Martha removed their suitcases and followed Rebecca over to the parking terminal to wait. "Here it comes," Martha commented.

"There are two of them, no three. Why so many?" Sarah wanted to know.

"They are shuttles," Rebecca told them. "A couple run the route for the parking agency, and then some for the airlines and rental car companies. With more than one, the wait is not so long."

"Isn't that expensive?" Sarah wondered out loud.

"It's all figured in the price somewhere, I suppose," Rebecca told her. "I never really thought of it."

A jet thundered over their heads, coming in to land. "It's all expensive, I think," Martha commented. "Don't worry about it, Sarah."

Rebecca smiled, "Here's our ride."

After the shuttle arrived, Rebecca led them through the terminal to the upper level. From there, she pulled a piece of paper from her purse with instructions, and directed them towards Concourse C. Next to the Frontier Airline gate she paused, checked the paper again, then walked up to the single attendant waiting. "Is the plane ready for the Ryan party?"

"Yes, Ma'am. You may board when you are ready."

"That would be now, thank you," Rebecca said and motioned for the girls to follow her.

Walking down steps, the door opened onto the open air of the Indianapolis, Indiana airport docking zone. Before them sat one of the unmarked Cessna Citation 5's owned by "Maxey Jacobs".

"It's not a big plane," Martha said, stopping up short. "It's just a little one."

"I'm sorry you're disappointed," Rebecca told her, "but it's what we're going in."

"Well, that's okay," Martha quickly assured her. "A big one would have been nice, but this works too."

"You ought to be thankful," Sarah chided her.

Rebecca chuckled, "You girls are a strange sort, aren't you? I guess this way it won't be going to your heads."

Both of them looked at Rebecca with questions in their eyes, but she simply headed for the ramp. Rebecca did not feel like explaining this one.

"I guess we're supposed to follow," Martha said, putting words into action. Sarah followed her up the ramp. At the top they were shown seats and instructed to buckle in. Fifteen minutes later they were airborne.

"It's not too bad," Sarah told Martha.

"Of course, I never thought it would be anything else," Martha replied. "This is great, even if it isn't a big plane."

"You like it?" Rebecca asked them from across the aisle, clouds visible from her window.

Both girls hung on to their seats as the plane bounced slightly in turbulence, but nodded their heads in affirmation.

"So, shall we plan what we will be seeing in New York?" Rebecca got a small paper tablet out of her purse. "What would you definitely like to see?"

"The Empire State Building," announced Martha, "then the Statue of Liberty. I want to see the top of it. Then ride the ferry to Staten Island."

"Okay," Rebecca made some notes, "what about you, Sarah?"

"When are we meeting Phillip?" she asked.

Martha looked at her with her mouth open as Rebecca replied, "We are going to the offices tomorrow."

Martha found her voice. "Wait a minute, wait a minute. You are meeting a boy? An English boy in New York? What is going on here, Sarah?"

Rebecca grinned, which did not help matters much as far as Martha was concerned.

"It's nothing," Sarah told her sister, looking calmly at her.

"Come on now, don't do that to me. What is going on? Sarah tell me, and tell me right now. Does Mom know about this? What about Lamar?"

"Calm down," Sarah told her, "I can explain."

"That's what they all say," Martha said sarcastically. "You had better start explaining real fast."

"It's like this," Sarah started, and was interrupted by Rebecca.

"Why don't I just tell her, since you are not really at fault in this?"

"Fine with me."

Martha was glaring at both of them. "I can't believe this conspiracy by the two of you! What are you doing anyway? Is this why I was not to come along? Are you leaving the Amish, Sarah?"

Sarah laughed out loud but Rebecca held up her hand, "Let me start at the beginning." She drew in a long breath and settled back in her seat. "Your sister visited me that first time, you remember?" Martha nodded. "While she was there, my son, Marcus, saw her, and mentioned her to his friend, Phillip."

This was too much for Martha, who exclaimed, "That doesn't explain anything, it just makes it worse!"

Rebecca continued her explanation, "Phillip manages a women's design company, 'Maxey Jacobs', which also models their own lines of clothing. It seems like Marcus and Phillip think Sarah would make an excellent model."

"A model, an English model?"

"I guess you could put it that way. I have never heard of an Amish model."

"She has seen this Phillip?" Martha asked.

"No."

"Then how does Phillip know she would make a good model? She looks ordinary enough to me."

"I don't know, unless he is going by Marcus's opinion.

"Anybody else's?"

"Well, maybe mine, too."

"But not Sarah's?"

"Of course not. She would never suggest something like that. You ought to know your sister better than that."

"I see." Martha was still glaring at them. "So this whole thing is about Sarah taking a job modeling for this company?"

"No, no," Rebecca hurried to say, "it's not just that."

"Then what is it?"

Rebecca took a long breath again. *Why did we bring her along*? "There is the trip, the sightseeing, and Phillip does want to meet her. Maybe take some photos tomorrow. From there, no one really knows. There is no commitment or anything like that." Suddenly, Rebecca had a moment of inspiration. "Phillip even came down one evening from New York, just trying to find Sarah. That's how badly he wants to see her."

Martha's mouth was open again. "An English boy, trying to see an Amish girl? Now I have heard everything! Did he manage to? Seeing Sarah, I mean? With all else she's pulling off, maybe she's dating him on the sly!"

"I told you, I have never met him." This came from Sarah.

"Why didn't you tell him where she lives?" Martha directed this to Rebecca.

"I didn't think it appropriate, plus I didn't want to do anything your sister would not approve of."

"So you asked her?"

"No, not directly, at least."

"Has Phillip got more in mind than just modeling photos?"

"He hasn't told me."

"Martha," Sarah exclaimed, "stop asking these questions."

Slowly a smile spread over Martha's face. "Whose plane is this?"

"Phillip's. Well, the Company's, probably," Rebecca told her, both of them ignoring Sarah.

"It's a private plane, then?"

"Yes," Rebecca nodded, looking inquisitively.

Turning to Sarah, Martha exclaimed, "Do you know what that means, Sarah? We are flying in a private plane!"

"Ya," Sarah muttered under her breath, the realization dawning fast, "here we thought it was just a small one." She blushed and turned to Rebecca. "We apologize, Mrs. Florence. We certainly did not intend to be ungrateful."

"It's nothing," Rebecca waved her hand slightly. "Phillip volunteered to make these arrangements. If it means so much to him, I would not worry about it."

"He's not expecting payment or something else, is he?" Sarah was worried now.

"No," Rebecca assured her, "nothing like that, I can assure you."

Martha finally found her voice again. "Sarah, do you really know what all this means?"

"Not really."

"It's your chance for great things. A model, Sarah, just think about that. What an opportunity!"

"You would do this?" Sarah questioned her sister.

"Well, I guess I would have to see the boy first, but yes, most certainly."

"Look, I'm not interested," Sarah informed her.

"So you're just going to stick with that loser, Lamar?"

"He's not a loser," Sarah said quietly.

"By the way, does he know all this?" Martha asked.

"Some of it."

"About Phillip?"

"Yes."

"Good, I'm glad. Let him stew in his juices. Worthless little nubbin. This one has a private plane."

"Don't say such things," Sarah said without much feeling in her voice.

Martha smiled, sitting back in her seat with a look of great expectation on her face. *What does this Phillip look like? My sister gets all the breaks. Well, let us at least enjoy them with her, even if she doesn't have enough sense to take advantage of them.*

Rebecca drew another long breath, glad the crisis seemed over. *These Amish people sure do create enough excitement!* Outside the clouds had cleared, leaving a huge expanse of clear blue sky. "We should be there soon," she observed. Neither girl responded, each apparently lost in her own thoughts.

Chapter Eighteen

BACK HOME, MALINDA's conscience was working with a vengeance. *What if something bad really did happen to Sarah? Could you live with yourself? How would you feel? Can you claim to be a Christian and take things into your own hands like this? Shut-up*, she snapped. It did no good. She had wrestled all night with these questions and fears and awoke bleary-eyed and sleepy. Something would have to be done, she knew. Her mother could only be expected to overlook this behavior for so long. Soon she would start to suspect that more was involved than her missing Lamar. Love could not be used as an excuse but so long in the Amish world.

You'd better go confess. It's best that way. Clear yourself of your guilt. Save Sarah quickly before she uses whatever is in that jar. Do something, and do it now. No, I won't lose him. If I give up now, I'll never get him back. It can't be like that. How will I live without Lamar? Please God, I was made for him. I know it. It can't be. It just can't be. She would have burst out in crying, but she felt like she was all cried out.

She left her room and went downstairs. Her mother would want to start canning peaches this afternoon. It was a little late in the day for that, but Malinda had just heard a truck pull in. The driver was long overdue with the scheduled drop-off. He came from the large fruit market in Washington that serviced several Amish families with their fruit orders. Naomi had called her order in two days ago, and was assured the route would be run early, as several other Amish families had also ordered peaches. Now it was almost noon.

As her feet touched the stairs, a fresh stab of pain hit her heart. Holding back the tears, she kept going. The afternoon and evening work would stretch well into the night she was sure.

You'd better confess rang in her head. *I won't. I can't lose him.* If this went on much longer she would go mad. Of this she was sure. *God help me? What am I going to do?*

⁂

The Cessna Citation 5 circled for landing over LaGuardia. "New York City," Rebecca told them.

"It's quite a city," Sarah observed, having watched the skyline for the past few minutes. She sat back in her seat as the pilot gently brought the small plane in for the landing.

"Yes, it is," Rebecca agreed. "Not some place I would want to live or work in, but it's quite something." The wheels touched down, bouncing slightly. "Here we are."

"Where are we staying for the night?" Martha wanted to know.

"The Beekman Tower Hotel," Rebecca told her, "will be our home for the next few days."

Martha made no comment, but Sarah looked expectantly. "That's close to the United Nations building. A lot of dignitaries use it, don't they? Sure we can afford the price?"

"Thankfully, none of us are paying for it," Rebecca grinned. "Just enjoy your stay. That's my advice. Such an opportunity might never come your way again."

Martha turned her nose up in Sarah's direction. "Think you know a lot? Then you ought to be smart enough to take advantage of your chance while you have it."

"I am," Sarah told her.

"I don't think so. Just think, Sarah, you could have this life all the time."

Rebecca smiled at these continued open exchanges. *They seem to have no problem letting people into their lives.* The conversation continued.

"I'm not leaving the Amish, and neither should you be thinking about it."

"How can I not think about it? Look around you, what a life this would be. Leave little weasel Lamar to his horse and buggy, Sarah. You can have the stars."

Sarah chuckled, "It's not all that it seems to be. Ask Rebecca if you don't believe me."

Martha turned to Rebecca, "Is it true?"

"Hey, I'm staying out of this," Rebecca told her emphatically. "I'm just the tour guide."

"There you go," Martha turned back to Sarah. "She likes her life."

"I'm sure she does," Sarah replied, "and so do I."

"I can't believe the girl," Martha muttered. "If I were offered this much, I sure would take it." Sarah only smiled while Martha was thinking. *Maybe she'll fall for the boy tomorrow. We haven't seen him yet. That's it. Once she sees him, she'll change her mind.*

"Quit looking at me," Sarah told Martha. "We need to go." Which was true, as Rebecca was already rising from her seat. In front, the plane door had been opened and a ramp appeared, rolled up by a little push-cart driven by a uniformed attendant.

They walked through the airport, collected their bags and caught a taxi outside the terminal by the sidewalk.

"Three Mitchell Place, the Beekman," Rebecca told the driver. He nodded and they were off, weaving in and out of traffic.

"Is this safe?" Sarah wanted to know. "Seems like we are going to crash at any minute."

"It's New York City," Rebecca told her. "If you look out your windows, there is Astoria Park on either side of us, a quite beautiful little park. Ahead is the Triborough Bridge."

"A park in the middle of the city?" Martha wanted to know.

"Yes, that's New York City for you. Central Park, in the center of Manhattan, is even larger."

"I will have to see that," Sarah spoke up. "It's more than 800 acres in size and takes up 6% of the island's land mass."

"Maybe you also know where we will be having supper?" Martha asked wryly. "I'm starving."

Sarah grinned, "How would I know that?"

"I don't know," Martha retorted, "I just thought you might have some useful information in that head of yours."

"Ah," Rebecca cleared her throat, "I'll show you in a minute."

The taxi driver was making a left hand turn off East 38th Street on to 1st Avenue. He then turned right onto East 50th street, a right on Beekman, another right on to Mitchell, and there it was, the Beekman Tower Hotel. The multi-columned face of the building with its lower-level oval windows stretched upwards for 26 stories. "Up there is where we are having supper."

"On the roof?" Martha exclaimed.

"Not really," Rebecca laughed, "there is a restaurant up there. Sort of on the roof, but with a roof on it."

Martha looked up as they climbed out. Neither girl said anything as they walked through the center door, its oval transom matching a set of windows on each side. Before them was the front lounge, its centerpiece a light gray couch done in modern décor. Wall-mounted glass fixtures were on either side of the couch flanked by two dark-blue sofas. An oval tile configuration made up the entrance with light-colored, angled hardwood floors joining from either side.

Both girls glanced nervously around, and Rebecca noticed their discomfort. "We're Amish," Martha exclaimed involuntarily, as if that explained everything.

"No one is looking. You're not that unusual," Rebecca assured her. When they looked skeptically at her, she added, "It's New York City. You can and will see any and everything in this city."

"That seems to be the explanation for everything around here."

"Almost," Rebecca chuckled.

Walking up to the front deck, she told the girl behind the desk, "Three rooms for the Ryan party."

"Certainly," the girl told her. Punching her computer keys, she announced, "Your rooms are on the tenth floor. Enjoy your stay."

"Thank you." Rebecca took computer card keys from the receptionist and looked around.

"The elevators are over there," the girl pointed. "Let us know if you need anything."

"I'm sure we will be fine," Rebecca told her.

Finding the elevators, they got off at the tenth floor, found their rooms, and settled in. If that is what it could be called. Sarah and Martha were both half afraid to move around lest they damage the artwork or the obviously expensive furniture.

"Makes you lonesome for the barn," Sarah commented dryly.

"I could get used to this," Martha decided.

Rebecca interrupted them, "You don't have to worry. This place is pet-friendly. It ought to be Amish-friendly, don't you think? Now, stop worrying. It's time to go for dinner."

Walking back to the elevators, they rode up with several other people who had also punched the 26th floor button. Once on top, they followed instructions and waited to be seated. Escorted to a table, they were given one with an open skyline view. Before them, the setting sun was beginning to color the sky. The financial district of Manhattan lay to the south with what was clearly Central Park to the Northwest.

"Do you like this now?" Martha asked Sarah.

"It's nice," she replied.

"Nice enough to stay here all the time, with someone you know?"

Sarah said nothing, looking out over the city, obviously thinking. She was still thinking when the waiter arrived with the menu. "Drinks?" he asked.

"Just water," they all said.

He looked somewhat disconcerted.

"He was surprised," Martha whispered, when he walked away.

"Not for the reason you think," Sarah told her.

"I know," Martha replied. "I just hope he comes back soon to take our orders. This has been a long day."

He was back soon enough and served them three glasses of water. Pulling out his tablet he took their orders. Twenty minutes later, they had their food. The girls ate slowly to savor the moment and the scenery of the city below them.

Riding back down the elevator after they were done, Rebecca suggested they get up at seven for breakfast. "That way we can get downtown by nine."

Both girls nodded, not really caring right now what time they got up. It had been a very full day of strange and new experiences and they were ready for bed.

"I will have the wake-up call for seven then," Rebecca told them.

They both nodded, not sure what that meant. A wake-up call was usually a holler up the stairs, but it was apparent other methods would be used here.

"It's a phone call to wake you," Rebecca told them as she recognized their questioning looks. "The phone is right beside your bedside. Good-night."

"Good-night," they said together, turning to go into their rooms.

"I'm here," Martha said. "Yours is the next door."

"I think so," Sarah agreed, running her card through the slide by the door she was standing in front of. The lock clicked open. "Yup," she said, "this is the right one."

❧

For Malinda, the evening was not going well. The peach canning made everything run late. It was ten by the time the last pressure cooker had boiled and cooled off. Her head still pounded furiously with anxiety. *How can I live through another night of this?*

Confess, the answer came. *Tell your sins to God and to the ones you have wronged.*

I can't. I'll lose him. Desperate to get away from people, she was finished cleaning the kitchen by eleven and she disappeared into her room. Throwing herself on the bed, the battle raged within her. Her conscience had a firm grip, and would not let go. *You have to tell. Clear yourself. You can't live a happy life with Lamar if something happens to Sarah.*

In the sheer agony of the struggle she got down and rolled on the floor, a pathetic figure, sobbing into her pillow to hide the noise from anyone else in the house. Finally, around midnight she had enough of it. *Okay I'll do it.*

All the energy drained out of her at the thought. The

years without Lamar stretched out in front of her as clearly as if she were looking at County Road 600 in the broad day-light. She would have to go on alone in life, no doubt an old maid, pitied and pampered, and the subject of secret disdain. Fresh sobs racked her body, as she pressed her face into the pillow.

She steeled herself to go on. *I have to do it, though. There is no other way out. I'll go in the morning. Please God, don't let anything happen before I get there.*

The big Ben rang out a single dong downstairs as Malinda climbed wearily back into bed and drifted off into troubled sleep. Her heart, though, felt its first peace since this troublesome problem began.

CHAPTER NINETEEN

A S HAD BEEN arranged, the wake-up call came at seven. Both Sarah and Martha lifted the ringing phones in their rooms, "Hello." *Who could be calling me in New York?* When there was no answer, they glanced at the clocks beside the beds, and put two and two together.

Rebecca insisted on breakfast at the *Zephyr Grill*, also on the *Beekman Tower* site. "The desk clerk told me it is excellent."

"Someplace we can pronounce would be fine with us," Sarah told her. "I am sure it would be cheaper."

"Money is not my concern right now," Rebecca replied. "Besides, with the taxi fare, any other place would be even higher."

"I see," Martha said, not used to such calculations when considering breakfast.

They had to admit that breakfast was, indeed excellent, with eggs any way you wished, and bacon or ham done up in ways no Amish person would have thought of.

By eight thirty, they were back in their rooms and Rebecca called for a taxi. Out on the street, they climbed in. "Eighty Pine Street", she told the driver.

You have a building number?" he asked, barely looking up as they rode down Mitchell.

"1-1-5-3-8-3."

The driver noted the number on his pad, still looking down all the time he was writing.

"Kind of dangerous driving," Sarah commented again, the situation making a fresh impression on her.

"New York City," Rebecca muttered.

"I think I'll be using that at home when I need a good excuse," Martha said dryly.

"It just might work," Rebecca chuckled, turning towards them. "I have a suggestion for when we arrive at the offices."

Both girls looked at her attentively.

"See, Phillip has never seen Sarah. He also does not know that Martha is coming along. How about if Sarah just hangs back a bit when we come to his floor? Then I will introduce Martha as Sarah."

"What is this supposed to do?" Martha asked skeptically.

"It will surprise him."

"How will he be surprised?"

Rebecca cleared her throat, suddenly seeing the pitfall of her suggestion. Why she had not seen it earlier she was not sure. "He will think," she started, but just could not say it, now wishing desperately for a way out of this.

Sarah was looking out the taxi window apparently unsure how to help. It was Martha herself who came to her aid. "I understand. I'm not as good-looking as Sarah. He will think you have all been selling him a lame horse when he sees me."

"I'm sorry," said Rebecca with sincerity in her voice, "it was most unkind of me. You really are good-looking, too, Martha."

"But not as good-looking as Sarah," Martha replied. "Look, you don't have to apologize. I understand. It doesn't hurt my feelings. Sure, I don't get chances like Sarah does, but maybe that is just as well. She seems to handle such situations better than I do. By all means, let's have some fun with this boy. It might do him some good."

"Are you sure?" Now it was Rebecca who was skeptical.

"Sure."

"What about you, Sarah?" Rebecca asked. "Are you okay with this?"

She grinned. "Martha will love it. She's real good at this kind of thing."

"Then let's do it," Rebecca said as she quickly went over some more details with them as they arrived at 80 Pine Street.

The building towered in the sky above them. Two-thirds of the way up the glass-sided complex, three tiers stair-stepped inwards. All around them were high-rise buildings of various sizes and shapes. They cast long shadows in the early morning sun.

"It's hard to see the sun from down here," Sarah commented.

"Here's where the money is made," Rebecca replied, "over there is the Trump Building and Wall Street Plaza."

"You have to marry this guy," Martha whispered to Sarah.

"Be quiet," she told her. "I haven't even met him."

Rebecca paid the taxi driver and they entered through the glass doors. Leading them over to the elevators, Rebecca consulted her instructions before the doors opened. Entering, she punched in the 25th floor. With a soft sucking sound they were on their way up.

"Now remember what to do when we get there," Rebecca told them. "You, Sarah, stay out of sight the best you can."

Malinda told Naomi she needed to visit the Schwartz's home that morning.

"Why right now?" Naomi wanted to know.

"Because it's important."

"You'll have to do better than that," Naomi said, looking intently at her daughter.

"I need to talk to Sarah."

Naomi looked at her. "You're going to try to talk Sarah out of dating Lamar or something? That would be really dumb."

"No, I wouldn't so something like that."

"The way you've been acting lately, I don't know anymore. You seem to be a person who would do almost anything."

Malinda was at a loss to know what to do now. If she did not say more, Naomi would not let her go. If she did tell more, it might just make matters worse. "I have to tell her I'm sorry for something I did," she tried.

"It can't wait until Sunday?"

"No," Malinda sighed. "I wish it could, but it can't. I need to talk to her this morning."

Naomi shrugged her shoulders. "If you hurry, it shouldn't take too long. I suppose you're not having a long talk once you get there."

"No, I'm not."

"Then go."

With that Malinda hitched up the horse and left. Each clop of the horse's hooves now weighed heavily on her. She felt tears welling up inside her, but she held them back. *I've got to stop thinking about Lamar, or I will cry. He's gone anyway, now.* She hardened her resolve and slapped the horse's reins.

Arriving at the driveway, she pulled in, tied the horse at the hitching rail and walked up the steps. *He's been here, with her. Right down these walks. Kissing her, I'm sure. God, how am I going to be able to bear this?* She took a deep breath, stepped up on the front porch and knocked.

Thankful that Deborah answered, she asked in a shaky voice, "Can I speak with Sarah?"

"Oh, my, you don't know?" Deborah told her.

Malinda paled and covered her mouth with her hand, "Oh, no!" The world started to swim around her. *It's already done. It's over.*

Deborah looked closely at her. *The girl is clearly troubled. I guess she's still taking this whole thing with Lamar hard.* "Sarah's in New York City. Martha's with her, too."

Slowly the words penetrated Malinda's consciousness, "They are in New York City?"

"Yes," Deborah stated with pleasure in her voice, "they will be back on Monday."

Malinda, struggling to recover, was at a complete loss as to what course of action to take now. "I guess I will talk to her when she comes back," she finally managed.

Deborah looked sharply at her again. *The girl is downright pale. I'm surprised Naomi lets her wander about in such a condition.* "That will be fine," she stated. "I will tell her you want to talk to her."

Malinda nodded, taking her leave, and headed back out to the buggy. When she arrived back home, she told Naomi that Sarah and Martha were visiting in New York City. "I will have to go back later," she managed to get out, now thoroughly frightened of what might happen between now and Monday.

Naomi thought of asking her what was troubling her, but decided against it. Saying apologies could be hard, but this one looked like a big one to her. *I hope she hasn't gone and done something really bad.*

The elevator doors opened onto the 25th floor. Rebecca and Martha walked straight towards the desk in front of them. Sarah kept her face turned sideways and moved away to the right. "Good morning," Rebecca said as they approached.

"Good morning, the girl behind the desk said, looking at them with a bland expression on her face.

"We are looking for Phillip Ryan," Rebecca told her.

"You have an appointment?"

"Sort of. Tell him Rebecca Florence is here."

"Oh, so you are Rebecca? I'm Camellia," she said extending her hand. "I believe we have spoken on the phone."

"That we have," Rebecca replied.

"I will get Phillip," she said, pausing to give Martha a long look from top to bottom. A slight smile spread across her face as she turned to go. *So this is the great Amish beauty? Not too bad, but no danger. I'm afraid the little twerp has been greatly overrated. Congratulate yourself, Ms. Camellia! You can do better than that.*

By now, in front of Phillip's office door, she knocked and opened it all in one motion. "Mrs. Rebecca Florence is here to see you."

She felt like slapping him for the look of delight that came across his face. At the same time the feeling of smugness was still in her stomach. *Wait until he sees her face, the little farm creature. A beauty? Right? How stupid to think that someone from there could make it in New York City.*

"I'll be right out," he said.

"He's coming." She took her seat ready to enjoy the show when Phillip saw this girl.

Phillip came out of his office. He had the well-kempt look of an attractive New York executive. His hair had been cut the day before, his blue eyes were shining, and his nose was accented by his chiseled face. Martha's mouth dropped open. "Oh, my," she said, her hand flying to her face.

Camellia grinned in satisfaction. *Falling all over herself. Clearly out of her depth.*

Phillip offered his hand, turning his head slightly to the side. "Phillip Ryan," he said, "and you are Sarah?"

Martha could not bring herself to carry this any further. This boy was any girl's dream. She could not hurt him. "No," she said, "I am Martha. Sarah is over there." She pointed to where Sarah was standing with her back turned.

Hearing Martha make the switch this soon surprised Sarah, but turning around she followed her lead. Had it not been for the company present, Camellia would have used barnyard language. Phillip shook his head slightly as if to clear it. Before him stood a girl who, even without makeup and with having that white thing on her head, was stunning. Her face radiated warmth in a way he was not used to seeing. Walking towards her, he said the first words that popped into his mind, "You are an angel!"

"I'm afraid not," she told him, laughing softly, "but I'm glad to meet you. I hear you were looking for me the other night?"

He searched for words, while Camellia ground her teeth in fury. *Sweeping him right off his feet. She can have anything she wants now.*

Phillip found his voice, "Yes, I did. I ran into some boys who didn't want me there, but I survived alright, I guess."

"One of them was my boyfriend," Sarah told him simply.

Martha cringed. *Don't be telling him you have a boyfriend. You can get rid of the creep.*

Camellia brightened up. *She has a boyfriend.* Then darkened again. *She'll dump him for this.*

"Well, I'm sorry for the trouble I caused," Phillip said with genuine emotion. "I really meant no harm. I suppose Rebecca has told you about what I wanted?"

"Yes, she did."

"What do you think of it?"

"I'm not sure."

"I see." Phillip was not sure where to go from here. "Would you consider doing a few test photos? Just to see. It would tell us if we are on to something. Might answer some questions if nothing else."

Sarah seemed to hesitate. Martha felt like screaming at her. *Don't throw away your chance.* "That would be okay," decided Sarah. "I owe you that much for all you are doing on this trip."

"Now, now," Phillip's face turned red, "that's not why I am doing this. If you say 'no', then that is okay, too."

"Let's do it," Sarah told him. "I would like to know, too."

Martha beamed. *Good girl. She'll like him yet.*

Camellia scowled but she was careful that no one was looking at her when she did.

Chapter Twenty

"COME UP TO the next floor, and I will show you what we have." Phillip told them, "Our latest line for this year is still fresh. We'll take the stairs. It's only one floor and faster than the elevator."

Leading the way, he made sure Sarah was beside him, while Martha and Rebecca followed. Camellia stayed at her desk. "So what do you think of New York City?"

"It is very nice," she said, smiling. "You really didn't have to do all this for us."

"Oh, it is my pleasure," he assured her.

Coming to the top of the stairs, he swung open the glass doors for Sarah, and then waited until Martha and Rebecca had entered. "This," he said with a motion of his hand, "is some of what we have."

Before them were racks of dresses and pant suits. "All women's clothing. I know they look better on the models, but you can get some idea as they are. This is a light gray outfit, matching slacks, blouse, shirt, with and without a scarf."

Sarah and Martha nodded their heads. "Here is another light gray, in a dress this time, frilly border, knee-length, sleeveless with a high top. Over here is a light brown dress, more casual, full high top collar, belt, and the break on the front. This is a black leather jacket, open in the front with a gray blouse and slight scarf, black slacks, with high top stringed boots. What do you think?"

The girls only nodded. "Then this is what I would like you to try on, Sarah. We will take a few test shots and see what happens. Okay?" he held up a dark blue mid-calf skirt, wide black belt, long-sleeved, dark gray, plain blouse with ruffled neckline. "Try this on," he held it towards her, "The changing rooms are over there. The girls will help you, and then the photographer will be in. Over there by the mirrors," he pointed.

Sarah took the offered clothing, not sure what to say. "Do it," Martha whispered from behind her.

"How can I?" she whispered back.

Martha made a face before Phillip turned around. "Is there a problem?" he asked.

Sarah made her mind up quickly. "Oh, no. Where are the rooms?"

"Over there," he said. "It says 'dressing rooms' on them. We will wait here."

Walking towards the other end of the floor, Sarah wondered how she was going to get into this clothing. As if in answer to her question, two attendants appeared, summoned by Phillip on his cell, unbeknownst to Sarah. They showed no surprise that an Amish girl would be modeling one of Maxey Jacob's dresses.

It's New York City, she told herself.

"Let's see what we can do," the lead attendant said, taking the dress from her.

"Makeup, maybe?" the other asked her partner, ignoring Sarah.

"Ah, no," Sarah said forcefully, inserting herself into the conversation.

"Excuse me?" the first girl looked curiously at her.

"No makeup," Sarah told her.

"As you wish. At least some facial cream, though. It softens the skin."

Sarah nodded her head, "I have some along." Opening her purse, she produced the jar of Pond's scented face cream that had been given to her by Malinda. "Will this work?"

The girl took the jar, cocked her head to the side and then opened it. She sniffed it, holding her nose directly above the jar. "Smell this." She held the jar out for the other girl. "It smells old or something," she said. "No offense, Ma'am." She addressed this to Sarah.

The second girl took the jar and smelled it. "I use this kind but this one is more than old. Where did you get this?"

"It was given to me by a friend," Sarah told her.

"Have you used any of it yet?"

"No," Sarah told her.

"It's been tampered with, I would say."

"That's not possible," Sarah told her.

"It can happen, Ma'am. Why don't we find out what's in this jar? Here, take this to Phillip and have him get it tested. People do try to mess with beautiful women's faces."

Taking the jar from her partner, the lead attendant headed towards Phillip. "In the meantime, why don't we get you into this dress?" the girl with Sarah said.

Sarah shrugged, "Fine with me."

Holding the door open, the girl motioned for her to enter the dressing room. Chairs were set along a long table on one side that was filled with lotions and makeup, with mirrors above the table. On the other side were the changing rooms. "Let's start with the lotions for your face and then we will do your hair. The dress comes after that."

Sarah wondered about the hair comment. "You're not cutting it off, are you?"

"No, Ma'am. We'll just brush out what you have. I assume it is long."

"Yes," Sarah nodded, as the door opened and the other girl came back in.

Before she could protest, they removed her white head covering, the hair clips and dropped her hair. Moving her back, they washed, blow-dried and brushed it out to its full silky length. "Now the dress," the lead attendant told her.

Numbly, Sarah took the offered dress to the dressing room to change. When she came out, they made adjustments and pronounced that she was ready to go.

"I'm not going out there," she told them flatly.

"You have to so the photographer can take the photos."

Sarah shook her head firmly, "I'm not going out in front of men."

They looked at each other. "Then we must get rid of the men." Opening the door, the lead attendant left but returned in a minute. "There are no men around now," she announced. "Let's get the photos."

Sarah walked cautiously through the door. Martha's eyes got bigger than saucers when she saw her, "My, you look English," she gushed.

"Don't say it," Sarah replied. "I feel bad enough already."

Leading her over to where the photographer was standing, and giving her instructions, the photos were quickly taken. Ten minutes later, Sarah was back in her Amish clothing and sighing with relief.

"How did it feel?" Martha asked when she came out.

"Really strange," she said.

Phillip reappeared and escorted them back down to the 25th floor. "I will see all of you tonight at the 21 Club Restaurant, then. Is that okay?"

The two girls looked at Rebecca who nodded her head. "We will see you then. By the way, what is the street address?"

"West 52nd Street," he said without looking up from his desk.

On the elevator down it dawned on Sarah what had just transpired. "He is coming tonight to supper with us?"

"Yes," Rebecca replied. "Is there a problem with that?"

"No," Sarah hesitated, "I guess not. There are just so many things happening so fast."

"I understand," Rebecca replied.

On the 25th floor, Phillip was looking at the photos that had just been taken. "What do you think?" the lead attendant asked him.

"As good as any we have," he told her.

"Have you signed her?"

"No," he said, "and I have a feeling we won't be able to, but I will try. It's a real shame."

"It certainly is," she said, chuckling at the look on Camellia's face. Then, for added emphasis, she added, "She's a real beauty."

After spending several hours of the afternoon walking around Times Square with its traffic congestion and brilliant neon signs, Rebecca, Martha, and Sarah arrived that evening at the 21 Club on 52nd Street. They were ushered upstairs where Phillip was already waiting at the table that had been reserved for them. Surrounding him were murals of Times Square and other high-rises of downtown New York City. A large chandelier hung from the ceiling of the 32-seat capacity, upper room of the restaurant, complimented by accented wall lighting.

"Good to see all of you again," he said with a smile, as he rose to his feet. "Please be seated."

No one mentioned it, but Sarah knew what was expected. She took the chair beside Phillip. Martha sat on the other side of him, with Rebecca between the two girls. Not to her surprise, Sarah found the entire experience pleasant.

But that was the problem, at least from her point of view. Martha was smiling from ear to ear.

"Our day has gone well," Rebecca spoke for them all. "I took the girls to Times Square."

Phillip nodded his head and then motioned to the waiter that they were ready to order. "What will it be?" he asked when the menus had been brought over.

Bending over their open folders, Martha and Sarah quickly decided on salad with a chicken filet side for Sarah and fish for Martha. Rebecca ordered the house special, while Phillip asked for the porterhouse steak and a soup appetizer.

When the waiter had left, Phillip turned to Sarah. "The photos turned out great."

Sarah blushed, while Martha asked eagerly, "Have you brought them along?"

"No, but they are really good."

"Good enough to use?" Martha continued.

"Yes."

"Will you?"

Phillip smiled, "We can't do that without Sarah's permission."

"Then I give it," Martha pronounced.

"It's not yours to give," Phillip chuckled. "That is up to Sarah."

"Tell him 'yes', Sarah, please," Martha begged.

Sarah was still red in the face, but she kept her voice from wavering. "I don't think so."

"I thought you might feel that way," Phillip said, "that's why I didn't bring them."

"Are you sure?" Rebecca turned to Sarah.

"I am sure," Sarah stated calmly. "It's best this way. Unless Phillip needs the photos as payment for all the money he has spent on us, but that would be a onetime deal."

Phillip saw his opening, but overcame the urge to take it. "No," he said, "I don't expect repayment. It was my pleasure."

"That is most considerate of you." Sarah was blushing again. Briefly, she wavered, but then held her ground. "Please accept my gratitude for everything," she told him.

"Accepted," he said softly.

Their talk then turned to lighter topics. The girls shared their impressions of New York: a subway ride they had been on today, the masses of people in New York City, and the driving habits of the taxi drivers.

It was not until the end of the evening that Phillip casually mentioned, "By the way, it's good you didn't use any of that cream, Sarah."

"Why is that?" she asked him, lifting her blue eyes to study him. With a pang he felt the full force of her beauty, and somehow felt that he would never get closer than this to her heart.

"The cream had been spiked with sodium hydroxide," he said calmly.

"What is that?" she wanted to know.

"It is a strong chemical used in pulp, paper, and drain cleaner. If you had put any of it on your skin, in a minute or so it would have burned your skin severely before you could have gotten it off."

"Who would have done something like that?" she asked, her mouth now open in amazement.

"Where did you get it?"

"A friend gave it to me."

"Who was this friend?"

"I don't know. It was left on our buggy seat, addressed to me."

"Probably someone who is jealous of you. Do you know anyone like that?"

"No, we are Amish," she said indignantly.

He looked at her closely. "I don't think you're that different from anyone else. You might want to keep your eyes open from now on. It's a good thing our girls caught this."

"Thank you," she told him. "I can't believe this."

"I have turned the matter over to the Pond's people. *Unilever* is the company. They will no doubt be contacting you to investigate whether this was a single case or a more widespread problem."

"You didn't have to do that!" Sarah exclaimed.

"They would have wanted to know," Phillip assured her. "We could be liable if we had not reported an act that might endanger other people."

Sarah had her hand over her mouth. "Oh, my. This is terrible!"

"Just answer their questions when they contact you and I'm sure everything will be okay," Phillip assured her. "Now, please excuse me," he turned to the others, "I must go. I hope you enjoy the rest of your stay in New York City. It has been a pleasure for me."

"We are so thankful for this experience," Martha gushed.

"Thank you," Sarah told him simply.

Rebecca also nodded, "I'll see you in Indiana sometime."

"Good night to you, ladies." He pushed back his chair and was gone.

CHAPTER TWENTY-ONE

Back at the hotel, Martha vented her frustration. "Why did you turn him down, Sarah? You had him eating out of your hand."

"I'm not modeling for him," Sarah stated firmly.

"There might be love involved," Martha raised her eyebrows.

"You really want to know why I can't go there?" Sarah retorted, without glancing at Rebecca who was also in the room. These girls' candor in discussing their problems in front of her still surprised her.

"Yes, I would."

"He believes in divorce," Sarah pronounced without hesitation.

"In divorce? Now what in *tarnation* has that got to do with anything? He's not going to divorce you, even if you would marry him."

Rebecca was all ears as Sarah paused as if to think. "Maybe not, and then maybe he would. I just can't consider marrying someone who has that as an option. Just picture yourself in that condition. Let's say we had a fight, or things got tough. Would you want to be married to someone who just might be thinking that it's too much for him, and he's bailing out on you?"

Martha took that in for a moment and then said, "Now, *that* I hadn't thought of, but at least model for him."

Rebecca thought she had better speak up here. "Ah, I'm sure he doesn't believe in divorce unless there is adultery involved."

Sarah shook her head. "That's still no comfort for me. Even nice people like Phillip can change their minds about marriage."

"I don't think he would," Rebecca assured her. "He's a good Christian man. You really shouldn't let something like that stand in the way of love."

Sarah still shook her head. "There are, of course, our cultural differences, but those could be overcome. He does have quite an attractive lifestyle. It is the fear of divorce that really keeps me from considering him."

"I agree with her on the marriage question," Martha pronounced, for once in agreement with her sister. "But why isn't she considering modeling for him?"

"I don't want to," Sarah stated simply.

"That is your choice, of course," Rebecca replied. "Just be sure about it. You may not get a chance like this again."

"I am sure, at least for now," Sarah replied, after some thought.

"Too bad you have to go back to old *weasel bag*, Lamar. He may not divorce you, but he sure isn't much," observed Martha flatly.

Sarah grinned, not offended in the least. "We will have to see about that."

"Surely you're not dumping him, too?"

"We will have to see," Sarah said, no longer grinning.

"An old maid-in-the-making, for sure," Martha dead-panned. "Dumping that many boys isn't good for any girl."

"We will have to see," Sarah repeated herself.

Rebecca concluded that the important part of the conversation was over, so she interrupted, "We need to plan tomorrow and Saturday, girls. Sunday we'll go to the Brooklyn Tabernacle for church, and then I want to visit the Bowery Mission in the afternoon. Fanny Crosby's old piano is located there."

"Are you playing it?" Sarah wanted to know.

"If they let me," Rebecca replied.

"She plays the most beautiful music," Sarah told Martha. "Maybe you'll get to hear it."

"I would like that," Martha said.

"Let's plan now," Rebecca told them, and they did. They simply made up a list and spontaneously followed the items as it suited them: Ellis Island, the Statue of Liberty, flying over the Statue by helicopter, and riding the ferry, visiting Chinatown, Hispanic Street, Greenwich Village, Little Italy, and TriBeCa. They stopped to sample the foods and sights of each new culture they encountered.

When there was still time left on Friday before returning to the hotel for the night, they took the taxi through Harlem, Washington Heights, and drove across the George Washington Bridge.

On Saturday, Rebecca concentrated on the Bronx, taking them through Van Cortlandt Park and the New York Botanical Gardens. They then drove through the neighborhood of Riverdale overlooking the Hudson River and the Palisades Cliffs. Then there was still time to sneak a look inside of Yankee Stadium. No one was playing, but the girls found it as interesting as if a ball game had been going on. The last stop of the day was another little Italian restaurant, since Martha and Sarah had both liked the Italian food so much the previous day. It was another very full day.

On Sunday, they beheld the Brooklyn Tabernacle Choir in its glory. Both Martha and Sarah were moved to tears. A visiting preacher, the Reverend Eli Mathis, Jr., was speaking. His booming voice on the platform sounded throughout the building. The title of the sermon was, "We Must be Born-Again of the Spirit".

Afterwards, Sarah asked Martha, "Do you think what he was saying was true?"

"It was in English," was her comment.

"I'm going to read it in German when we get home," Sarah informed her. "If it says that, we had better do it."

"I think so, too," Martha agreed.

In the afternoon, as promised, Rebecca stopped in at the Bowery Mission on 227 Bowery Street. The director was more than happy to let Rebecca play Fanny Crosby's piano. With the girls singing along, Rebecca played *O Save Me at the Cross*. There was a hush on those gathered around when they were done.

Returning to the hotel, they got a good night's sleep before the flight home the next morning. After landing in Indianapolis, Rebecca had them home two hours later.

Deborah met them at the door. "How was the trip?"

"Just fine," they assured her, exhaustion already beginning to set in.

"You will have to tell me all about it. Be sure and thank Mrs. Florence."

"We already did," they told her. That evening with Ben and Mark listening they recounted the whole story. Everything, that is, except the part about Phillip. Without saying it, they both felt that that would best be left untold, at least for the time being.

Before retiring, Sarah took out her German Bible and read the passages in John, Chapter Three. It said the same thing. Calling Martha over, she showed it to her.

"What do you think?" Martha asked her.

"We had better do it," Sarah told her.

Making sure the door was closed, they knelt together

by the bedside, and asked the Spirit of God to birth in them a creation that only He could form.

"We had better get baptized," Sarah said, still on her knees.

"I think so," Martha agreed, "I suddenly want to."

≈

Greatly to her surprise, the next morning Sarah saw Malinda going past the window on the front porch. Deborah saw her too. "Oh my, I forgot to tell you, Sarah. Malinda wants to talk to you."

"To me?"

"That's what she said last week."

There was no time for further conversation as Malinda was already knocking on the door. Opening it, Deborah said, "Good Morning".

Returning the greeting, Malinda asked for Sarah. "She's right here," Deborah said, turning back into the house and motioning for Sarah to come. Although Sarah was hesitant, there was no choice but to obey. *What in the world does she want with me?*

Out on the porch, Malinda would not look directly at her at first and only cleared her throat repeatedly. *The girl is really troubled*, Sarah thought, and she relaxed a little. "What do you want?" she managed to ask, gently.

Looking close to tears, Malinda asked, "Can we talk somewhere alone?"

"Sure," Sarah said. "There is the swing," she pointed out in the yard.

Malinda followed Sarah to the swing. Once they were seated, Sarah waited for Malinda to start. "I have something to tell you," she began. "Hopefully, it is not too late." She glanced nervously at Sarah's face.

"You got a package of face cream a while back." Malinda

waited until Sarah nodded her head, then continued, "I gave you that package." She now gave up the effort to hold back her emotions and sobbed openly.

"There was something in it. I don't know what but it was meant to hurt you. I am so sorry. Can you forgive me, please?"

Sarah put her arms around Malinda's shoulder. She didn't move. "I already know," Sarah told her.

"You do? Were you hurt?"

"No, but I could have been. Why did you do it?"

"Because I wanted Lamar back so badly," Malinda sobbed again, then collected herself. "But I am willing to give him up now. I'm just really sorry I did this."

"Did you put the stuff in the cream?" Sarah asked her, watching her face.

"No."

"Who did then?"

"I can't tell. She's my friend. I'll just take the blame myself."

Sarah smiled, "That's okay. It'll all work out."

"You are okay, then?" Malinda asked, looking intently at Sarah's face again.

Sarah nodded. "I have a question though."

"What is it?"

"Why did Lamar leave you?"

Malinda looked perplexed. "He didn't. I told him to leave."

"I see," Sarah said softly, not overly surprised.

"Is there something wrong?" Malinda asked now, alarmed again.

"I don't think so," Sarah assured her. "I think everything will be just fine."

Malinda sighed in relief, "I am so glad you are okay. Well, I had better be going. Mom needs me today."

"You have a good day," Sarah told her gently and she stayed on the swing until Malinda's buggy was out the driveway.

Well, I guess you are a weasel, my boy. We will have to see about this. She got up and walked towards the house.

❧

That afternoon a long black Suburban with tinted windows pulled into the Schwartz driveway.

"*Vass in de Velt?*" Deborah exclaimed. "Where is your father?"

"He's out plowing in the back field," Sarah told her calmly. "I'll go out and see what they want."

Deborah looked strangely at her. "What has come over you?"

"Nothing, Mother," she told Deborah. "Let me see what they want."

Walking briskly out the walk, she waited until the door of the Suburban opened to reveal a well-dressed businessman in a dark blue suit and matching tie. "Ms. Schwartz, I presume?" he asked.

She nodded, not offering to move or shake his hand.

"Could we have a word with you?" he asked as another man appeared on the other side of the Suburban similarly attired.

"The swing?" she pointed across the yard.

He looked, shrugged, "I guess that will do."

She walked over and sat down, but offered them nothing. They remained standing. Deborah was beside herself, watching from the front window.

"What are they doing? Who are they?" she asked Martha.

"I don't know," Martha told her, then slowly a thought

occurred to her. "It has something to do with New York City, I think." She said this without a trace of concern in her voice.

"With New York City?" Deborah was not satisfied with the answer.

"A small matter, nothing serious, I think," Martha dismissed the subject with a little wave of her hand.

Deborah glared at her. "You call this no big deal. That's a big vehicle."

Martha saw that the subject was not easily explained away. "Sarah had some facial cream with her, Pond's I think. The jar was contaminated with something. These are the people from the company. Sarah told them there was no need to worry, but they said it needed to be checked into lest other people get hurt."

"Well, that's nothing," Deborah huffed. "The English are always making a bigger deal out of things than they really are. I hope they don't keep her too long. We have work to do."

"It probably won't take long," Martha ventured, hoping she was correct.

Out in the yard the first man had already established who he was and that Sarah was the owner of the contaminated jar of Pond's facial cream. "The Unilever company takes this very seriously," he told Sarah. "Were you hurt in any way by this contamination?"

"No," Sarah shook her head.

"We have checked this lot number in five states already and there is no other contamination anywhere else."

"I am glad to hear that," Sarah told them.

"Are you sure you are okay?" the man asked again. "We can have a doctor examine you, if you wish."

"There is no need of that," Sarah assured them.

"Would you be willing to sign a statement then that the

Unilever Company is not liable for anything related to this incident?"

Sarah nodded and reached for the paper and pen the man had produced. She carefully signed her name.

When they were gone, she walked back into the house. "Was it the face cream thing?' Deborah demanded to know.

"Yes," Sarah said, relieved that Martha had obviously already done some explaining.

"What did they want?"

"That I sign a paper that states they are not responsible."

Deborah was satisfied. "Sounds like the English. Just concerned about themselves."

Sarah thought of saying more, but decided to leave well enough alone. Some things only got worse for the telling, she figured.

CHAPTER TWENTY-TWO

REMEMBERING MALINDA'S VISIT, Sarah suddenly had a strong urge to see Lamar. Not wishing to wait until Sunday to talk to him, she cast about for some way to see him. Then it occurred to her that he might soon stop by. Smiling, she felt confident her hunch was correct. At 7:30 that evening, a buggy rattled up the driveway.

"Who is it now?" Deborah demanded to know. "Are we to have no peace anymore?"

"It's Lamar," Sarah told her as she headed for the door.

"Well," Deborah said to her as she turned to go out, "that's different, of course."

Smiling, she met him on the walk where he already was standing after tying up his horse. Seeing her face, he brightened considerably. "Good evening," he told her.

She returned the greeting, motioning toward the swing. Gladly following her, he sat beside her without an invitation. "I see you're back," he announced.

"Yes," she said.

"No English boy came along?" he asked point-blank.

Sarah suddenly remembered how much his jealousy irritated her. "That's the least of your worries," she told him.

"Oh?" he stammered.

"You lied to me."

"Oh?" he said again.

"You did not break up with Malinda. She told you to leave."

Firmly caught in his tangled web, his face reddened. "Well, that's a small matter. I'm sorry," he said. "I could have explained myself better, perhaps."

"No," she told him, "you lied. Now go."

"Go?" he asked, unbelieving. "I can't leave you."

"Have you lost your legs?" she asked him.

"I mean," he searched for words, "I can't lose you."

"You already have, now go."

"Now?"

"Yes, now."

He looked stricken, his handsome face pale with beads of sweat appearing on his brow. "I'm really sorry. I will make it up to you."

She simply pointed toward his buggy, and he got up slowly and walked towards it. Waiting until he drove away she got to her feet and walked towards the house. Now that it was over, she felt the tears coming.

Deborah noticed them when she walked in the door. "Is there something wrong?"

"I told him to leave," she said simply.

Deborah gasped, "You did not?"

Sarah simply nodded.

"You're going to be an old maid yet, even if you are beautiful," Deborah said, horror in her voice.

"I have to do what's right," Sarah told her. "What happens, happens."

"I suppose that's true," Deborah agreed, then shook her head as Sarah disappeared up the stairs. *I hope the girl knows what she's doing.*

Once he was on the road, Lamar's fury was great. *How dare she do that to me? Now what am I going to do? All the world will know that I have been dumped by two girls.*

For a time, deep in thought, he let his horse have its head. His anger slowly faded out of him, replaced instead with fear. *How will I ever live this one down?*

⌇

Two Sundays later was Preparation Sunday, two Sundays after that Communion, and then a new instruction class for baptism was announced. Both Martha and Sarah joined. The next six months would be a time of proving themselves for the applicants, both in instruction and in judgment upon their character and actions. Those who were found wanting would be approached and offered correction. Depending on the offense and response of the applicant, instruction might or might not proceed to baptism. Neither Martha nor Sarah expected any trouble.

Soon after instruction class started, Sarah and Martha decided they wanted to attend the mid-week youth outing at the community center. That was not an easy matter, since it involved using horse and buggy and driving a considerable distance.

"If we can go to New York City, we can go to the youth center," Martha proclaimed.

"But we didn't go to New York by horse and buggy," Sarah reminded her.

"Let's plan out what we need to do. It can be done," Martha assured her.

So they did and ended up taking Mark into their plans as well. They could leave early for the anticipated hour-long drive, spend some time there, and still be home by eleven. That would not be too bad for a weeknight.

Martha's biggest concern was Mark's horse, "Can he make it?" she made a point of asking him.

"I'll give him extra oats and he'll be fine," he assured her.

So they took off on a Thursday night. It took longer than expected, but they got there by 7:30. The place was already full of young people when they arrived. Sarah and Martha immediately began looking for girls they knew, some of whom they had not seen for a long time. The Amish community was widespread and the different districts did not often have contact with each other.

As the evening wore on, Sarah was sitting on the bleachers in deep conversation with one of her cousins, when a boy cleared his throat behind her. When she turned around he asked, "Are you, Sarah Schwartz?"

She nodded, not paying that much attention to him.

"Hi," he announced, a confident tone in his voice.

That irritated her, but also caused her to take a closer look at him. He was not that tall, not ugly, but also not what she would have considered handsome. His hands were those of a farmer, he was muscular and had brown eyes that shone softly with the same confidence his voice revealed. He was obviously not afraid of her. "Who are you?" she asked him.

"Melvin Yoder," he said without offering any additional explanation.

"Have I met you before?" she asked him.

"We were in the same fifth grade class," he told her. "My parents moved up to the northern district after that."

She searched her mind for memories of the fifth grade class, and finally remembered a curly-headed nondescript boy who sat two seats behind her. "Your curls are gone," she said, surprised by her own boldness.

He nodded in acknowledgement. "Yep, that's right. I heard you just came back from New York City?"

"Yes," she told him, "is that any of your business?"

He chuckled, calmly taking a seat beside her on the bench. "It is if I make it."

Sarah was sure her red face glowed in the dark. *The nerve of this guy.* Inside though, he had her full attention. "Have you ever been to New York City?" she asked him, trying to keep the emotion out of her voice.

"We've never stopped there," he said. "We have family in upper New York State. We drive close by on the interstate. It looks nice."

"I see," she said, not sure what else to say.

He solved that for her. "Are you looking for someone to take you home on Sunday evening?"

"No," she told him.

"Good," he said, "then I will take you."

"Oh, you will?" Sarah stared at him as her attempt at anger utterly failed. *What is it about this fellow?*

"If you agree, of course," he said with that same confidence in his voice. "One wouldn't want to take a girl home against her will."

"I would have to know you better first," she said, "and maybe some other things," her voice steady now. "But it's no, for now."

"Maybe I'll see you, then," he calmly stated, nodding his head before getting up and walking away.

"You just got asked for a date," her cousin gushed beside her. "Have you ever met that guy before?"

"No," Sarah told her.

"My, you are something," her cousin said with awe in her voice.

On the way home, Sarah admitted that she had been asked out for Sunday evening by a Melvin Yoder.

"Did you accept?" Mark asked her.

"No, I don't even know the boy."

Martha started laughing. "I got asked out, too. Well, sort of. His name is Silas Mast, a Mennonite."

"You bunch of low-down, slime buckets," Mark said in

mock horror. "I take you out for one night, and you both start getting hitched up, just like that."

The girls ignored him.

"You can't date a Mennonite," Sarah told Martha.

"Well, I'm not going to until after I am baptized, and then we will start. I wouldn't want to cause too much hurt to Mom. She really wants to see me baptized Amish. Makes it easier on everyone, too."

"I can't believe this!" Mark exclaimed.

"Well, believe it," Sarah told him. "I don't know how it happened, but it happened, so keep it under your hat until we know which way the wind blows."

"Agreed," he said, "both of you can tell Mom and Dad when you are ready. I'll keep my mouth shut."

"Thanks," they said together.

⌒

Later that evening, Lamar stopped by the gas station in Montgomery. Tying his horse to a convenient telephone pole, he went inside. When he came out, he had a copy of the "USA Today" in his hand. A little late in the day for any up-to-date news, but Lamar wanted to see it anyway.

Climbing back in the buggy, he checked the sports pages first, then glanced through the A section. Towards the back, his eye fell on a full-page advertisement for women's clothing. Usually, half of the page would be men's clothing, while the other half would be for women. However, this spread was entirely for women.

Nothing interested him much, especially when there were evening gowns and casual dress with sporty cuffs and collars. He was more interested in looking at the models. *None of them are as beautiful as Sarah.* A pain went through him. The face of one, half-way down the page on the left, made him do a double-take. It was Sarah Schwartz!

"It's not possible," he told himself.

He looked again. *It is Sarah. Now what has she been up to? So that is why she told me off. Oh, this is interesting. She's in English dress.*

Tucking the newspaper carefully on the buggy shelf behind him, he let out the reins to get his horse going. *This will sure help me out!*

CHAPTER TWENTY-THREE

IT WAS STILL early Saturday evening when the sound of buggy wheels could be heard in the Schwartz's driveway. The sun was still an hour from setting and had just begun to cast shadows from the tall oak trees across the front yard.

"Someone's coming," Deborah told her girls. Ben was still in the barn finishing some chores before supper. The three women were in the kitchen putting the rest of the supper on the table.

"I wonder who it is on a Saturday evening?" Sarah spoke her question out loud.

"Dating time perhaps, except you're not dating, nor am I," commented Martha.

"You don't suppose?" Sarah continued with her questioning out loud.

"He wouldn't dare," Martha said, following her train of thought.

"Would you girls start making sense?" Deborah snapped. "Nothing you are saying makes any sense. I don't know who it is. If either of you do, then say so."

"We don't," Martha told her.

"Then why don't you go look?" Deborah said, reaching for the bowl of mashed potatoes to set on the table. "I have my hands full here."

Sarah shrugged her shoulders and, without saying anything else, left for the living room with its front window

and view of the hitching post. She was back almost immediately, her face flushed. "It is him," she whispered.

"Would you make sense," Deborah was at the end of
her patience again. "Who is he?"

"Lamar," Sarah whispered again.

"You don't say?" Martha's mouth dropped open. "How
does he dare?"

Deborah set the bowl of corn down a little too roughly
in her hurry. She turned to Sarah. "I thought you quit this
boy, and now he shows up? Maybe God is trying to tell you
something. He's a real nice boy, got a good job and plenty of
money. If this really is him, maybe you ought to think twice
about your decision."

"I wonder what he wants," Sarah was still whispering.
"This can't be good."

"Did you hear what I just said?" Deborah tried again.

"Yes, Mother," Sarah said.

"You had better go out and see what he wants," Martha
suggested, glancing nervously through the kitchen to the
front door.

Sarah's face was no longer flushed, but now drained of
blood. "I suppose," she said, "but this can't be good."

"Sarah," Deborah's voice broke through to her, "this
could be your chance. Go out and make up with him, if
that's what he wants. He's a good boy."

Martha almost said something, but decided against
contradicting her mother. "Just be careful," she told Sarah.

"You girls don't make a bit of sense," Deborah's exasperation returned. "Now go, Sarah."

Numbly, Sarah walked across the living room towards
the front door and slowly turned the knob.

Melvin Yoder was spending his Saturday evening doing last-minute chores around his parent's place in preparation for Sunday. The second to the youngest of four boys, he still lived at home with his parents. His younger brother would be the one to take over the family farm. Melvin had been of age now for two years, and although it was time he found his own farm and a girl to marry, he had not yet dated seriously.

"It's time," his mother had told him many times. "We have nice girls here in our district who would have you, Melvin."

"I don't like any of them," he had told her.

"Then go look in the other districts," she instructed him. "Visit around, it is time you got married and bought your own farm."

Tonight he was thinking of those words again. This week he had finally seen a girl who had captured his imagination, and he was sure would easily capture his heart. She lived in the southern district around Glendale. News spreads around Amish circles mainly through talk. He had heard the boys talking about her and he had decided to go see for himself. Last Thursday night had been that night.

Once he had seen her sitting there on the bleachers, he was sure that his memory was correct. He knew her from the fifth grade, before his parents had moved to the northern district. With that knowledge and his natural self-confidence, he walked right up to her and introduced himself.

She was beautiful, beyond any girl he knew, but it was more than that. Her blue eyes were warm with a kind of inner beauty. When she spoke, he felt at home with her, even when she was obviously irritated with him.

This was worth pursuing he decided, and he asked her out then and there. She had said 'no', or 'maybe', or something like that. He was not entirely sure. Even if it had been a solid 'no', he knew he would have asked again, unless she was going with someone. He was sure she was not going with someone. His questions to one of the boys had confirmed that she had just quit with a Lamar Wagler. There was also talk that sounded to Melvin like rumors of an English boyfriend.

"Interested in her?" the boy had asked him teasingly.

"Yes," he said without hesitation.

"Well, you must be new around here," the boy told. "Most of us without girlfriends are interested. And," he said with a chuckle, "some like Lamar, who was almost married, are interested. She's the most beautiful Amish girl in the area."

"It's more than that," Melvin told him. "She seems like a real nice girl."

This produced another chuckle. "Whatever you say. Nice on the outside would be good enough for me."

Melvin had nodded his thanks and moved on his way. *I am going to visit her district Sunday. See where she lives.* This he decided at once, and now his resolve had only grown. He wanted to see her at church and the singing. He was not sure why, but it seemed important to him.

Phillip Ryan was working this weekend. It was already past midnight at the Paris office where his dad had been based for the last week. Their last conversation had been an hour ago. Wearily he flipped through Sarah Schwartz's file. Her face and profile in the test photos of the outfit from the *Densine Line* looked as good as they did when he had first seen them. *Sure would help if she came to work for us. Even these would be nice to run.*

Walking over to the secretary's front desk he picked up the stack of papers Camellia had left for him. He liked to go over all the print copies of the newspapers where Maxey Jacobs ran ads. Reports were not good enough for him.

About mid-way down the pile, he glanced at a copy of "USA Today" which had run that week. Everything seemed to be in order. Just as he was about to go on, he took a second look. It was Sarah in the dark blue mid-calf skirt, wide black belt, long-sleeved, dark gray, plain blouse, with ruffled neckline.

Disbelieving, he opened her file and compared the photos. One matched perfectly. *Where did this run?* His mind whirled. Checking, he soon had the answer: it had run nationwide. *Do the Amish buy newspapers? Has she seen it? We had no permission to do this. How did this happen?*

Phillip ran possible scenarios through his mind of how this photo could have been used without his authorization. There was only one person who could have authorized its use besides him. That was his father. *But Dad wasn't here all week. He would not have gotten involved at this level anyway.*

Then he knew. There was no way he would ever prove it, but Camellia could have done it. She knew everything about the business at the level of day-to-day operations here at this office. Overriding his permission, or even somehow using his name was certainly within the realm of possibilities.

Why would she do it? To find that answer took only a little imagination and intuition. If Sarah found out they used her photo without permission, she would hardly believe it was an accident. It would look like a deliberate attempt to profit from her, after making a show of not doing so. He had no doubt as to what Sarah would think of that.

There was also little doubt as to how Camellia thought she would benefit from Sarah's reaction. He reached for the phone and dialed the Florence's residence in Washington, Indiana.

"Hello," Rebecca answered.

"This is Phillip," he told her. "I think I need your help with something."

~

Sarah faced Lamar on the sidewalk with her hands on her hips. "What are you doing here?" she demanded to know.

He was grinning from ear to ear. "I think you need to talk to me."

"No, I don't," she told him. "We are through, and there is no use discussing it."

"You need to look at this." He took the "USA Today" from behind his back where he had been holding it. "Maybe this will have something to do with your decision?"

"I can see no way that it would. An English paper does not affect me."

"The swing over there," he pointed. "Sit down and I will show you."

Something about the way he said it made her comply. They walked over together, and he sat down first and unfolded the paper. She was still standing when he held the page with the Maxey Jacob's ad towards her. "Have a seat, and take a look."

Recognition came slowly as she descended onto the swing. It was her photo with the outfit from New York City. "I don't understand," she managed to say.

Lamar grinned again, "It's simple, isn't it? You go to New York City on a trip with an English lady. You meet this English boy, and who knows what all else you did? There you are in that evil city without any ministers to guide you.

No bishop to watch your back and this is what you do. You pose for an evil business corporation for your picture. How much did they pay you? Does this explain how you could fly up there in a private jet? Someone said you did. We all know that's expensive. What else did you do while in New York City?"

She was numb, not because of Lamar's words, but from a deep and aching sense of betrayal. *Phillip lied to me. It was all about the money. To think that I even thought of him as something more.* She blushed deeply at the thought.

Lamar took her red cheeks as an admission of guilt. *Good, she admits she's guilty. This will even make it easier.* Out loud he proclaimed, "I can't believe you did this. This is something, not only so terribly wrong, but so against the *Ordnung!*" (Church disciplines)

She was reliving the scenes in New York City and that final night with Phillip. So charming, he was. Didn't even bring the photos because he knew she never would allow him to use them. So this is what his plans were? Run them without her knowing it. *Why didn't I see this coming?* In the distance she heard Lamar's words, but they made no impact.

"So, what have you got to say for yourself?" he asked triumphantly leaning back in the swing, as if he planned on staying a long time.

"I didn't do it," she told him.

He laughed out loud, "Pictures don't lie."

"Neither do they tell the whole truth."

"So what is the whole truth?"

"They talked me into posing with the dress, just to see how it would turn out, but I was promised the pictures would not be used."

"Do you expect anyone to believe that?"

"Yes."

Lamar laughed heartily, "Well, think again then."

"If you don't believe me, then why are you still here?"

He grinned, "That does bring up the point of why I came. This thing could be a big problem for you if the bishop and deacon find out about it. I have a proposal."

She almost didn't ask, but then changed her mind. "What is that?"

"Let's say you forget about the story I told you about leaving Malinda, if I promise, of course, not to do it again? Then, if you promise the same, I will forget about this. It's not likely that anyone else will buy Thursday's paper. They probably won't run it twice. What do you say?"

Chapter Twenty-Four

"I see," Rebecca said into the phone. "Is there some kind of problem?"

"Yes," Phillip told her, "it involves Sarah."

"Sarah? How can that be?"

There was a long sigh at the other end of the line. "I just saw our ads for Thursday."

"You mean you had not seen them before?" Rebecca interrupted.

"Sure, I saw the proofs of what was supposed to run, but I now have in my hands what actually ran."

"I don't understand."

"They are different."

"What has this got to do with Sarah?"

Phillip drew another breath. "She is in our Thursday's ad spread of 'USA Today'."

Rebecca said nothing.

"I did not authorize this to run."

"Who did then?"

"The only other person would have been Dad, but he was not here."

"Are you hiding something, Phillip?"

"No."

"Then who gave the authorization?"

"I have a feeling it was Camellia."

"Can she do that?"

"I'm afraid so. I just never thought she would."

"What are you going to do if Sarah finds this out?"

"That's why I'm calling you."

"I see, and what am I suppose to do?"

"Should we contact her, and tell her what happened?"

Rebecca thought for a moment. "I don't think so. Amish don't read newspapers much and the chance of someone recognizing her is slim. I'll see her the Monday after next when I pick her up for the cleaning day. That might be a good time to break the news."

"Thanks," said Phillip, "that takes a load off of my mind."

"Glad to help. I'll let you know what her reaction is."

"Thanks," Phillip told her again, hanging up the phone.

Rebecca placed the receiver on the hook gently. *Men do get themselves in a lot of trouble.*

❧

"I will have nothing of it," Sarah told him with clenched teeth, looking him straight in the eye.

Lamar wrinkled his brow. "You're not serious, are you? I will go straight to the deacon with this."

"Why do you still want me, if I did all the things you think I did?" Sarah was still glaring at him with her piercing blue eyes.

Lamar only glanced at her. "That's some question. We all do things we shouldn't. It is just that I like you. Why wouldn't I want you?"

"Well," Sarah told him, "I don't like you, and I'm not going to take you back regardless of how much trouble you make for me."

"Come on now," Lamar pleaded, "it doesn't have to be this way at all. We can settle this peacefully."

"Then settle it by believing me and by not saying anything."

"Will you take me back then?"

"No," she told him, "I will not take you back regardless."

"Then I will have to go to the deacon." He rose to his feet.

She got up and, without another word, walked towards the house. His buggy wheels were rolling on the gravel by the time she shut the front door.

"What was that all about?" Martha confronted her.

"Phillip ran the picture," Sarah told her simply.

"I don't believe it."

"Lamar has the ad, and he's going to the deacon's house right now."

Martha's hand was over her mouth. "How can this be? Phillip told you he would not run it."

"I have no idea."

"We can't let Mom and Dad find this out."

"They will if the deacon does."

"We should at least wait until then."

"I suppose," Sarah sighed, "they won't believe me either way."

"Maybe, maybe not. You do have to admit it's a hard story to buy. Even I would have problems with it if I hadn't been there, you know."

"I understand," Sarah told her. "We will just have to see what happens."

❧

Lamar never had a doubt as to what he would do next. He would never get Sarah back now, but he just might save his reputation. It might also help him get what clearly was the best choice now available. If he couldn't have Sarah,

Malinda was still the best looking girl around. It was a miracle no one had already snatched her up.

This news would sew the whole thing up just fine. His tattered feelings and pride would be restored with this on the record. Sarah Schwartz had been to New York City, doing, God knows what, with the English boyfriend she was keeping on the sly. Her modeling picture was in one of the main papers of the country. No one could fault him for dumping her. They would, in fact, admire him for it. Yes, he knew what he would do.

Pulling into Deacon Stephen's driveway, he tied his horse and knocked on the door. Stephen, a short, middle-aged man, came to the door. He was used to people calling on Saturday nights, either with their own troubles or with reports of other's troubles. It really made no difference to Stephen. These were all matters he would have to handle himself or report to Bishop Amos if they were serious enough. Stroking his beard, he opened the door. "Good evening, Lamar. I'll be out in just a minute."

Lamar nodded his head and stood waiting on the porch. Stephen came back out quickly enough. "The children are still up," he explained. "We might go out to the barn."

"The buggy's fine," Lamar told him. "It shouldn't take too long."

"Fine with me," Stephen said, following Lamar out to where his horse was tied. Leaning against his buggy, Lamar produced the newspaper. "As you know, I have been dating Sarah Schwartz," he began.

A look of concern crossed Stephen's face. "You have surely not been inappropriate. That is a nice family she comes from, very upstanding in the church. I hope you have not caused trouble for them."

Lamar clutched his paper, feeling angry all over again. *So this is what this girl does to me? Am I glad I have some evi-*

dence against her! "No, not at all," he said quickly to Stephen. "I hope you don't think such ill of me?"

Stephen looked at him sharply then relaxed. "That's good to hear. What is it then?"

Lamar held out the newspaper, glad he had hard evidence. He would need it to make his point. "This is Sarah," he announced letting Stephen have the paper and fully study it for a moment. He continued, "I bought the paper on Thursday. As you know, she and her sister were just on a trip to New York City. Before she left, she told me that she has been keeping an English boyfriend."

Stephen looked at Lamar in disbelief. Only the paper in his hand kept him listening.

"I tried to reprove her of this sin, but she would not listen to me. Only my love for her kept me silent this long. I thought when she came back from the trip, maybe I could talk to her again. Now I see that she has been modeling for this clothing company, and I could not go on any longer. We broke up."

"I see," was all Deacon Stephen could get out.

"I felt it my duty to come and tell you of this. This is surely a serious church matter."

Stephen cleared his throat. "Yes, yes, it is. Lamar, are you sure about all this?"

"There is the picture," was all Lamar had to say.

"I will look into this," Stephen finally said. "This comes as a great shock to me."

"Yes, it did to me, too," said Lamar as he untied his horse. Stephen folded the paper and silently walked towards the house. Lamar drove out the lane with a big grin on his face. Stephen did not see Lamar's glee since his eyes were on the ground. *I can't believe the Schwartz family would be involved in something like this. Ben is the most upstanding of church members. Always a great help to the church.*

Stephen sighed as he entered the front door. His wife saw him come in with a burdened look on his face. Serious church troubles were troubling, she could tell, but as was her custom, she stayed out of it.

"Your supper," she told him, "is still warm on the stove."

He nodded silently in thanks.

Melvin got up early for the long drive to church. He pulled into the yard, already full of buggies. Out by the barn, a long line of men was forming. Women, in their black bonnets and shawls, disappeared into the door of the summer kitchen. As he pulled into line to unhitch, no one paid him undue attention. Visiting boys were not uncommon.

After church got started, he noticed the long line of baptismal applicants seated on the front rows. Boys were on one side and the girls on the other. It was only after the ministers rose to leave for the council meeting, followed by the applicants, that he noticed Sarah among the girls. *I would have figured she had already joined church. At least she's getting it done.* Melvin had joined two years ago.

By the third song, with the ten o'clock hour well underway, a sign of movement finally came from upstairs. Filing down, the boys leading, the applicants all took their places on the benches. Melvin got the distinct feeling they all looked uncomfortable. Another song followed so that it was ten-thirty before the ministers reappeared. *Must just be an extra long instruction class, or was there trouble afoot?*

It was closing time before Melvin learned the reason for the lengthy instruction class. At quarter after twelve, the bishop rose to his feet and announced that all members were directed to stay seated. Melvin, as a visitor in good standing at his home district, would be allowed to remain. In any voting, though, his vote would only be considered for advisement purposes.

"A serious matter has been brought to our attention," Bishop Amos began, when all the non-members had filed out. He stood in front of them all, his white beard falling straight down his chest. "This involves a very serious charge against one of our baptismal applicants." He cleared his throat before continuing, "A grave error has been revealed to us. It is our great desire that this thing not be true, but yet, we believe it to be. A sister, who is among the instruction class, has been found in sin.

"I would not ask you to believe this, if I did not believe it myself. Deacon Stephen has seen the photo of this evidence himself. Sarah Schwartz," here Bishop Amos paused as if weighing his words to the silent audience before him, "has been modeling for an English company in New York City. There have also been reports that she is keeping an English boyfriend. We tell you this with great sorrow in our hearts, yet as our duty to keep the people of God pure from the world. As you know, Sarah is not yet a member, so we will not be referring her to you for any punishment, but she will need to be removed from the instruction class until she makes a full confession and repents. Her answers to us this morning were not satisfactory at all. To this all of us ministers agree, so we simply tell you of this and of our decision. I will now let the others express themselves, also."

With that Bishop Amos sat down, as the other ministers basically went over the same points, with the deacon giving a first-hand account. He did not show the paper as evidence since such a display of photos in church would have been considered sacrilegious. There was no one who doubted his word in any case.

When they were finished, Bishop Amos rose again and dismissed the congregation. No one said a word as they filed out.

CHAPTER TWENTY-FIVE

MELVIN'S HEAD WAS buzzing. Never had he heard of anything like this. You don't just get up and accuse an Amish girl of modeling and of keeping an English boyfriend in front of church unless there was some truth to it. The ministers cared too much about their credibility to do such a thing without some basis. *How could she do that? I don't believe it,* he told himself on the way out to the barn. All around him, the boys were beginning to buzz with conversation.

Melvin overheard one of the boys, "Isn't that something? She's keeping an English boyfriend."

"So that's why she wouldn't date any of us."

"How did Lamar get a hold of her?"

"Ya, why is Lamar dating her?"

"Ask him, he's over there."

"Hey, Lamar," one of them hollered, "come over here and explain yourself."

This was what Lamar had been waiting for. It was his chance. He knew every word he said would be repeated from now on in any conversation on the subject and he planned to make the most of it.

"*Ya,*" he said and walked over to where they were standing. "What do you want?"

"Explain yourself," the boy told him. There was no reason to say on what since it was clear what they meant.

Lamar cleared his throat. "I only found out myself just before she left on her trip to New York." They all nodded, knowing to what he was referring. "I tried then to persuade her what she was doing was wrong, but she wouldn't budge. The only reason I kept silent was my hope that I could still talk sense into her when she came back, but now I see it was in vain. She was already having her picture taken and selling it." Lamar shrugged, "Who knows what else she was doing? I had no choice but to drop her and go to the ministers with the matter."

"Why was she dating you?" the boy asked.

Lamar had anticipated that question and was ready. "It must have been as a cover. That way no one would get suspicious."

"Has she been doing this for long?"

"I don't know, but how would we know? It's not like we read the papers all over the country."

They were all nodding when Melvin spoke up, "I think there must be some mistake. Sarah wouldn't do something like this."

Lamar turned to him. "Who are you? You're not from around here."

"I'm Melvin Yoder," he stated simply.

"Do you know Sarah?"

"No, not really," Melvin replied, "but I don't think she would do it. What is her side of the story?"

Lamar glared at him. "If you don't know her, then what do you know about it? Just mind your own business. The ministers wouldn't be telling us this unless there was something to it."

Melvin shrugged his shoulders. "Usually, but sometimes they can be wrong."

"Why don't you go tell them," Lamar laughed. "Maybe they might look into whether you are receiving any of the money Sarah has been making selling her pictures."

Melvin made no reply since it was clear to him that it was of no use anyway. He did resolve, if at all possible, to speak to Sarah about it. If necessary, he would risk his own reputation by being seen with her.

"Well, this has been interesting," commented the boy who had posed the questions to Lamar. Already the crowd of boys was breaking up to get in line for the second seating of the noon meal.

Dropping towards the end of the line, Melvin saw his chance on the way into the house. He caught a glimpse of Sarah by herself in the back of the kitchen. Moving out of line, he made a pretense of wanting something and then slipped over behind her. He cleared his throat.

She jerked at the sound of a male voice and whirled around to face him. "Excuse me," he said softly. "You remember me?"

She did. He was the boy who wanted a date, but at the moment what struck her most was his friendly face. "Yes," she nodded.

"Did you do it?" he asked without accusation or any sound of anger in his voice.

She almost burst into tears, but managed to control her voice. "No," was all she could manage to say.

"How did all this get started then?" Again he asked gently as if he really wanted to know.

She glanced around to see if anyone had noticed them talking. No one was observing them so she quietly whispered the basics of the story to him. Later she would be greatly astonished when she realized that she had told a strange boy all about it, but at the time it seemed like a great relief to tell him.

"I see," he said, when she was done.

"You don't believe me," she stated, watching his face.

"Oh, I do," he assured her. "It's just that it will be a hard story to sell."

"That's what Martha said, and she was there."

"Martha?" he asked.

"That's my sister."

"Well, I hope everything turns out okay," he smiled, knowing that he must get back out before someone noticed.

She turned away quickly lest he see her tears. For some reason she did not want to cry at the moment.

He left as quietly as he had come.

Mark said nothing as he drove his two sisters home. They offered no comments either, knowing full well there was a storm brewing at home. There would be plenty of time for words then.

Deborah was sitting in the living room rocker, wiping tears away. Ben was sitting stone-faced on the couch, waiting for them when they walked in the door.

"What have you done, Sarah?" Deborah wailed.

"I haven't done anything," Sarah told her, "except let them take a picture of me in that dress which they said they would not use."

"An English dress?"

Sarah nodded.

Deborah broke into fresh weeping. Ben slowly found his voice. "This is a very serious thing which you have done, Sarah. I hope you know that. Our family will not live this down in a long time."

Now Sarah could not hold back the tears. "I really wasn't doing anything wrong," she said, although this would probably not help her cause any.

"Maybe she ought to tell us the whole story," Mark suggested.

"That would be good," Ben agreed, leaning back on the couch. "It is no doubt a long story. Why don't you start at the beginning?"

So Sarah did, telling them as many details as she could remember. When she was done, Ben turned to Martha. "How much of this can you verify?"

"Most of it. I was with her."

"You are sure of this?"

"Yes," Martha was irritated, "why would I lie for her?"

"There could be many reasons," her father told her. "Even if it is true, it's still very serious. Going to New York City on a company's private jet. Having supper with a young English man. I am really disappointed in both of you. I just don't see how this story, even if it is all true, will help anything."

"It's true," Sarah insisted.

"Lamar's word will be hard to disprove. I suppose they also have the picture somewhere. It's just bad," Ben concluded.

Deborah, her tears about all wept out, proclaimed, "I'm going to call Rebecca right now. I thought she was a friend. How could she have done this to our girls?"

"No, don't, please Mother, she meant no harm," Sarah begged.

"I'm going to call right now," Deborah said without much emotion in her voice. "It is best to deal with this right away."

Martha made as if to speak, but her father stopped her. "Let your Mother call her friend. Not much of a friend she is, but it is best this way."

They watched as Deborah walked down to the phone booth by the end of the driveway. She must have known the number by heart, for she took nothing with her. It seemed like a long time before she retuned, but they were all still waiting for her. "Well, what did she say?" Ben asked.

"About the same thing as the girls," Deborah said numbly. "It still doesn't help much."

"Anything different?" Ben wanted to know.

"No," Deborah said, then changed her mind. "She did say that the model picture was run without the company's permission."

"Phillip said that?" Sarah asked, instantly attentive.

Ben also looked with interest. "Would that be the reported English boyfriend?"

Sarah blushed which caused her father to comment, "So that part is true, then?"

"No, no, he's not my boyfriend, but he promised me he wouldn't run the photo. Who did Rebecca say ran the photo then, Mother?"

"The secretary, he thinks. It was all a mistake. Rebecca seemed real sorry for the trouble this is causing. She said she would have come and told you sooner, if she known it would cause so much trouble."

"So she already knew about the photo?"

"Yes, Phillip called her on Saturday when he discovered it. But what has this all got to do with anything, Sarah? You are in a lot of trouble with the ministers."

Sarah was absorbing this new information quickly. She was also quickly reaching her own conclusions. "They can't ex-communicate me," she announced to the family.

"That is true," her father concurred, "but you are no longer in the instruction class. It will be very hard to get back in, plus all this will have to be explained to everyone's satisfaction."

"I'm going back to New York," she said, without any hesitation. They all looked at her puzzled.

"How is that going to help?" her father wanted to know.

"I don't know, but I don't really care right now. I tried to do the right thing. I turned down a lot of money Phillip offered me. I also turned down the possibility of his love and this is what I get for it. Maybe I ought to reconsider."

"You shouldn't get bitter," her father told her. "We must accept what God has for us."

"That's all well and good," Sarah said, "but right now, no one really believes my story. They all think I was trying to sneak off and do things when I was not. How am I going to convince them otherwise? It could take years."

"That's true," her father agreed, "but running away won't convince anyone either."

"I'm going," stated Sarah. This caused her mother to begin crying again.

"So, there is more to this than we thought?" stated her father simply. "I am glad you cannot be ex-communicated because you surely would be if you were a member."

"I am glad, too," Sarah told him. "It will spare you a lot of sorrow."

"When are you leaving?" Deborah wailed.

"As soon as I can talk with Rebecca, maybe the next time I clean for her."

Ben walked over and put his arm around his weeping wife's shoulder. "We must let her go, Deborah. It is in the hands of God now. He will give us grace to bear the burden."

Martha and Sarah left the room. Mark followed. They were all sober at the sight of their father bent over Deborah's rocker holding her.

"Are you sure this is the right thing to do?" Martha asked her sister.

She nodded, "There is no other way out of this."

The following week was a weary one for the Schwartz household as they prepared for Sarah's departure. Sarah went to call Rebecca, and later received confirmation through her, from Phillip, that she would be welcome to return to New York City. Plans were made for the next Monday.

Lamar took it upon himself to show up at Malinda's place in the middle of the week. He was confident of a positive reception, now that the word had had time to get around.

"Can I talk to Malinda?" he asked Naomi when she answered the door.

"Sure," she said, confirming his feelings of a good reception.

Naomi left him at the door while she went to call Malinda. When Malinda came down the stairs, she stopped when she saw him. Expecting to see a smile light up her face, Lamar experienced his first disappointment of the evening.

"Can we talk?" he asked quietly.

She nodded and followed him out onto the porch. Her heart was screaming inside of her, "He's back. Take him in your arms." However, another part of her she had known little about until recently was also making itself heard. "He's being dishonest. Don't let him get away with it."

"What do you want?" she asked still unsmiling.

It's just her disappointment at my leaving her. She doesn't know that I want to come back. Lamar gathered all his courage. "I just wanted to tell you that I am sorry for the way things have been between us. I know that you told me to leave, if I couldn't get my mind off of Sarah. Well, now I have my mind off of her. She is not the girl either of us thought she was. It is terrible what she has been doing."

"Sarah is a wonderful girl. Whatever you are saying about her makes no difference," Malinda told him, looking grim.

Lamar could not believe his ears. "Maybe you have not heard what she is doing?"

"I have heard," she told him.

"But," he started, "you don't understand."

"I understand perfectly. You are the one who does not understand. I know you, Lamar, and I don't believe what you are saying about Sarah. Don't think you can come sneaking around here to have me save your face just because you need a girl! As far as I am concerned, you aren't telling the truth about Sarah. Until you tell the truth I don't want to see you."

Lamar's mouth was open in astonishment. "You can't mean that!"

"That is the way it will be," she told him as she turned to go into the house.

With her hand on the doorknob, he figured there was no other choice. He headed down the steps and out to his buggy. He felt as if his world were crashing in on him.

Now I will be the laughingstock of the community, was his thought. As he drove away, he glanced at the front porch. It was empty.

Upstairs Malinda was sobbing into her pillow.

CHAPTER TWENTY-SIX

REBECCA CAME BY on Monday to drive Sarah to Indianap-olis. The pain of Sarah's departure was intense. Deborah sat in the rocker in the living room, crying softly.

"Take care of yourself," Martha told her. Her feelings about her sister leaving ranged from sorrow to excitement. "Don't forget us."

"I won't," Sarah told her.

As they drove to the airport, Rebecca seemed intent on making things as easy for everyone as possible. "I am really sorry about all this. I hope your mother will not blame me too much."

Sarah smiled, "She blames everyone, I think."

"I'll have to stop by and visit her soon. I really meant no harm."

"She knows it was my decision," Sarah told her.

"Well, be that as it is, I will see if I there is anything I can do to make it easier."

"It probably won't help since there is only one thing they want, and that is for me to come back."

"Any chance of that?" Rebecca wondered.

"I suppose."

"What about you and Phillip?"

Sarah nodded her head, "I'm going to consider it."

"I think that's wise." Rebecca glanced at her watch. "We

should be at the airport soon. Are you ready for New York City?"

"No," Sarah laughed. "Do you think I will survive?"

"Phillip will take care of you."

"This is all a big step," Sarah ignored the assurance. "But I will just take it one day at a time and see what happens."

"I'm sure you'll be fine," Rebecca said as they pulled into the short-term airport parking lot. "I will see you to the plane, but then you're on your own."

Sarah said nothing but took a deep breath.

They made their way through security and entered the terminal where the Cessna Citation 5 was parked. Sarah walked down by herself but stopped to wave at the window before boarding. The flight was uneventful and the landing was at LaGuardia soon after lunch. Not to her surprise, Phillip himself was waiting.

"Nice flight?" he asked, not sure where to go with this relationship now that he was actually alone with her. Her Amish dress hit him hard, for some reason. *Must be that she's by herself. We have to get her out of that clothing.*

"It was fine, thanks," she said as she smiled and looked intently into his face with her blue eyes. He felt himself relaxing and soon forgot how she looked. The innocence and sincerity with which she approached him moved him deeply.

"You are working for me now," he told her. "As they say, 'No more free lunches'."

"I know that," she said. "When do I start?"

"Tomorrow. No need to wait since we really do have great need for you. Let me tell you again how sorry I am for the ad that ran without your permission. I guess the positive part was that we got excellent feedback when it ran." Then he added, "The other good part is that you are here now." From his smile, it was clear how pleased he was about that.

As they walked through the airport she asked, "Was it really Camellia who ran the photo?"

"Yes, I think so. I can't prove it 100 percent, but she had both the motive and the opportunity. I fired her immediately."

"Oh," Sarah was shocked. "All because of me?"

"I think it was time for her to go anyway," he shrugged. "Now, are you ready for New York City?"

"I think so," she said, although it did not sound very convincing to either one of them.

He looked skeptically at her. "We will have to do better than that. Here is the plan. I have a condo for you. That is where you will be staying. One of our girls will stay with you for a week or so. That way you can come to work together, and she can show you around evenings. Of course, you might go out with me sometimes, too."

She blushed slightly, "Whatever you say."

Calling for a taxi, he held the door open for her before climbing in on the other side. "Continental Towers," he told the driver who looked strangely at them. Phillip felt himself getting tense again. *This has to stop. She has to get out of that clothing.*

As if she had read his thoughts she asked, "Where do I get some English clothing?"

It amused him to hear her ask for English clothing. "Why do you call them that?"

"Because that's what they are for us."

"Well, I guess," he agreed, "you could look at it like that. So are your clothes considered 'German clothing'?"

"Yes," she nodded, "but we just call it Amish."

"Makes sense to me," he told her. "There are some clothes for you at the condo. After all, we are designers so we have plenty to choose from. The girls picked out different sizes. If they don't fit, you can talk to Marci who will be staying with you."

"Thank you," Sarah told him.

"Don't worry," he assured her, smiling. "It all comes out of your wages now."

"By the way, how much am I being paid?" she asked.

Phillip quoted some figures which he explained were dependent upon sales and distribution figures. Sarah's mouth fell open. He chuckled at the look on her face. "So what do you think?"

"That should be plenty."

He nodded and smiled, "Good, I was hoping it would be. Marci will also help you set up a checking account and any other banking needs you have. From then on, you should be able to take care of it yourself. Think you can do it?"

She nodded her head, "I will be fine. You have done much more than is necessary."

"It is really my pleasure. Now here is the condo. I will see you to your room, then we can get to work tomorrow morning. Marci will be here sometime after five." As the taxi came to a halt, he climbed out and opened her door. Together they walked in, making for a strange-looking couple — even for New York City.

❧

Marci showed up at six, introduced herself, and helped Sarah get settled in. "Have you been to New York before?" she asked Sarah.

"Once."

"Well, I think you will get the hang of this quickly."

"I need some help with these dresses first," Sarah told her, pointing to the closet.

"That is where we will start then," Marci declared, walking over to see what had been sent over from Maxey Jacobs. "Looks like they sent over only the best."

"Really." Sarah was surprised. "I'm just wearing these to work, aren't I?"

"I guess Phillip wants you to look your best all the time."

"I suppose so." Sarah wished she could stop blushing every time Phillip's name was mentioned. English boys still felt strange to her.

What followed was a crash course in English dressing customs. Sarah insisted, to Marci's astonishment, on wearing only what she called modest dresses. Sarah's judgment on what she considered appropriate meant that about half of the selections were rejected before they even got started. The next problem surfaced when Sarah tried on her Amish head covering with one of the new dresses.

"That's not going to work," Marci announced.

"Why not?"

"It just doesn't."

"I'm not going out into the public with nothing on my head."

Marci pondered the problem for a time, then came up with a compromise. Sarah would wear a matching scarf with each outfit. Sarah was not sure she liked that idea, but decided to go along with it. It was better than nothing, and her Amish covering obviously would not work for her new position.

With that decided, they settled in for the night. In the morning it was down to the Pine Street offices for work. The first day was spent teaching Sarah the intense routine of fashion modeling. Here again, her customs and beliefs got in the way of some things. She steadfastly refused to be seen with her hair uncovered in the presence of men. If not for Phillip's intervention, this preference would not have been tolerated. "Humor her," he instructed the manager. "She might come around."

Life quickly became a blur of dressing rooms, poses, clicking cameras, and learning the ways of the City. In the evenings for the first few weeks, Phillip often took her to restaurants he liked: Emily's, the Manhattan Café, Christo's, and O'Lunney's were among the places they frequented. Finally Sarah found herself longing for a simple supper table with meat, corn, and potatoes, and windows she could open to let in fresh country air.

"So how are you doing?" he asked her, late one evening. They were at the Café Bondi after she had requested Italian food.

"Okay, I guess," she told him, weary to the bone.

"Are we working you too hard?" he asked, concerned.

"No, no," she assured him, "it's just there never seems to be time enough to rest."

"After you get used to life in the City, it gets better."

She was not that sure of his reasoning, but tried to go along. "I suppose so."

"Are we paying you enough?" he asked.

"Enough?" she exclaimed, "I can't believe the amount of money you give me."

He chuckled, "We are doing okay. Sales of the Densine Line are excellent. Reviews have been very positive. I have no complaints and I should probably pay you even more."

"No, you should not," Sarah stated emphatically. "It's plenty already."

What he did not know was that she was sending a large portion of the money home. No one could hold her to Amish rules in New York City, but she wanted her parents to have some of the money. It was a matter of conscience and for other, more subconscious reasons she felt without being able to articulate.

Phillip was looking at her with an expression of wonderment on his face. "You are an amazing girl."

"Really?" she asked. This time she was too tired to blush.

"Yes," he said. "You are amazing in so many ways. I am glad to have met you and even more glad you are here."

"Thanks," she said simply and waited to see if he would continue. He seemed to want to but hesitated. Instead, he motioned for the waiter. "Time to get some rest, don't you think?"

She nodded, feeling a sense of relief, as if this were ground for which she was not yet prepared.

"Let's go then," he said, rising to his feet. She followed him out to the sidewalk, and she was suddenly in awe of how much and how quickly life had changed for her. Here she was freely associating with an English boy, working for him, and..." she abruptly stopped there. *No, I am not his girl-friend. Not yet, at least.*

As if he had read her thoughts, Phillip reached for her hand. She felt his fingers slip into hers, smooth and without calluses. Her reaction was instinctual, "We can't do that," as she pulled her hand away from his.

He could not have been more astonished. "You can't do that?"

"I'm Amish," she said simply.

"The Amish don't hold hands?" he asked.

"Some do, but we don't," she explained.

"I see," he said, not seeing at all. "Here is the taxi."

Getting in, they drove to her condo in silence, both of them puzzled by the gulf between them and what could be done about it.

"See you tomorrow," he told her, opening the taxi door for her as he always did.

"Tomorrow it is," she told him and she walked in without looking back. Right now, she was too tired to think. However, Sarah suddenly knew that that time was coming.

CHAPTER TWENTY-SEVEN

MELVIN WAS VISITING Sarah's district this Sunday morning. He watched the ministers file upstairs as the baptismal class followed. That Sarah was not among them was now old news. Yet, there were some people, Melvin among them, whose Sarah's absence still bothered. At present, there was little information available about her, other than that she was in New York City. Her family was staying tight-lipped about the situation.

This did not surprise him, as he expected he would have done the same in similar circumstances. Why give out information that could be detrimental? If New York City had been closer, or if there had been any Amish living in the city, the family's silence would have been useless. News would have been obtained. As it was, the lack of news bode ill. It must mean things were not going well from the Amish perspective.

The week after her departure, a sense of relief swept the community. Not that Melvin shared that feeling but he understood its meaning. A tremendous problem had been presented by the accusations against Sarah by Lamar, supported by the photo in the "USA Today". The fact that nothing could be proven definitively only added to the gravity of the situation.

If Sarah were to have stuck to her denial, or even if she had produced a letter from "Maxey Jacobs" stating her case, it would not have helped. The underlying accusation of violating tenets of the Amish faith, as well as the general Amish suspicion of human nature, would have prevented the issue from any satisfactory conclusion.

Years of friendships and hard-won church loyalty could have been lost if everyone had been forced to take sides. This way was much easier. To them, a real sin was more forgivable than an imagined one. Moreover, this conformed to their view of what young people do. It was now a manageable problem. The lines had been clearly drawn, just as they all liked them to be.

Melvin wondered if any of this had had anything to do with Sarah leaving. Whether it had meant nothing one way or the other as far as the church people were concerned. It was un-provable, and made no difference. What counted was what one did.

To Melvin, however, it did make a difference. He wished he could know for sure. It might have a lot to do with whether she was coming back. That question mattered to him. Coming back would not simply be enough either. She must come back willingly, untainted by what she was experiencing. Otherwise, there might always be the risk of her leaving again.

These were matters of grave concern, he knew. Although they were too much for him, Melvin pondered them nevertheless. Only this morning, he overheard Bishop Amos talking with *Bloh* Jonas in the line of men outside the barn.

"She is?" *Bloh* Jonas asked.

"Yes, that is what my wife told me."

"Sending her money home?"

"Yes, at least part of it."

"This is good news, then, don't you think?"

"I believe so."

"My Malinda has good things to say about her also. Maybe the time will come when the wild oats are out of her?"

"We hope so," Bishop Amos had said quietly.

Melvin was sure the conversation was about Sarah. No other girl fit the description. If she was sending her money home, it had tremendous meaning in the Amish world. Money, to them, was what turned the waters of many a stream.

The time had come for Melvin to make a decision. He realized this and also knew the consequences of a wrong decision. Waiting to see how things turned out would be an option, he guessed, but it was not in his nature to do so. He would make his decision now, and live with the consequences. The wrong decision could cost him a lot but he was willing to put his money where his heart was.

After church, he drove home, made the conscious choice to attend the singing in his own district. The next morning the conversation came up naturally enough to allow him to tell his parents.

"Were you visiting again in Glendale yesterday?" his mother asked him.

He nodded, "Yes."

"You didn't stay for the singing there, though?" his father asked.

"No," he told them, "I decided to come on back to our own district for the singing."

"So it's not a girl," his mother said to no one in particular.

"I wouldn't be so sure," his father remarked.

Melvin saw his chance. "I am buying a farm in the area."

His father was not totally surprised. "There are better prices down there, but are you sure it is wise? If you ever decide to sell, the sale will not be as good. Most of us stay north of the highway."

"I think I'll do it," Melvin told them simply. "I've thought about it a long time, and I think it's time."

"You could buy closer to us," his mother said, not totally pleased.

"Yes," he told her, "but I think around Whitfield would be a good spot. I like the area down there."

"Like anything else?" his father asked him.

Melvin said nothing. It would be hard to explain this, even if he tried. So he simply fell back on the Amish defense of saying nothing.

"Well, it's up to you, I guess," his mother told him, looking at his father. "You are getting older, but you are still welcome at home."

"I know that," he said. "You have done a lot for me."

They both nodded their appreciation of his gratitude.

After breakfast, Melvin left to start his real estate transaction in Worthington. The agent driving him around looking at available farms took most of the day. When he left the office in Worthington that evening, he carried with him a contract on 120 acres just outside the town of Whitfield. The closing date was in sixty days.

Lamar's world had improved little. None of the honor he had been expecting from disclosing Sarah's photo materialized. He was also without a girl. There were many girls he could have dated, but none he wanted. To make matters worse, he had already heard of two boys who had asked Malinda for a Sunday evening date. That she had declined was obvious. What was not so obvious was whether she would continue to do so.

His conscience, an entity with which he had little contact prior to all this, also made its debut. He hated it, but it would not be silent. It popped up at the most inconvenient times. When he most wanted to forget his troubles, it only made matters worse. His physical surroundings in matters of his heart now matched the desolation of his soul. The eternal love of God, which surpasses the understanding of human beings, was making its appearance.

He would not yield, though. To do so would involve too much. Some girl he liked would come along. He was sure of it. Visitors would come through from time to time. On this he pinned his hopes for a while. When nothing happened, he fell into despair again.

Rallying his spirit, he resolved to go on. *Something will come up,* he told himself.

❧

It was Millie Anderson who worked in the costume department who showed the article to Sarah. "It's just a gossip column," she assured Sarah. "They are known for their nastiness."

Sarah took the offered New York paper gingerly: "What is Phillip up to?" the headline of the article read.

"It's really nothing," Millie offered, shrugging. "They do this all the time."

"What is it about?" Sarah asked.

"Silly, about you and Phillip, of course."

Sarah only looked blankly at Millie.

"Did you think it would stay a secret forever? You can't date the owner of one of the top designer firms for women's clothing in New York City and expect no one to notice."

"I'm not dating him," she protested.

Millie chuckled, "See what the article says."

Concentrating, Sarah scanned the words, "What is Phillip up to?...the young, part owner of Maxey Jacobs...

company whose stock soars higher each day, it seems…has been spotted around New York's trendiest restaurants with his new girlfriend…is she his girlfriend?…they have never been seen holding hands or trading other affections, yet he is with her often…is this romance without love?…the mystery only deepens…it seems young Phillip is also using her as his top model in his *Densine Line* of designer women's clothing, which, one might note, is soaring in sales…. My question, is Phillip dating a nun…. I personally checked after noting this curiosity…. The girl always appears in public with a headdress, although never in the ads…. What has Phillip found the rest of us have missed?…. Her name was difficult to come by, but it is Sarah Schwartz…could there be other mysteries about this girl?"

Sarah felt weak in the knees, and almost let the paper drop from her hand. Millie chuckled, "Don't take it too hard. It's just gossip."

I have to talk to Phillip about this, was her first thought. But what was there to talk about? *Am I his girlfriend? Oh, no, I can't go there, but I have to talk to him.*

"You'll be okay," Millie chuckled again. "This job pays enough for some bumps and bruises, don't you think?"

Sarah nodded numbly, but she was not thinking about bumps and bruises. She was thinking about Phillip. *I will see him tonight.* She carefully folded the paper and placed it in her bag.

When Phillip picked her up at the condo she asked him where they were going. She did not really care where they went, but asked because she was nervous.

"Mulholland Drive," he told her. "Or do you want to go somewhere else?"

"No, no, that's fine," she told him quickly.

Making small talk, she kept her nerves under control until they got to the restaurant. After ordering, she produced her copy of the New York paper. Glancing at it, he laughed, "Don't take it seriously."

"But I do," she told him.

"Well, I guess it does reveal a problem we should deal with," he finally admitted.

"And that is?" she asked him.

"You and me," he said, turning his chair to face her.

She held his gaze. "How are we?" she asked.

He paused, thinking for a moment. "It is like this. We are neither here nor there, it seems to me. I am who I am. You are who you are, but neither of us has moved much towards the other. Shouldn't we be doing that? Also, we don't define things, for some reason. I am not used to that."

"What do you want to define?" she asked him.

"It's not that I really want to, maybe that bothers me. Take, for example, you working for the company. You still have no contract with us."

"Does that bother you?"

"No, but it's not normal. No one else in my world would think of working without a contract."

"Have you heard me complaining?"

"No, and that is good, but it still bothers me how we do things. I ask you out for evenings, yet are we dating?"

"The papers say we are."

"That is because the papers are normal. They live in the usual world."

"So, we don't?"

He shook his head, "Of course we don't."

"I'm sorry," she told him.

Her hand was on the table, and he reached over and gently took it. She made no effort to pull away. "We need to decide. What are we? Am I going to be like you, or are you going to be like me, or," he sighed, "are we just going to make things up as we go along? Just hoping it turns out right?"

She let her eyes fall to the table and to his hand still wrapped around her fingers. Her training was screaming for her to pull away, but she overrode it to speak from her heart.

"I understand, Phillip," she said. "I guess some of it is my fault. I have just been letting things go along without much thought. It hasn't been fair to you."

"No," he shook his head, "I am as much at fault as you are. That is why I am glad this conversation has come up. There are so many things I like about you, Sarah Schwartz," he smiled gently at the playful formality, "but I have to be true to what I am also." She nodded, as he continued, "You do things that don't bother me that much, but yet they are not where I live."

She nodded in agreement.

He continued, "These are things from your upbringing, no doubt, and they are good things, but they are not my world: your insistence on certain dresses, your wearing of that head covering in public, and other little things that I had hoped would change."

"But they haven't," she finished for him.

He drew his hand back, and settled back in his seat. All around them were other couples and singles engaged in conversation like theirs, in public but, at the same time, totally private. Sarah was suddenly struck by the contradiction as she waited for him to continue.

CHAPTER TWENTY-EIGHT

Thinking of himself was Lamar's habit. He had never thought of the necessity of changing that. On his own, he would not have changed that habit now either, if he had not been nudged in that direction by a totally unexpected chain of events.

Bloh Jonas held a work frolic for the young people one Friday night. Those who wanted to could come and husk corn by the full moon. It was not expected that much work would be done, or that it needed to be. Jonas had other methods of harvesting his corn crop, but this provided needed diversion and fun for the young people.

Not attending was Lamar's first inclination. He discarded that thought, however, when he thought about how it might look. "Can't keep the girl, and now afraid of her place," was what the story among the boys would be.

So he went and even enjoyed himself. The moon had just risen, and about twenty-five young people followed the wagon through the corn patch. Full ears of corn made rhythmic thumps on the wagon's sideboards to the patter of their conversation.

It was when he drifted towards the back of the group that he heard Malinda and her cousin talking. In the semi-darkness, they were not paying attention to him.

"Did he ever ask to come back?" the cousin asked.

"Yes," Malinda's voice answered.

"Why didn't you let him?"

Lamar was sure he heard a slight sob before Malinda answered, "I couldn't because he is not telling the truth about Sarah."

"But why are you worrying about Sarah? She's gone."

"I'm not worrying about her. I'm looking out for myself. I can't go with a boy who is lying."

"So you still like him?"

"Of course," Malinda said, "more than I can say."

Lamar moved forward quickly down the corn row, afraid they would notice him and realize he had been listening. This put things in a totally different light. She was putting him off, not because she wanted to, but because of her principles.

He pondered that the rest of the evening and into the rest of the week. The guilt of his own position became ever more evident to him. By Saturday evening he was ready. With his conscience firmly in place, he harnessed his horse. He stopped first at the deacon's place.

"So part of your story was not true?" the deacon asked him from where they were standing on the front porch.

"Yes," Lamar told him.

"The picture was real, though?"

"Yes."

"Well, I don't see how this changes anything. You shouldn't have lied and you need to make that right with those you have harmed."

"I think I have done that by telling you," Lamar told him. "Well, there is someone else I need to tell this to," he added.

"That is as it may be," the deacon said. "Sarah is in New York City. She went there by her own choice. We will take all this into account if she ever comes back."

"I'm sorry," Lamar muttered, making a move to leave the porch.

"It is good that you came," the deacon told him.

Lamar walked out to the horse, untied it and drove out the lane. His next stop was *Bloh* Jonas's place. By now it was late, but he hoped Malinda would still be up. Pulling in the driveway, he saw that lights were still on in the living room and in her upstairs bedroom.

Naomi answered the door. "Can I see Malinda?" he asked.

"Sure," she told him, "I will get her."

Moving out to the porch to wait, he did not turn around when the front door opened and closed. He felt her presence behind him as she stood waiting.

"I have come to say that I am sorry," he said without turning around.

"Sorry for what?" she asked him.

"For the lies I told about Sarah," he said turning around.

She drew her breath in sharply, "Have you told anyone else about this?"

"I just came from the deacon's place," he said. "I told him the truth this time."

"And?" she waited.

"He said he was glad I came, but it did not make that much difference."

"Was the photo a lie too?"

"No, just the things I added about it."

Lamar felt greatly humbled by all this, but at the same time cleaned and cleansed. He decided the feeling was desirable. It also made him refrain from asking what was uppermost on his mind, namely, whether he could date her again.

Turning, he made as if to go, but she stopped him with a move of her hand. "Does your question from last time still stand?"

Surprised, he looked at her, "Yes, of course."

"Then you may," she said smiling deeply.

He was overcome with a feeling to which he was not accustomed. Tears threatened to come to his eyes. "I don't know what to say," he finally said, coming close to her and placing his hand on her shoulder.

She gently removed his hand. "This time, none of that, okay? Not until we're married."

Again he was surprised at his feelings. He was not angry with her. Instead he felt relief, gladness even, at the new world of goodness he found himself in. "We had better start talking about those wedding plans, then," he told her.

She was smiling again. "I'll see you Sunday night then."

"Yes," was all he could manage to say as she turned and left him standing in the front yard.

❧

"I like you Sarah, very much. It is just that things can't go on like this. Excuse me for wanting things my way, but I do."

"What is your way?" she asked him.

"That you come to my world," he said softly, looking intently at her face. "Could you do that?"

"Would you want that?" she asked, meeting his gaze.

"Well, a part of me does, but I'm not sure."

"Are you comfortable with me doing it just for your sake?"

He pondered that. "I would almost say 'yes', but no. That would not do. I would not feel right about it, knowing you had given up something you desired for me."

"I could do that," she told him. "Is that not what wives are supposed to do?"

He chuckled at that. "Maybe in your world, but even

there this would be stretching it. No, Sarah," he paused as if becoming clear himself. "For us, it would never work. Our hearts are not in the same place."

"And if they are not?" she asked him.

"Then we must face reality."

"I see," she said.

"I'm sorry," he took her hand again.

"It's not your fault," she told him. "I know it is true. You have been wonderful to me, Phillip."

He dropped his eyes to the table.

"There is another girl," she said softly, "isn't there?"

"Maybe," he raised his eyes to meet hers.

"It's okay," she assured him. "Remember we have no agreed arrangement."

"But you have led me to her, and for that I am grateful," he told her quickly.

"Well," she said, "that's something to be thankful for."

"You showed me what I wanted."

"Don't go comparing her to me," Sarah told him force-fully. "That's not fair to the girl."

"I know," he said, "I don't, but one still values the begin-ning of the road which leads to the desired destination."

"Is she in your world?" Sarah asked in a weak voice.

He smiled slightly, "I think so. Is there not someone who is in yours?"

Sarah thought about that for a moment, surrounded by the soft lighting and the murmur of voices. "Not that I know for certain," but then her eyes shone with a faraway look. Her memory was of a confident Amish boy who was not afraid of her.

"There is," he said with a twinkle in his eyes.

"Well," she wrinkled her forehead, "I told him off. By this time he's probably long gone."

"You never know," he told her. "Life leads us in strange

directions. Who would have thought I would ever meet an Amish girl and be so much better off for the experience?"

"Thank you," she told him, her voice breaking. "You have been very kind to me."

"It's been a pleasure, Sarah Schwartz, Amish beauty. You have been an angel. To many happy years with your Amish beloved."

She laughed out loud at his pronouncement. "I am not an angel."

"I know," he said, "you just look like one. Now, we must be going. Can we make some final arrangements? It might be best that way."

"You mean I can't keep working for you?" she asked, trying to sound hurt.

He chuckled, "You can work as long as you want, but I have a feeling you will be wanting to get back soon."

"Two weeks," she told him without thinking long.

He thought about that. "Make it three, please. We will have run the final photos for the Densine Line by then. The season will be over, and for the next round we can start over again with a new lead model."

She smiled, "Three weeks it will be then."

"Agreed," he said, as they rose from the table.

⟨≋⟩

Sarah wrote another letter that evening to Martha. At first, she had thought of addressing the letters to her mother when writing home, but concluded that the tension of opening a letter from her would be less if Martha received the mail.

"Dear Ones," she wrote: "Things have wrapped up here in New York, and I will be coming home in three weeks. Don't worry about picking me up at the airport. Rebecca will take care of that. I look forward to seeing all of you."

SARAH

When the letter arrived, it caused the usual level of interest in the Schwartz household. Deborah sat in the rocker in great anticipation as Martha opened and read the letter silently first. News from Sarah was talked about for days.

This time, Martha's face drained of color as she read silently.

Deborah gasped from her rocker, "Oh, no, she's marrying that English boy. Please, *Gott im Himmel*, help us!"

"Mom, she's coming home," Martha said loudly to break through her mother's thoughts of disaster.

"She is what?" Deborah sat bolt upright.

"The letter says she will be home on the 24th."

"Oh," Deborah cast her eyes around frantically for the calendar, "that's in two weeks."

"A little more," Martha corrected her.

"Do you think she's changed?" Deborah's eyes were clouded with worry.

"I don't know, Mother." Martha was not sure what to say. As a matter of fact, she was worried herself.

"Oh, we will never live down the shame if she comes home looking like an English girl," Deborah moaned in agony at the thought.

Martha did not tell her mother her own thoughts, but if Sarah came home in that condition it would really make life more difficult for her, too. Now that the baptismal class had been completed and the applicants had been baptized, she was seriously considering announcing her secret talks with the Mennonite, Silas Mast. That way she could openly court him, instead of only sneaking a few words with him now and then. Two daughters leaving the Amish faith at once might simply be too much sorrow for her mother. *Please, let her come home decent, at least.*

"We must get ready," Deborah announced. "The house has to be cleaned. We must make some cherry pies. Sarah just loves those. Oh, my, what in the world are we going to do? Is she really marrying that rich English boy?"

"I don't think so, Mother," Martha calmed her down, hoping against hope it was true. *Surely she wouldn't do that and not tell me.*

CHAPTER TWENTY-NINE

PHILLIP SAID HIS goodbye to Sarah on her last day at work on Pine Street. He called her into his office and closed the door. Taking her hands in his he kissed her gently on the cheek. "All happiness to you, angel. It is best this way," he told her softly.

She nodded, wishing he hadn't kissed her, but she understood. It was his way. "May God give you a good life," she told him. "As our preachers say, 'May He cause His light to shine upon you.'"

He laughed, releasing her hands. "You are something, aren't you? Well, I am glad to have met you. The plane will be ready when you get to the airport. If you ever need anything, let me know."

She looked intently at him, "Are you serious?"

"Sure, why not?" he replied. "If there is something I can do, I will."

"I'll be going then," she told him, turning to go. She left him standing there, straight and erect by his desk, his arms folded. Momentary regret passed through her mind, but her heart steadied her. She was going home.

Taking the taxi to LaGuardia, she found the correct terminal and ten minutes later the Cessna Citation took off. On the flight, she removed her English dress and changed into her full Amish clothing. When they landed in Indianapolis an Amish girl walked down the steps onto the tarmac.

Rebecca was waiting inside, and hugged her when she saw her. "It's so good to see you."

"You, too," she told her. "How is Mom?"

"I haven't seen her for a few weeks, but she was okay then. I suppose they will be glad to see you." Rebecca looked carefully at Sarah. "You haven't changed much."

"No," Sarah laughed softly. "New York was good, but I am glad to be home."

"Well, let's get you there, then," Rebecca said, leading the way out of the terminal to her waiting car.

On the drive down, Sarah told Rebecca all about her time in New York. Even the part about Phillip. "I can see the point," Rebecca told her. "I had high hopes for the two of you, but it's probably best this way. Are you telling your Mom about this?"

Sarah shook her head in horror, "No."

"Even if she asks?"

"No details," Sarah emphasized. "It is best that way."

When they pulled into the driveway, both Martha and Deborah were waiting on the front porch. "Oh, my, how does she look? Can you see, Martha? Can you see anything?"

"We will have to wait," Martha told her mother calmly.

When the car came to a stop, Sarah opened the car door and got out slowly. All around her the sounds and smells of home swept over her. She savored the wind in the trees, the background smell of the barn, and the simple white house.

On the porch, the color was returning to Deborah's face. "Oh, *Gott sei dank* (God be thanked) Martha, she looks normal."

"Yes, she does," Martha smiled, walking down the sidewalk to meet her sister.

The rest of the evening and the next day were a flurry of activity and talk. Mark and Ben participated as much as they could, but it was mainly the women who talked. Since

Sarah showed no signs of English dress or mannerisms, their hearts flowed together without fear. Even Ben let himself go and laughed at her stories of New York City.

On Saturday morning, though, he approached her with a worried look on his face. Clearing his throat, he told Sarah, "You will need to go see the deacon this evening. I will take you myself. It will be better to make your things right before we go to church on Sunday."

Expecting an outburst from her, he was greatly surprised when she immediately agreed. "What time?" she asked him.

"Around six," he told her. So that was how they found themselves pulling into Deacon Stephen's driveway a little before six thirty. He could not have been more astonished to see Sarah. He looked her up and down sharply, while his wife came forward to shake Sarah's hand. He must have seen nothing amiss because he seemed to relax. "Let's step out on the porch," he said after his wife finished greeting Sarah and welcomed her back.

When they got out, Ben cleared his throat. "We have come to make things right with the church concerning Sarah's matter. Hopefully this can be done without too much trouble."

"You are back to stay?" the deacon asked, looking at Sarah.

"Yes," she stated simply.

The deacon cleared his throat. "Since you left we have had confirmation that your story was correct about the photo in the paper. Why did you leave for New York City then?"

"I had to see this matter through for myself," Sarah told him. "I have seen the big city, but now I am back. I want to join the next instruction class, if I can settle my things with the church."

Ben sighed in relief. *She was saying all the right things. Where did the girl get it from?*

Stephen was smiling, "That is good to hear. I will tell this to Bishop Amos tomorrow, and I believe this matter can be settled very quickly."

"I am willing to make a confession," Sarah offered.

"Oh," the deacon waved his hand, "that most likely will not be necessary. We have heard good things about you since you left. I am sure that this matter is already settled. If not, I will let you know."

"Thank you then," Sarah told him and turned to go.

On the way home Ben could not stop looking at her. "How did you do that?"

"It was the right thing to do," she told him, refusing to comment any further.

Deborah wept openly when Ben told her how it went. "My daughter is back again," she sobbed.

⟨≋⟩

He found her, later the next week. She had gone to spend some time at the park, east of Dogwood Lake, having driven down by herself with the old driving horse. She was standing looking out over the water when he came up quietly behind her.

"Good evening," he said.

She knew who it was without turning around. "You have come," she stated simply.

"You were expecting me?" he asked, already knowing the answer.

She shrugged her shoulders, "Yes."

"It's a beautiful evening," he stated. "This is a nice place."

"Yes," she said, offering no more.

"I was hoping you would come back," he told her. "It is good that you did."

His characteristic confidence and boldness moved her, as it had that first night when he approached her at the ball field. "Really?" she responded, not knowing what else to say.

He nodded his head. "You are one of us, Sarah. Your home is here. I am one who has been glad for a long time that it is so."

Sarah smiled at him. "Well, I am back."

Melvin's hands hung at his side, palms rough from farming. His eyes did not flinch or seek to overwhelm her. They were simple in their directness and calm assurance. She felt comforted and at peace. This was indeed home. He could not have said it better. More than that, he could not have corresponded better to her vision of what home was. "I am glad to be back," she told him.

Together they walked along the lakeshore. She told him about New York City, about the modeling she did, of all the money involved, and she told him about Phillip. He said little, only listening. "It is right that you came back," he stated simply when she was done.

She looked at him again, the shadows of the evening now wrapping themselves around the landscape. His form was still outlined against the water as it rippled slightly when stirred. "I would not have had it any other way," she stated, meaning every word.

"I will see you Sunday night then?" he stated more than asked.

She nodded her head, barely seeming to move against the dark background of the land.

"Let's get you home, then," he said, leading the way to their buggies.

The next Sunday was already the second one for which Sarah was home. Things had already greatly calmed down from the curiosity expressed when she first returned. Word had had time to get around that the ministers had accepted her. Melvin was well-known by this time because of the farm he had purchased in the area. By the time he drove Sarah home, her place in the community had been fully restored.

Esther, though she mentioned it to no one, was not all that happy. Not that she could do anything, but it all seemed a little too improbable to her. Sarah seemed capable of pulling off stunts that would have entangled others for years. Sarah had somehow managed to clear everything up in a matter of days. This served to increase Esther's suspicions of what could be behind all of this.

As she and Melvin drove home in his buggy after the singing, Sarah exulted in the feeling of the buggy wheels humming on the pavement and the wild pull of a horse on his reins. The darkness accelerated the impression of speed as she laughed out loud for joy.

"Happy tonight?" Melvin glanced in her direction, hanging on to the reins with both hands.

"Glad to be back," she said quickly, lest he read too much into her joy.

He chuckled, "Not quite like a plane, but still fun."

"Actually, better," she said without hesitation.

He shrugged his shoulders. "God has given each of us his pleasure. It is wise that we walk in the joys that we have."

She was a little astonished at his pronouncements, but decided that it fit his personality well. She also decided again that she liked it.

"You have bought a farm in the area?" she asked him.

"Yes," he allowed, "are you dating me for my farm?"

She laughed again, thoroughly amused at the thought. "Not exactly."

"That's good," he told her, "glad we have that straight."

When she laughed again, he allowed himself a few chuckles. "You could probably pay off my farm in a year doing work in New York City."

"I suppose so," she said, wondering where he was going with this line of thought.

"It's better this way," he said softy, "much better."

"You really think so?" she asked, wanting to see what he would say.

"Yes," he said, "It is better for a man to work with the sweat of his brow. That is our way."

His words soothed her and confirmed her own feelings. A fresh feeling of belonging swept over her. As he turned his horse into her driveway, she was sure she had come home in more ways than just coming back to this house.

The evening passed quickly. At the end of it, Melvin suggested they sing a song together before he left. Not sure what to expect, she agreed. She could not have been more surprised. When he led in the song, he sang with a beautiful deep baritone. She had no problem joining in.

"You can sing," she told him when they were done.

"You're not too bad yourself."

"I love music," she told him.

"It is one of the most beautiful things on this earth," he stated simply. "God Himself must have wanted us to sing."

"Good-night," he said, his hand on the doorknob, "see you next Sunday?"

She simply nodded as he stepped into the night.

CHAPTER THIRTY

THE MONTHS PASSED quickly. Sarah and Melvin saw each other every Sunday night, and grew ever more comfortable and at ease in the relationship with each other. After communion in the fall, another baptismal class began which Sarah joined.

Now that she had been baptized, Martha took it upon herself to break the news about Silas to her mother. "I like a Mennonite boy," she announced one afternoon without any introductions.

It was Martha who was surprised when her mother showed no astonishment. "I figured something was up," she said, without looking up from her work.

"How did you know?"

"I didn't, at least not the details."

"Who told you?" Martha demanded to know.

"Look," Deborah gave her a look, "it's not your place to be asking the questions, but if you want to know, Mandy Esh said her young people mentioned they saw you talking to a Mennonite boy. Several times now, they said."

"Well," Martha decided to make the plunge, "I want to date him."

"You should have done that before you were baptized. You know you can't now."

"I didn't want to hurt you," she said softly.

"So why are you now?"

Martha sighed, "I like him."

"In that case, you will have to join the Mennonites. You can't date him while you are Amish."

"You don't care if I join the Mennonites?"

"Of course we care. That's why you're not dating any Mennonite until you are twenty-one. After that, maybe you'll have some sense in your head."

"That's two more years," Martha wailed.

"Then it's time to start liking a nice Amish boy. You could be married by that time."

Martha gave up, knowing that further pleading was useless. *I hope Silas waits for me that long.*

"He will, if he's worth anything," her mother smiled as if she knew her thoughts.

"It's not fair," she proclaimed.

"No one said it was. We just have to deal with what God gives us."

"Why does Sarah have all the good things happening to her?"

"She's staying Amish," Deborah gave her a look.

Martha decided it was time to stop talking again.

⌇

As they were driving home on the Sunday of her baptism, Melvin asked Sarah whether she would marry him. He asked it casually enough, a natural extension of where both their thoughts had already gone.

She said simply, "Of course," as she moved over in the buggy seat until she was fully leaning against him. He kept his hands on the reins. In the darkness with the buggy wheels humming on the pavement, they simply enjoyed each other's presence.

Unbeknownst to them, that week was when Esther

decided to check up on Sarah. Still curious how Sarah had done it, Esther stopped by the *Bloh* Jonas' residence on Tuesday night. Arriving at suppertime, she was not considered an intruder, but invited to join the meal.

Esther waited until the meal was over, and the older children were cleaning the dishes in the kitchen, before she mentioned the subject of her visit.

"So, Sarah Schwartz got baptized last Sunday?"

Jonas and Naomi were both still lingering at the table anticipating that Esther had something on her mind. They both nodded.

"I am uneasy about her."

"Really?" Naomi was surprised. "Malinda has so many good things to say about her."

Jonas was pretty sure he knew where Esther's questioning was going. "The ministers have approved of her fully," he said calmly.

"But how is that possible?" Esther probed. "Did you fully research all that she did in New York City? Maybe now that she is a member would be the time to have her confess fully and do repentance?"

Normally Jonas would not have divulged such ministerial information to a woman without her husband present, but since there was no husband, he told her, "Both Deacon Steven, Bishop Amos, and I have asked the questions we wanted to ask, and we feel nothing else is necessary. Now if you have new information that she has done something since she came home, that might be different. Otherwise, the past must be left in the past."

Esther shrugged her shoulders, "Well, if that is how it is, then that is how it is."

"It is," Jonas nodded, "and we will just leave it at that." Rising, he excused himself and headed to the barn to do some last-minute chores.

Esther chatted awhile with Naomi and then left, her horse plodding out the driveway.

❧

The wedding was to be a huge affair. The first daughter of Ben and Deborah Schwarz was to be married. Sarah chose a light cream-colored cloth for her dress, and matching darker brown for her attendants. Martha was chosen for Sarah's side and one of Melvin's brothers for his side. The brother already had a girlfriend, so that was simple enough for him. Martha had Silas, but only informally. Because of Deborah's prohibition, they were not dating yet. Now, Deborah would have nothing of this either.

"She is not sitting with that boy," Deborah declared. "It will be an Amish boy. Maybe if she is around a decent one, she will get some sense in her head."

Martha loudly protested, to no avail, "It's not fair to Silas."

"It's got nothing to do with him. We owe him nothing," Deborah silenced her. "Now *behayf dich selvaht*" (behave yourself).

"We'll find someone," Sarah added her voice to the mix in the hopes of calming her sister. "It's only for one day."

"Okay," Martha said, trying to calm down, "I guess I can make it, but I want to make my own pick."

"That's fine, whatever you want," Sarah told her.

She thought for a moment. "I want Mark's friend, Will Stoll."

"That's a good choice," Deborah declared. "Now, if you have any sense you'll marry him."

Martha made a face discreetly in no one's direction.

The invitations were sent out. Sarah took her mother aside and asked whether she could send one to Rebecca and also to Phillip, by that same route.

Deborah hesitated for a moment but then relented, "You have been real good since you came home. I guess you deserve that."

Sarah took one of the invitations, made a note in one for Rebecca and stuck it in a larger envelope. Adding another invitation for Phillip, she wrote on the small cover envelope, "Please pass on to Phillip." On the inside of the card she wrote, "Bring her, too." Smiling, she sealed and dropped it on the pile to be mailed out.

❧

The sun rose on a perfect day that Thursday. Bishop Amos was to perform the ceremony, while one of the ministers from Melvin's home district would hold the main sermon. Ministerial functions, even in Amish weddings, are performed at the request of the bride and groom.

Phillip could not resist the invitation and arrived promptly at nine o'clock with Rebecca and Bill. Phillip's wife was with him, too. Long lines of men in black hats, white shirts, and black dress suits were filing into the house.

There were no parking attendants, but it was clear what was expected. Vehicles were segregated into English and Amish sections. The buggies were on one side and the automobiles on the other side of the barn. Mostly there were vans bringing in the visiting Amish relatives.

Cautiously the party of four got out of Rebecca's Toyota. The air was completely still, except for the last-minute sound of an Amish attendee's horse clopping down the road.

Walking up to the house, they were met by what appeared to be an usher, although he was dressed like everyone else. They were taken inside and were told to sit in a room with a clear view of the rest of the house. They were allowed to remain seated as couples although the rest of the house was set up clearly into male and female sections.

Phillip's back ached for support before the first song had ended. In spite of his pain, the soaring sound of German singing continued with the voice of the entire congregation rising and falling in perfect unison. The experience was slightly disconcerting. He held onto his wife's hand when he noticed her looking strangely at him. About his age, she was a tall dark-blond country girl with good looks. Her name was Megan and she had grown up on her father's horse farm in Kentucky. It was clear to any who saw her looking at Phillip that she adored him. "They are normal," he whispered to her.

Afterwards there were sermons and then another one, and finally the ceremony. After a leisurely closing, Phillip checked his watch and saw that the whole service had taken more than three hours.

Everyone filed out of the house and the men congregated in the yard. Across the driveway, the double doors of the pole barn were being pushed open. The inside revealed that tables had been set along the outer walls with two rows down the center. Three men began giving directions for the seating. Phillip and his party were seated at one of the center tables.

After the tables were filled, the time for grace was announced. A prayer was read by *Bloh* Jonas as heads were bowed. Servers then began scurrying to their assigned tables. Starting at the end of each long table, plates of food were passed down and then quickly refilled by the watchful servers.

There was baked chicken, mashed potatoes, brown gravy, dressing and noodles, vegetable sides and cole slaw. After the main course dessert followed: date pudding; cherry, pumpkin and pecan pies; and then sheet cake. Bowls of canned fruit and celery sticks had been placed on the tables, as much for decoration as anything. Phillip had thought about taking some peaches, but after he had fin-ished with the food that had been passed to him, there was no longer any room for anything else.

After the meal, while people were milling around, Sarah and Melvin got up from their corner table. Taking Melvin's hand she made her way through the crowd towards Rebecca and Phillip. Greetings and introductions were exchanged all around.

"So glad you could come," Sarah smiled.

"Good to be here," Phillip told her. "How much would they charge for food like this in New York?"

"They don't make this food in New York," she told him.

"Oh, you are right about that," he agreed.

"Phillip has told me all about your experiences in New York City, and modeling for the company," Megan told Sarah. "You ought to write a book about it. There are not that many times that an Amish girls goes all that way, and then comes all the way back."

"I suppose so," Sarah mused, "but I don't think there is anyone who would publish something like that."

Megan smiled, "I am an editor at Simon & Schuster. When you have it written, try me."

Phillip grinned, "That would be some book, I'm sure."

"Well," Sarah told them, "I'm not a very good writer."

They continued exchanging information about New York and Amish life until it became obvious that other people needed to meet the bride and groom. Excusing themselves, Phillip and Rebecca's party left. The afternoon unfolded with chats with aunts, uncles, first and second cousins, nephews, nieces, and various other people who were connected to the wedding party as relatives or simply friends.

At five-thirty supper was served for the young folks, and afterwards the singing and visiting continued. It was past one o'clock when Sarah and Melvin were finally alone. With only a kerosene lamp burning in the bedroom, they stood looking at each other, both half giddy with happiness and weariness. Outside, the moon shone in full glory.

Melvin took her hands in his calloused ones. "God has been good to us," he said softly. "His ways are indeed the best."

"Yes," she said shyly, "they are."

As the moon beams played in her hair, he gently kissed her for the first time.

Jerry Eicher lives with his wife and
four children in central Virginia.
He is the author of *A Time to Live*.